ANCIENT GLASS
IN THE YALE UNIVERSITY ART GALLERY

343

Ancient Glass in the Yale University Art Gallery

Susan B. Matheson

YALE UNIVERSITY ART GALLERY

This catalogue was made possible by a grant
from the National Endowment for the Arts, a federal agency,
and by a donation from the Barker Welfare Foundation
in Memory of Catherine Barker and Charles V. Hickox.

TABLE OF CONTENTS

FOREWORD

THE sizeable collection of ancient glass of the Mediterranean region in the Yale University Art Gallery is notable for both its quality and its breadth. The greatest strength of the collection is in glass from about the time of Augustus, that is, the end of the first century B.C. and the early part of the first century A.D. Our mold-blown glass of this period is especially important, as is the mold-pressed and mosaic glass of the late Hellenistic and early Roman periods. Considering the diversity and relative completeness of the collection, it is noteworthy that only a small fraction of it was purchased by the University. The earliest glass to enter the collection came as part of the Whiting Palestinian Collection, acquired by Yale in 1909. Only one other ancient glass object was purchased, an inlay of a princess from the Amarna period of Egypt, purchased for Yale in 1936 (cat. no. 4). The reason for the strength of the collection, therefore, is not an aggressive purchase policy on the part of the Yale Art Gallery. It is, rather, the result of a series of generous gifts from alumni and other friends of Yale who were themselves collectors of ancient glass. By far, the largest and most important gift came in the form of the Hobart and Edward Small Moore Memorial Collection, the bequest of Mrs. W. H. Moore in 1955. This collection contained over 350 vessels, beads, and other objects. More than half of the material in the present catalogue comes from the Moore Collection. Other donors and gifts in memory of other Yale alumni include: the Anna Rosalie Mansfield Collection, gift of the Hon. Burton Mansfield, 1875s, of New Haven, in memory of his wife (1930 gift); Robert Lehman, B.A. 1913 (1953 gift); Edward B. Greene, B.A. 1900 (1930 gift); Carleton H. Stevens, B.A. 1906 (1932 gift); 1940 bequest in memory of Thomas Sedgwick van Volkenburgh, B.A. 1866; Henry F. Pearson, B.A. 1928, B.F.A. 1933 (1943 gift); E. Francis Riggs, B.A. 1909 and T. Laurason Riggs, B.A. 1910 (1929 gift); Shepherd Stevens, B.F.A. 1922 (1947 gift); Elmer D. Keith, B.A. 1910 (1960 gift). In addition, a small group of vessels came as an exchange of archaeological material with the Oriental Institute of the University of Chicago in 1940. From these various sources, our museum has gradually been able to assemble a comprehensive teaching collection of great quality.

The preparation of this catalogue would have been impossible without the aid of the National Endowment for the Arts, a federal agency. It provided funds not only for basic research and much needed photography, but also for a large share of the actual printing costs of this volume. Dr. Sidney M. Goldstein, curator of Ancient Glass at the Corning Museum of Glass, and Professor David Grose, Department of Classics, University of Massachusetts, kindly agreed to read the trial catalogue entries and to comment upon their form and content.

This catalogue was first proposed by Susan B. Matheson, who carried out all the extensive preparatory research and wrote this exceptionally lucid and informative catalogue while simultaneously carrying out her normal duties as associate curator for Ancient Art and Dura-Europos. Many of the objects presented in this catalogue have not been published previously. Although the Moore Collection was published in 1927, much new archaeological evidence has emerged subsequently, giving rise to new interpretations, identifications, and dates. We are proud of this publication which calls attention to an excellent, but little-known collection at Yale.

Alan Shestack, *Director*

ACKNOWLEDGEMENTS

THIS CATALOGUE would not have been completed without the help and encouragement of many friends and colleagues, and I am grateful for the opportunity to acknowledge their contributions here.

From the beginning the idea of publishing the Yale collection was endorsed by Andrew Oliver, Jr. and Donald Harden, and it was their encouragement which prompted me to undertake the project. I am especially grateful to Alan Shestack, Director of the Yale Art Gallery, for his enthusiastic support throughout the process of research and writing. His encouragement of "excavations" in our storage rooms and his willingness to support publication of little known parts of the collection have provided the incentive for this and a number of other undertakings.

A Museum Professional Grant by the Smithsonian Institution, under the provision of the National Museum Act (Public Law 91–629) as amended, and the National Endowment for the Arts provided the funds for a research trip to the major glass collections in Europe in 1973. I am grateful to the many colleagues in European museums who were particularly generous in sharing their knowledge and access to their collections: Alfonso de Francisis (Naples), Donald Harden (British Museum), Ulrich Gehrig (Berlin), Miriam Guise (Louvre), Clasina Isings (Utrecht), J. H. C. Kern (Leiden), Richard Nicholls (Cambridge), Kyrios Nicolau (Cyprus), Nicholas Yalouris (Athens). In this country, Susan Auth (Newark), Sidney M. Goldstein (Corning), and Kurt Luckner (Toledo) were especially generous with their time and collections, for which I offer sincere thanks. I am also appreciative of the many helpful discussions shared with visitors to the Yale collection, especially Dan Barag and Mrs. Yael Israeli, as well as grateful to those scholars and collectors with whom I have corresponded about individual objects: John D. Cooney, Waldemar Haberey,

Paul Hollister, Dr. Leonard Rakow, and Isabelle Raubitschek. Andrew Oliver, Jr. freely shared his knowledge of glass and related objects, and I have benefited greatly from his generosity. The manuscript was improved considerably by the suggestions of Sidney M. Goldstein, David Grose, and Jerome J. Pollitt, and I am deeply grateful to these three scholars for their time and concern.

Many colleagues and friends have rendered invaluable assistance in the production of the catalogue. I am particularly grateful to Joseph Szaszfai, who with extraordinary patience photographed and rephotographed the collection to comply with myriad special requests, and to Geri Mancini, who has consistently produced fine prints and helped in many other ways. Special thanks are also due Melissa Stern for her careful execution of the drawings. The editorial work was done with the utmost care and precision by Elise K. Kenney, to whose eagle eye and command of detail I owe a considerable debt. Dorothy M. Hooker typed a large portion of the manuscript with impressive accuracy, saving me considerable time and effort for which I am indeed grateful. My thanks are also offered to Estelle Miehle and Fernande Ross, who have both played a major rôle in bringing order to this project, and to Diane Hoose, Jane Krieger, Melissa Kroning, and Elizabeth Sinnott, who have been immensely helpful with innumerable details.

The catalogue was designed by Klaus Gemming, whose talent speaks for itself. I am especially grateful to Mr. Gemming for his patience, his interest, and his consistent good humor. Production was supervised by Greer Allen, University Printer, of the Yale University Printing Service, without whose firm hand any result would have been impossible.

Susan B. Matheson

HISTORY OF GLASSMAKING
IN THE ANCIENT MEDITERRANEAN

THE ORIGINS of glassmaking are now placed on the basis of archaeological evidence in Mesopotamia in the third millenium B.C.[1] The earliest glassmakers produced beads and other small objects, and it has been suggested that the making of true glass developed from the manufacture of faience, a glassy-surfaced material consisting primarily of quartz, which was popular for similar objects in Egypt and Mesopotamia at this time.

The first glass vessels appeared in Mesopotamia around 1500 B.C.,[2] and soon thereafter in Egypt from which the majority of the surviving early glass vessels have come. During the Eighteenth and Nineteenth Dynasties (1570–1197 B.C.) the Egyptian glass industry flourished, producing large numbers of core-formed cosmetic containers (cat. nos. 1–3)[3] as well as inlays and amulets (cat. nos. 4–6)[4] in colors which imitated semiprecious stones such as lapis lazuli, carnelian, and jasper. Glass inlays were used in the jewelry and funerary equipment of royalty, as in the gold funeral mask of Tutankhamen, and for eyes, jewelry, and other details of stone and wooden sculpture. Remains of glass factories have been found at a number of Egyptian sites including Tell el-Amarna and Lisht, the earliest being that at Thebes which dates from the reign of Amenhotep III (1410–1372 B.C.).[5]

Outside Egypt, finds of glass from this period include core-formed vessels from graves and temple sites in northern Mesopotamia,[6] mold-cast beads from graves at Mycenae,[7] and molded plaques with figures of nude women found at various temple sites in the Near East and thought to be dedications to the fertility goddess Astarte.[8] The earliest mosaic glass vessels were made in Mesopotamia and also date from this period.[9]

Some literary evidence for the technology of glassmaking in the late second millenium B.C. is provided by cuneiform tablets from the library of the Assyrian king, Assurbanipal I (668–627 B.C.) at Nineveh.[10] The tablets contain recipes for a basic mix of silica or quartzite pebbles and plant ash, the use of metal compounds for coloring,

and instructions on heating, cooling, and grinding the glass. Ritual sacrifices and other special preparations were also considered necessary for success in glassmaking, and some of these are outlined on the tablets. References on the tablets to "lapis lazuli from the kiln" clearly indicate that Mesopotamian glassmakers, like the Egyptians, used glass as a cheaper imitation of semiprecious stones.

In the Aegean, the palace civilizations of Crete and Mycenaean Greece, and the glassmaking industry that they had supported, died out completely by circa 1100 B.C. The end of the Kassite Dynasty in Babylon and the weakening of Assyria in the eleventh and tenth centuries B.C. seem to be responsible for a general decline in Mesopotamia which resulted in the drastic reduction of glassmaking for nearly three hundred years. In Egypt, the end of the Ramesside period brought a cultural decline, and here also luxury industries such as glassmaking suffered. Very little glass has been found in excavations of sites dating from 1200 to 900 B.C., although some evidence for the continuous if very limited production of mosaic glass throughout this period has come to light in Mesopotamia.[11]

Glassmaking resumed on a larger scale in the ninth century B.C. with the production of glass inlays and mosaic glass vessels. Among the most important discoveries from this period are the intricate fragmentary mosaic glass beakers from Hasanlu, Iran, decorated in two registers with a frieze of ibexes and date palms and a procession of men.[12] Core-formed vessels begin to occur again in the eighth century,[13] and a substantial industry for this type continued in both Egypt and Mesopotamia from the sixth century through the Hellenistic period (cat. nos. 7–33). Although closely resembling second millenium core-formed vessels in technique and in the use of color and opacity to imitate semiprecious stones, these vessels occurred in new shapes, derived from the forms of contemporary Greek pottery.

Other properties of glass, such as translucency,

were explored at this time in cast vessels and vessels cut from blanks, and new types of decoration including cutting, engraving, and painting were used. Both closed forms, such as an alabastron from Nimrud in Assyria inscribed with the name of King Sargon II (722–705 B.C.), and open forms, such as a cut ribbed bowl from Gordion in Phrygia and other bowl fragments from Nimrud, were produced in the eighth century.[14] Cast bowls have also been found in larger numbers in seventh and sixth century contexts. A notable example is the handsome blue bowl from the Bernadini tomb at Praeneste, apparently considered a luxury object since it was found with a treasure of gold, silver, and ivory objects.[15]

During the fifth century cast and core-formed vessels continued to be produced, and glass was also used for a wider range of decorative purposes. Glass ornament was used, for example, on Pheidias's famous cult image of Zeus at Olympia and on the column capitals of the North Porch of the Erectheum in Athens.[16]

Core-formed and cast or mold-pressed vessels still dominated glass production in the Hellenistic period. Simple cast bowls in pale blue green or brown with wheel-cut grooves as decoration were produced and traded in great numbers (cat. nos. 34–37). Often their shapes imitated metalware, and the simple banded decoration may derive from metal prototypes as well. Toward the end of this period, in the second to first century B.C., mosaic glass techniques were revived, possibly in Alexandria. Bowls (cat. nos. 40–41, 53), plates (cat. no. 54), and cups (cat. nos. 48–52, 55) were the most common mosaic glass vessels of this period, often echoing the forms of the monochrome mold-pressed (cat. nos. 34–37, 39, 42–47) and cut bowls with which they coexisted until the end of the first century A.D. In the early Roman period, some of these shapes imitated contempory forms of Arretine ware, a red glazed pottery from around the time of Augustus (cat. nos. 48–52). After the discovery of glassblowing, mosaic glass was adapted to bottles as well.

Glass was still considered a luxury in the Hellenistic period. The techniques used to make core-formed and mosaic glass vessels were especially laborious, and consequently far fewer objects could be produced by a given craftsman than was possible later when the technique of glassblowing was invented. The use of vivid colors and even gold in many vessels increased the richness of their appearance, an aesthetic predilection which continued to be applied to vessels of the early Roman period. Glass tableware seems to have been produced for the first time in this period, and although monochrome, it too was probably a luxury item, destined for the wealthier classes in much the same way as was the black and red-figure pottery of sixth and fifth century Athens.

The discovery of glassblowing seems to have occurred in the mid-first century B.C. Archaeological evidence points to the Syro-Palestinian coast as the place where this new technique was developed. A small blown bottle found with first century B.C. pottery in a grave near En-Gedi and a sealed deposit containing glass found in the Jewish quarter of the Old City of Jerusalem (dated on the basis of coins to no later than 50/40 B.C. and containing both cast bowls and blown bottles as well as the glass rods, cullet, and wasters normally associated with glassmaking workshops) are the earliest finds of blown glass in the Mediterranean area.

The consequences of this invention were revolutionary. Glass, which had once been a luxury, could now be produced so quickly and in such great numbers that every household could afford not just one vessel, but entire sets of glassware. Tables were set; commodities were shipped; and the ashes of the dead were buried in glass vessels throughout the Roman Empire. Excavations at well-preserved sites like Pompeii and Herculaneum have shown that glass was used for windows by the first century A.D., and glass vessels appear in still-life compositions in the wall paintings of houses in these towns.

Rome is described as an important and innovative center for glassmaking by Strabo in his *Geography*,[17] written around the time of Augustus, but glassblowing is not mentioned specifically in the literary sources until the third quarter of the first century A.D. Finds in the Roman Forum and the House of Livia on the Palatine, however, demonstrate that blown glass was being used and presumably made in Rome by the end of the first century B.C. or the start of the next century.[18]

Most of the earliest blown vessels were small bottles of simple form (cat. nos. 56–58, 78), but glassmakers soon branched out into drinking cups, tableware, and storage containers. The interest in variations in color cited by both Strabo and Pliny the Elder[19] is borne out by the large proportion of early vessels in rich hues of dark blue, purple, red, and green (cat. nos. 56–65, 106). Many of the shapes of these early vessels imitated the pottery vessels they were rapidly replacing.

Mold-blown glass quickly followed the discovery of glass blowing. The aesthetic effect of the relief decoration produced with these molds clearly derives from the molded and stamped relief pottery of the late Hellenistic and early Roman periods. Mold-blown vessels provide us with the first signatures of ancient glassmakers.[20] Artists such as Ennion (cat. no. 118) and his workshop were master craftsmen whose works were known and influential throughout the Mediterranean area.

By the end of the first century A.D., glass vessels had become thoroughly commonplace and inexpensive.[21] Most of the intentional coloration, surface patterns, and mold-blown decoration characteristic of first century vessels had been abandoned in favor of natural bluish green glassware in basic utilitarian shapes. Glassware of this type was widely produced throughout the Roman and Byzantine periods, and it forms the nucleus of the Yale collection, as it does of most others. The minimal decoration and variation among these vessels includes pinched ribs, knobs, indents, applied blobs, and trailed thread decoration, the last becoming elaborate and often overpowering in eastern Mediterranean vessels of the late Roman and Byzantine periods (cat. nos. 327–29).

Some first century decorative techniques did survive and even expand during the Roman Empire, however. The Romans seem to have preferred colorless glass for wheel-cut decoration, and once methods of decoloration were perfected, wheel-cut decoration became especially popular.[22] Elaborate figured scenes showing mythological and religious subjects (cat. no. 258) and views of circuses and of Roman towns were produced in Italy, Cologne, Alexandria, and elsewhere; simpler vessels with geometric (cat. no. 203), plant, and animal motifs (cat. no. 287) have been found throughout the Empire. Less common but equally important were painted

glass, with subjects often similar to those of wheel-cut vessels,[23] and gold-glass, best known from the portrait medallions and early Christian and Jewish gold-glasses found in the Roman catacombs and elsewhere.[24] Mold-blown glass was also made throughout this period; but although often of interest for its subject matter, which replaces the earlier decorative motifs with vessels in the shape of heads (cat. no. 283), fish, and even a famous statue (cat. no. 276), its workmanship is of lesser quality than that of its first century predecessors.

Towards the end of the Roman Empire, specifically from the fourth century onwards, local variations in style and form can be distinguished with somewhat greater frequency. These distinctions are relatively minor, however, and do not alter the basic consistency of glassmaking in the Roman period.

The decline of the Roman Empire in the west in the mid-fifth century A.D. and the Moslem conquest of the eastern Mediterranean in the seventh century A.D. brought changes to glassmaking which mark the end of the Roman tradition. Roman forms, and, with the exception of trailed thread decoration and mold-blowing, Roman decorative techniques were totally abandoned by western glassmakers. In the east, wheel-cut glass survived under the Sassanian Empire in the fifth and sixth centuries A.D. and was eventually adopted and widely used by Islamic glassmakers. Mold-blowing, trailed thread, and pinched decoration continued, but all were adapted to new vessel forms. Lustre painting, gilding, and enamelling were introduced, and it is primarily these techniques, along with many of the new shapes, that were carried back to Venice in the Middle Ages to begin the revival of glassmaking in Western Europe.[25]

NOTES

1. Dan Barag, "Mesopotamian Core-Formed Glass Vessels (1500–500 B.C.)," in Oppenheim, *Glassmaking* 132–33; H. C. Beck, "Glass before 1500 B.C.," *Ancient Egypt and the East* (1934) 7–21.

The best introduction to the history of ancient glass remains D. B. Harden's three articles in the *Archaeological Journal*: "Ancient Glass, I: Pre-Roman," 125 (1969) 46–72; "Ancient Glass, II: Roman," 126 (1970) 44–77; "Ancient Glass, III: Post-Roman," 128 (1972) 78–117.

2. Barag, "Core-Formed" 133.

3. For a thorough study of these vessels, see Nolte, *Glasgefässe Ägypten.*

4. For a selection see Riefstahl, *Glass and Glazes.*

5. Lucas, *Egyptian Materials* 184.

6. Barag, "Core-Formed" 131–98.

7. Harden, "Pre-Roman" 49, pl. II, E, with additional references.

8. Dan Barag, "Mesopotamian Glass Vessels of the Second Millenium B.C.," *JGS* 4 (1962) 21, note 68; Barag, "Core-Formed" 199, figs. 98–99.

9. Axel von Saldern, "Mosaic Glass from Hasanlu, Marlik, and Tell al-Rimah," *JGS* 8 (1966) 9–25.

10. Translated with commentary by Oppenheim, *Glassmaking* 4–101.

11. Axel von Saldern, "Other Mesopotamian Glass Vessels (1500–600 B.C.)," in Oppenheim, *Glassmaking* 203–28; von Saldern, "Mosaic Glass" 19–23.

12. von Saldern, "Mosaic Glass" 10–15.

13. von Saldern, "Mesopotamian Glass Vessels" 210.

14. For these and other examples, see von Saldern, "Mesopotamian Glass Vessels" 210–11, figs. 14–17.

15. C. D. Curtis, *The Bernadini Tomb, Memoirs of the American Academy in Rome* 3 (1919) 65, cat. 60, pl. 43, no. 1; von Saldern, "Meospotamian Glass Vessels" 211.

16. For the glass inlay molds from Pheidias's workshop, see Alfred Mallwitz and Wolfgang Schiering, *Die Werkstatt des Pheidias, Olympische Forschungen* 5 (Berlin 1964) 141; glass beads were used in the guilloche of the capitals of the columns on the North Porch of the Erechtheum, for which see L. D. Caskey, H. N. Fowler, J. M. Paton, G. P. Stevens, *The Erechtheum* (Cambridge, Mass. 1927) 85–86.

17. Strabo 16.2.25.

18. Evidence for the origins of glassblowing in both the eastern Mediterranean and Italy is discussed by Grose, "Early Blown Glass."

19. Strabo 16.2.25 and Pliny, *N.H.* 36.198.

20. For other signatures, in both Greek and Latin, see Trowbridge, *Philological Studies* 112–28.

21. A fact mentioned in the ancient literature: Strabo 16.2.25; Pliny, *N.H.* 36.199; Petronius, *Satyr.* 50, cited by Grose, "Early Blown Glass" 15, note 30.

22. For representative examples, see Harden, *Masterpieces* nos. 94–99 and 101–5.

23. Not represented in the Yale collection, but see Harden, "Roman" pl. IX for some of the most important pieces.

24. Morey, *Gold Glass*; more recently Irmgard Schüler, "A Note on Jewish Gold Glasses," *JGS* 8 (1966) 48–61.

25. For further reading on glass after the decline of the Roman Empire, see Harden, "Post-Roman," with additional references.

ANCIENT GLASSMAKING TECHNIQUES

Our present understanding of the processes used in the manufacture of ancient glass is based largely on archaeological evidence and analysis of the glass itself.[1] Some ancient literary evidence is provided by descriptions and formulae recorded on cuneiform tablets from the library of the Assyrian king, Assurbanipal I (668–627 B.C.) and later, in such works as the *Natural History* of Pliny the Elder (A.D. 23/24–79), although this material is far from complete and omits, prior to the Byzantine period, such critical information as the formulae for coloring glass.[2]

From literary sources and modern scientific analysis, we know that sand (silica), soda (alkali), and lime (possibly from shells) were the basic components of ancient glass.[3] Different metal oxides were added to color or decolor the glass.[4] Broken or ground glass was also added to the batch, as is the practice in glassmaking today, and a substantial trade in broken glass grew up as a result.[5]

Little is known about ancient glass furnaces, although they appear to have been wood-fired and to have had two chambers, one for heating and fusing, the second for cooling or annealing. Excavations have yielded some ground plans of furnaces in Roman Britain and near Cologne, and these, along with some Mediaeval book illustrations and a first century A.D. lamp from Dalmatia showing a glass furnace, provide evidence for the basic design of ancient furnaces.[6]

Three basic techniques were used in the manufacture of ancient glass vessels: sandcore, molding or casting in a mold, and blowing. Decorative techniques can be divided into those applied after the vessel had cooled, such as painting and wheel-cutting, those applied while the vessel was hot, such as trailed threads, blobs, and pinched decoration, and decoration which occurs as part of the manufacturing process, as in mold-blown and mosaic glass.

The following list of terms used in glassmaking includes those most frequently cited in the catalogue. Representative examples from the collection of the techniques described have been cited where possible.

Manufacturing Techniques

Color Band Glass: see Mosaic Glass.

Core-Formed: see Sandcore.

Fire-Polishing: smoothing the surface of a cooled vessel by reheating in the furnace; also used to finish rims.

Free-Blown: The vessel was inflated from a gather of molten glass through a long hollow metal rod or blowpipe. After inflation, the vessel was transferred to a solid rod called a pontil rod or punty, where it was shaped with such tools as pincers, given handles and feet, and decorated. The pontil rod often left a mark on the base of free-blown vessels known as a pontil mark.

Gold-Glass: A thin layer of gold leaf was sandwiched between two layers of glass, with details of figures or floral patterns incised into the gold layer. A variant technique apparently used gold dust or powder in suspension as a paint. When used as one of the bands of color band glass, the gold often "crackled" when the mold was heated.

Lathe-Cut: The form of the vessel was carved out of a molded or cast glass blank, using the same tools and techniques that produced carved stone and rock crystal vessels.

Marvering: rolling the vessel on a flat surface to shape it or smooth its surface. Trailed thread decoration was often embedded in the surface by marvering.

Mold-Blown: The vessel was blown into a reusable wood or terra cotta mold of two or more parts, whose seams show up on the finished vessel as "mold marks" (cat. no. 118).

Mold-Pressed: A casting process using open or closed molds. Most mold-pressed vessels were cast in a two part mold, using ground or broken glass heated in the mold until it fused or using molten glass poured into the mold cavity by the lost wax method employed in antiquity for casting bronze. After cooling, the surface was wheel or fire-polished. Decoration was generally wheel-cut (cat. no. 34).

Mosaic Glass: A variant mold-pressed technique. Fused glass rods whose cross-sections formed geometric patterns, flowers, birds, etc., were sliced into discs which were laid in a two part mold. The mold was heated until the discs fused, then cooled, and the vessel was finished by wheel-polishing or fire-polishing (cat. no. 48). Variations included fused bands of solid colors (color band or ribbon glass, cat. no. 38), twisted spiral threads which were also often used for rims (cat. no. 53), and marble or onyx pattern glass (cat. no. 40).

Optic-Blown: The vessel was blown through a metal ring with ridges that formed ribs. The vessel was generally further inflated, resulting in a softened, less distinctly ribbed surface (cat. no. 217).

Pattern-Molded: The vessel was first molded, then blown, producing a distended effect in the surface pattern (cat. no. 284).

Sandcore or Core-Formed: A core of sand, mud, or clay was formed around the end of a metal rod. Molten glass was trailed onto the core to form the body of the vessel. Decorative threads of contrasting colors were trailed on and dragged into zigzag or feather patterns, and the surface was smoothed by marvering. Handles and bases were formed separately and added. The core was removed after cooling (cat. nos. 1 and 7).

Wheel-Polishing: smoothing the surface of a cooled vessel on a wheel using an abrasive powder such as emery; also used to finish rims.

Decorating Techniques

Indented: Pressure was applied to the hot vessel with the tips of the pincers to make indentations in the sides of vessels (cat. nos. 214 and 249).

Painted: Painted decoration was applied after the vessel had cooled (cat. no. 111).

Pinched: Pincers were used while the glass was still hot to form raised knobs and ridges (cat. no. 225).

Splash Glass: Small glass chips were scattered over the surface of the gather of molten glass, then the vessel was inflated, resulting in a surface design of thin distended drops or splashes (cat. nos. 109 and 110).

Trailed Thread: Molten glass threads, often in contrasting colors, were wound or trailed onto the body of the hot vessel in a spiral (cat. no. 75), abstract patterns (cat. no. 304), or serpentine patterns (cat. no. 184). Sometimes the threads were dragged to form a zigzag, feather, or festoon pattern (cat. nos. 2, 27, and 31 respectively), while in later examples a festoon pattern was created by applying a trailed thread before inflating the vessel (cat. no. 65). The trailed thread decoration on sandcore and early blown vessels is often marvered, while that of late Roman and Byzantine vessels is not.

Wheel-cut: Once the vessel had cooled, a metal wheel and an abrasive powder such as emery could be used to cut or engrave bands (cat. no. 34), facets (cat. no. 100), inscriptions (cat. no. 292), deco-

rative motifs (cat. no. 287), or figured scenes (cat. no. 258). Cameo glass was also produced in this manner.

Color

In its natural state, glass made from the soda, lime, and silica mixture used by ancient glassmakers is bluish green because of the iron oxide present in the silica or sand. Most Roman glass is of this natural color. Some Hellenistic glass, although made from the same components, was heated in a reducing atmosphere which produced a golden brown color.

Egyptian and Roman glassmakers added certain metal oxides to the glass to vary its color. Copper oxides produced blue, red, or green, depending on the atmosphere in the furnace; cobalt produced dark blue; antimony and lead were used to make yellow; manganese produced purple or yellowish glass; and tin was used for opaque white.

Antimony and manganese were also used as decolorants by the Romans to produce the colorless glass favored for wheel-cut decoration.

Weathering or Devitrification

Very little ancient glass has survived with its original surface intact. Moisture and acids frequently present in the burial contexts in which glass is found act on the surface of the vessel to cause a chemical decomposition known as devitrification or "weathering." This chemical decomposition produces a change of color in the surface layers of the vessel, commonly turning them iridescent, white, or light brown. These decomposed layers have a tendency to separate in flakes from the stable unweathered glass underneath, with the result that surface details such as painted or lightly engraved decoration are often lost. In cases where the surface is not lost, the original color and transparent quality of the glass are frequently obscured. Although prized by collectors and imitated by modern glassmakers, the colorful iridescence and other effects of weathering were never intended by ancient glassmakers.

Shapes

At least eighty Greek and Latin names for the shapes of glass vessels are known from literary references. Although the functions of these vessels are often mentioned as well, it has seldom been possible to identify the names with surviving vessels. Among those that have been identified are the amphoriskos (Greek, small amphora, cat. no. 13), skyphos (Greek, two-handled drinking cup, cat. no. 109), pyxis

(Greek, small lidded box, used as a container for cosmetics and medicine, cat. no. 124), and calix or carchesium (Latin, goblet with concave sides, cat. no. 110).

Many glass shapes, including those listed above, as well as such basic shapes as plates, jugs, bowls, and bottles, imitate or derive from pottery and metal vessels. Among sandcore vessels, the alabastron (cat. no. 22) and the oinochoe (cat. no. 7) are both found in Greek pottery of the sixth and fifth centuries B.C. Late Hellenistic and early Roman pottery shapes imitated in glass include the pear-shaped flask (cat. no. 80), patella cup (cat. no. 45), plate (cat. no. 108), pyxis, and jug, while bronze and silver skyphoi (cat. no. 109), pyxides (cat. no. 124), jugs, and amphoriskoi (cat. no. 62) also have parallels in glass. The relief decoration of mold-blown glass vessels is also derived from Hellenistic and Roman pottery and metalwork.

NOTES

1. Good general introductions include Robert H. Brill, "Ancient Glass," *Scientific American* 209 (1963) 120–30, and Price, "Glass" 111–25.

2. On the cuneiform tablets, see Oppenheim, *Glassmaking* 4–101; Pliny, *N.H.* 36.190–200; for additional literary evidence in Greek and Roman writers, see Trowbridge, *Philological Studies*.

3. Pliny, *N.H.* 36.190–94.

4. For Egyptian glass, see Lucas, *Egyptian Materials* 187–91; for Mesopotamian glass, Oppenheim, *Glassmaking* 76–80, and R. H. Brill, "The Chemical Interpretation of the Texts," in Oppenheim, *Glassmaking* 105–28; for Roman glass, Price, "Glass" 116.

5. Price, "Glass" 116.

6. Price, "Glass" 114–15; Robert J. Charleston, "Glass Furnaces through the Ages," *JGS* 20 (1978) 9–33.

ABBREVIATIONS

AJA   *American Journal of Archaeology*

Amyx, *Echoes*   Amyx, D. A., ed. *Echoes from Olympus*, exhibition catalogue. University Art Museum, Berkeley, California, 1974.

Augustan Art   *Augustan Art*, exhibition catalogue. Metropolitan Museum of Art, New York, 4 January–13 February 1939.

Auth, Newark   Auth, Susan H. *Ancient Glass at the Newark Museum*. Newark, New Jersey, 1976.

Barag, *Beth She'arim*   Barag, Dan. "Glass." In *Beth She'arim III The Archaeological Excavations during 1953–1958: The Catacombs 12–23*, edited by N. Avigad, pp. 149–60, pl. 48. Israel Exploration Society, Jerusalem, 1971.

Barag, "Pilgrim Vessels"   Barag, Dan. "Glass Pilgrim Vessels from Jerusalem: Part I." *Journal of Glass Studies* 12 (1970) 35–63; "Glass Pilgrim Vessels from Jerusalem: Parts II and III." Ibid. 13 (1970) 45–63.

Baur, *Gerasa*   Baur, Paul V. C. "Glassware." In *Gerasa, City of the Decapolis*, edited by Carl H. Kraeling, pp. 505–46, pls. 139–41. New Haven, 1938.

Berger, Vindonissa   Berger, Ludwig. *Römische Gläser aus Vindonissa*. Basel, 1960.

Brown, *Terra-Sigillata*   Brown, A. C. *Catalogue of the Italian Terra-Sigillata in the Ashmolean Museum*. Oxford, 1968.

Bull. Assoc. Fine Arts Yale   *Bulletin of the Associates in Fine Arts at Yale University*

Calvi, Aquileia   Calvi, M. C. *I Vetri Romani del Museo di Aquileia*. Aquileia, 1968.

Cambridge, Fitzwilliam   Bourriau, J. D., J. E. A. Liversidge, and R. V. Nicholls, "The Ancient World." In *Glass at the Fitzwilliam Museum*, pp. 11–57. Cambridge, 1978.

Clairmont, Dura   Clairmont, Christoph. *The Excavations at Dura-Europos, Final Report IV, Part V: The Glass Vessels*. New Haven, 1963.

Crowfoot and Harden, "Glass Lamps"   Crowfoot, G. M. and D. B. Harden. "Early Byzantine and Later Glass Lamps." *Journal of Egyptian Archaeology* 17 (1931) 196–208.

Crowfoot, *Samaria-Sebaste*   Crowfoot, G. M. "Glass." In J. W. Crowfoot, G. M. Crowfoot, and K. M. Kenyon. *The Objects from Samaria (Samaria-Sebaste III)*, pp. 403–22, pl. 25. London, 1957.

Davidson, *Corinth*   Davidson, Gladys. *Corinth XII: The Minor Objects*. Princeton, 1952.

Delougaz and Haines, *Khirbat al-Karak*   Delougaz, Pinhas and Richard C. Haines. *A Byzantine Church at Khirbat al-Karak*. University of Chicago, Oriental Institute Publications, vol. 85. Chicago, 1960.

de Ridder, *de Clercq*   de Ridder, André. *Collection de Clercq, Catalogue. Tome VI. Les Terres cuites et les verres*. Paris, 1909.

Doppelfeld, *Köln*   Doppelfeld, Otto. *Römisches und Fränkisches Glas in Köln*. Cologne, 1966.

Dragendorff   Dragendorff, H. "Terra Sigillata. Ein Beitrag zur Geschichte der Griechischen und Römischen Keramik." *Bonner Jahrbücher* 96–97 (1895) 18–155, pls. I–VI (pls. I–III have profile drawings).

Dura, *Preliminary Report*	Toll, N. P. *The Excavations at Dura-Europos, Preliminary Report of the Ninth Season of Work, 1935–1936. Part II: The Necropolis*, edited by M. I. Rostovtzeff, A. R. Bellinger, F. E. Brown, and C. B. Welles. New Haven, 1946.
Dusenbery, "Wheaton College"	Dusenbery, Elsbeth B. "Ancient Glass in the Collections of Wheaton College." *Journal of Glass Studies* 13 (1971) 9–33.
Eisen	Eisen, G. A. and Fahim Kouchakji. *Glass.* 2 vols. New York, 1927.
Fossing	Fossing, Paul. *Glass Vessels before Glass Blowing.* Copenhagen, 1948.
Fremersdorf, Denkmäler	Fremersdorf, Fritz. *Die Denkmäler des Römisches Köln.* Vols. 3–8. Cologne, 1958–67.
Froehner, *Gréau*	Froehner, Wilhelm. *Collection Julien Gréau, Verrerie antique . . . appartenant à M. John Pierpont Morgan.* Paris, 1903.
Goldstein, "Forgeries"	Goldstein, Sidney M. "Forgeries and Reproductions of Ancient Glass in Corning." *Journal of Glass Studies* 19 (1977) 40–62.
Grose, "Early Blown Glass"	Grose, David. "Early Blown Glass." *Journal of Glass Studies* 19 (1977) 9–29.
Grose, *Toledo*	Grose, David. "Ancient Glass." *Museum News, The Toledo Museum of Art* 20 (1978) 67–90.
Hamelin, "Bégram"	Hamelin, Pierre. "Matériaux pour servir à l'étude des verreries de Bégram." *Cahiers de Byrsa* 3 (1953) 121–23; 4 (1954) 180.
Harden, "Amman"	Harden, D. B. "Some Tomb Groups of Late Roman Date in the Amman Museum." *Annales du 3e Congrès des Journées Internationales du Verre.* Damascus, 1964, pp. 48–55.
Harden "Highdown Hill"	Harden, D. B. "The Highdown Hill Glass Goblet with Greek Inscription." *Sussex Archaeological Collections* 97 (1959) 3–20.
Harden, *Karanis*	Harden, Donald B. *Roman Glass from Karanis.* Oxford, 1936.
Harden, *Masterpieces*	Harden, Donald B., K. S. Painter, R. H. Pinder-Wilson, and Hugh Tait. *Masterpieces of Glass.* British Museum, London, 1968.
Harden, "Mould-blown Inscriptions"	Harden, Donald B. "Romano-Syrian Glasses with Mould-blown Inscriptions." *Journal of Roman Studies* 25 (1935) 163–86.
Harden, "Roman"	Harden, Donald B. "Ancient Glass, II: Roman." *Archaeological Journal* 126 (1970) 44–77, pls. 1–12.
Harden, "Yahmour"	Harden, Donald B. "Two Tombgroups of the First Century A.D. from Yahmour, Syria, and a Supplement to the List of Romano-Syrian Glasses with Mould-blown Inscriptions." *Syria* 24 (1944–45) 81–95.
Harden and Price, "Fishbourne"	Harden, Donald B. and Jennifer Price. "Excavations at Fishbourne 1961–69: The Glass." *Reports of the Research Committee of the Society of Antiquaries of London* 27 (1971) 317–70, pls. 25–28.
Hayes, Toronto	Hayes, John W. *Roman and Pre-Roman Glass in the Royal Ontario Museum.* Toronto, 1975.
Hayward, "Yale"	Hayward, Jane. "Roman Mold-Blown Glass at Yale University." *Journal of Glass Studies* 4 (1962) 49–60.
Isings	Isings, Clasina. *Roman Glass from Dated Finds.* Groningen, 1957.
Isings, *Limburg*	Isings, Clasina. *Roman Glass in Limburg.* Groningen, 1971.

Israeli, "Museum Haaretz"	Israeli, Yael. "Sidonian Mold-blown Glass Vessels in the Museum Haaretz." *Journal of Glass Studies* 6 (1964) 34–41.
JGS	*Journal of Glass Studies*
JIV	*Bulletin des Journées Internationales du Verre*
JRS	*Journal of Roman Studies*
Kern, "Glaskelche in Leiden"	Kern, J. H. C. "Zwei buntgefleckte Glaskelche des I. Jahrhunderts nach Christ in Leiden." *Archeologia Classica* 8, Fascicule 1 (1956) 56–63.
Kisa, *Glas*	Kisa, Anton. *Das Glas im Altertume.* 3 vols. Leipzig, 1908.
Kouchakji	Kouchakji, Fahim. "Catalogue of the Moore Collection of Glass." ca. 1940–45. Unpublished.
Lucas, *Egyptian Materials*	Lucas, A. *Ancient Egyptian Materials and Industries,* 4th ed. rev. by J. R. Harris. London, 1962.
Morey, *Gold Glass*	Morey, Charles Rufus. *The Gold Glass Collections of the Vatican Library, with Additional Catalogues of Other Gold Glass Collections,* edited by Guy Ferrari (*Catalogo del Museo Sacro della Biblioteca Apostolica Vaticana,* vol. 4). Città del Vaticano, 1959.
Neuberg, *Glas*	Neuburg, Frederic. *Antikes Glas.* Darmstadt, 1962.
Nolte, *Glasgefässe Ägypten*	Nolte, Birgit. *Die Glasgefässe im alten Ägypten.* Berlin, 1968.
Oliver, "Millefiori Glass"	Oliver, Jr., Andrew. "Millefiori Glass in Classical Antiquity." *Journal of Glass Studies* 10 (1968) 48–70.
Oppenheim, *Glassmaking*	Oppenheim, A. Leo. *Glass and Glassmaking in Ancient Mesopotamia.* Corning, New York, 1970.
Oswald and Pryce, *Terra Sigillata*	Oswald, F. and T. D. Pryce. *An Introduction to the Study of Terra Sigillata.* London, 1920.
Price, "Glass"	Price, Jennifer. "Glass." In *Roman Crafts,* edited by Donald Strong and David Brown, pp. 111–25. London, 1976.
Riefstahl, *Glass and Glazes*	Riefstahl, Elizabeth. *Ancient Egyptian Glass and Glazes in the Brooklyn Museum.* Brooklyn, 1968.
von Saldern, Boston	von Saldern, Axel. *Ancient Glass in the Museum of Fine Arts, Boston.* Boston, 1968.
von Saldern, Oppenländer	von Saldern, Axel, Birgit Nolte, Peter La Baume, and Thea Elisabeth Haevernick. *Gläser der Antike, Sammlung Erwin Oppenländer.* Mainz, 1974.
von Saldern, "Reproductions"	von Saldern, Axel. "Originals—Reproductions—Fakes." *Annales du 5ᵉ Congrès de l'Association Internationale pour l'Histoire du Verre, Prague 6–11 Juillet 1970.* Liège, 1972, pp. 299–318.
Sangiorgi, *Vetri Antichi*	Sangiorgi, G. *Collezione di Vetri Antichi dalle Origini al V sec D. C.* Milan, 1914.
Smith, Corning	Smith, Ray Winfield. *Glass from the Ancient World.* Corning, New York, 1957.
SPB, Constable-Maxwell	Sotheby Parke Bernet. *Catalogue of the Constable-Maxwell Collection of Ancient Glass.* London, 4–5 June 1979.

Spartz, Kassel

Spartz, Edith. *Kataloge der Staatliche Kunstsammlungen Kassel, nr. 1: Antike Gläser.* Kassel, 1967.

Toledo, *Glass*

Art in Glass, A Guide to the Glass Collections. The Toledo Museum of Art. Toledo, Ohio, 1969.

Trowbridge, *Philological Studies*

Trowbridge, Mary L. *Philological Studies in Ancient Glass.* University of Illinois, Urbana, 1930.

Vessburg, "Cyprus"

Vessburg, Olof. "Roman Glass in Cyprus." *Opuscula Archaeologica* 7 (1952) 109–65.

Weinberg, "Mold-Blown Beakers"

Weinberg, Gladys D. "Mold-Blown Beakers with Mythological Scenes." *Journal of Glass Studies* 14 (1972) 26–47.

Weinberg, "Notes"

Weinberg, Gladys D. "Notes on Glass from Upper Galilee." *Journal of Glass Studies* 15 (1973) 35–51.

Weinberg, "Tel Anafa"

Weinberg, Gladys D. "Hellenistic Glass from Tel Anafa in Upper Galilee." *Journal of Glass Studies* 12 (1970) 17–27.

Zahn, *Galerie Bachstitz II*

Zahn, Robert. *Galerie Bachstitz II: Die Sammlung Friedrich L. von Gans.* Berlin, 1921.

———

NOTE: Sidney M. Goldstein, *Pre-Roman and Early Roman Glass in The Corning Museum of Glass* (1979) arrived as this catalogue was going to press, too late, unfortunately, to permit incorporation of Dr. Goldstein's valuable research and conclusions.

NOTES TO THE CATALOGUE

THE CATALOGUE is divided into broad chrono-logical sections, and within these sections the entries are grouped typologically. Lacking archaeological provenances, it has not been possible, especially with the simpler forms, to determine a precise date for every vessel, so the chronology should not be regarded as absolute. Vessel shapes with long life spans have generally been grouped together and placed into the chronological development around the time of their introduction, even though some specific examples may be of considerably later date. The catalogue does not include glass from Dura-Europos and Gerasa, except as comparative material. Although this glass forms an important part of the Yale collection, it has been published elsewhere.

The *Descriptions* omit most details that can be seen in the illustrations. *Bibliography* refers to publications or illustrations of the object described in the entry, while similar vessels and other related references are listed under *Parallels*. "Cat. no." is used solely to refer to the entry numbers in this catalogue; entry numbers in all other publications are stated as "no." The archives of the Dura-Europos excavations contain a large group of photographs of glass in the Damascus Museum, referred to here as Damascus Museum (Dura photos); the numbers are written on labels in the photographs and may refer to an early published catalogue.

The following abbreviations have been used for museums which are mentioned frequently:

BM: British Museum, London
BMFA: Museum of Fine Arts, Boston
CMG: Corning Museum of Glass, Corning, New York
MMA: Metropolitan Museum of Art, New York
TMA: Toledo Museum of Art, Toledo, Ohio
VAM: Victoria and Albert Museum, London

Shortened forms of many credit lines have been used at the beginning of the entries. These short forms are listed here with their complete credit lines:

Lehman Gift: Gift of Robert Lehman, B.A. 1913
Mansfield Collection: The Anna Rosalie Mansfield Collection
Moore Collection: The Hobart and Edward Small Moore Memorial Collection
Oriental Institute: The Oriental Institute, University of Chicago, Chicago, Illinois, by Exchange
Stevens Gift: Given in memory of Egbert C. Fuller by Carleton H. Stevens, B.A. 1906
Van Volkenburgh Bequest: Bequest of Florence Baiz Van Volkenburgh in memory of her husband Thomas Sedgwick Van Volkenburgh, B.A. 1866
Whiting Collection: The Whiting Palestinian Collection
Yale University Art Gallery: provenance unknown

Catalogue numbers, left to right:

101: opaque white ribbed bowl, blown, first century A.D.

94: large pale green square jug, mold-blown, first-second century A.D.

200: pale green chain-handled jug, blown, third century A.D.

308: purple jar, blown fourth-fifth century A.D.

53: yellow mosaic glass bowl, mold-pressed, first century B.C.

184: pale green snake thread bottle, blown, second century A.D.

138: pale brown head flask, mold-blown, first century A.D.

136: olive green Dionysiac beaker, mold-blown, first century A.D.

41: blue mosaic glass bowl, mold-pressed, first century B.C.-first century A.D.

65: brown and white alabastron, blown, first century A.D.

Catalogue numbers, left to right:

55: purple mosaic glass beaker, mold-pressed, first century B.C.-first century A.D.

137: yellowish brown Seasons beaker, mold-blown, first century A.D.

17: dark blue amphoriskos, core-formed, sixth-fourth century B.C.

276: pale purple Tyche bottle, mold-blown, second-third century A.D.

257: gilded purple beaker with inscription, blown, third-fourth century A.D.

118: pale blue jar signed by Ennion, mold-blown, first century A.D.

284: olive green honeycomb beaker, pattern-molded, fourth century A.D.

121: opaque white pyxis, mold-blown, first century A.D.

343: yellow tall-necked amphora, blown, fifth-sixth century A.D.

ANCIENT GLASS
IN THE YALE UNIVERSITY ART GALLERY

1, 2, 3

2   EGYPTIAN GLASS

Egyptian Glass of the New Kingdom

CA. 1400–1200 B.C.

VESSELS

1 Column Flask

Egyptian
Late Dynasty XVIII–Dynasty XIX, ca. 1400–1200 B.C.
Moore Collection, 1955.6.1
H. 8.5 cm.

Among the earliest surviving datable glass vessels are the small sandcore perfume and cosmetic flasks made in Egypt during the New Kingdom. In the sandcore process, the vessel was formed around a friable earthen core held on the end of a rod. Hot molten glass was smeared or coiled around the core until it covered the surface, forming the basic shape of the body. Decoration consisted of threads of contrasting colors trailed in a spiral around the body, dragged, and marvered. Dark blue and turquoise were favored for the body and yellow and white for the decoration.

Small sandcore flasks in the shape of palm columns were used to contain *kohl*, a dark eye paint, during the late Eighteenth Dynasty and the Ramesside period. The medium blue of this example is unusual, as is the absence of zigzag decoration.

DESCRIPTION: sandcore; medium blue; yellow and white thread decoration encircles base and neck; capital leaves outlined with yellow thread. CONDITION: broken and repaired, fragment missing from body; one leaf of capital broken away, two others chipped; neck thread decoration partly missing. PROVENANCE: said to have been found at Luxor, Egypt; Khayat, 1922; Moore Collection no. 829. BIBLIOGRAPHY: *Eisen* 121, pl. 3c; *Kouchakji* no. 1; *Fossing* 22, note 1; Nolte, *Glasgefässe Ägypten* 150.

2 Lentoid Flask

Egyptian
Late Dynasty XVIII, ca. 1400–1350 B.C.
Anonymous Gift, 1937.180
Pres. H. 6.8 cm.

The dark blue body and yellow and white dragged decoration of this flask are a common color combination for New Kingdom vessels. Two dark blue handles from the neck to the shoulder and a trailed

white or yellow thread around the rim probably completed the flask.

DESCRIPTION: sandcore; dark blue with yellow and white decoration. CONDITION: handles, rim, and part of neck broken away; body cracked but not broken. PROVENANCE: Mrs. R. Berens, sale Sotheby's, July 1923. BIBLIOGRAPHY: Nolte, *Glasgefässe Ägypten* 99.

3 Fragment of an Amphoriskos

Egyptian
Late Dynasty XVIII, ca. 1400–1350 B.C.
Anonymous Gift, 1937.181
Max. Pres. H. 3.3 cm., Max. Pres. W. 5 cm.

DESCRIPTION: sandcore; neck and shoulder fragment, dark blue with yellow and white dragged decoration. CONDITION: surface virtually unweathered. PROVENANCE: Mrs. R. Berens, sale Sotheby's, July 1923. PARALLELS: Nolte, *Glasgefässe Ägypten* "Werkreis 1," especially pl. 4, no. 16.

INLAYS, NEW KINGDOM AND PTOLEMAIC

4 Amulet, Amarna Princess

Egyptian
Late Dynasty XVIII, ca. 1400–1350 B.C.
University Purchase Fund, 1936.50
Pres. H. 3 cm.

The head and upper torso of a princess are preserved in this fragmentary amulet. The ovoid head and drawn out features immediately suggest the work of an Amarna period artist. The princess, her hair tied in a sidelock, is in a seated position, dressed only in a skirt, a broad collar, and an arm ring. Holding her hand to her mouth, she is a well-known figure in the later Eighteenth Dynasty, especially during the reign of Amenhotep III and Akhenaten. Her gesture signifies that she is a royal child and is consistent with the traditional pose of the infant Harpocrates.

DESCRIPTION: molded with carved details; opaque medium grayish blue. CONDITION: fragmentary; lower body, left arm, and part of the upper torso broken away; surface dull;

  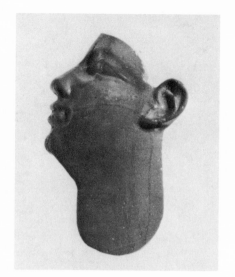

4, 5, 6

underside flat and smooth. PROVENANCE: G. C. Pier, sale American Art Association, Anderson Galleries, New York, 6 March 1936, no. 102. BIBLIOGRAPHY: *Egyptian Antiquities in the Pier Collection*, sale catalogue, American Art Association, Anderson Galleries, New York, 1936, no. 102, p. 24, pl. 12; Ludlow Bull, "Egyptian Antiquities from the Pier Collection," *Bull. Assoc. Fine Arts Yale* 7 (June 1936) 31–32, fig. 3. PARALLELS: for the pose and costume in relief sculpture, see for example W. M. F. Petrie, *Tell el Amarna* (London 1894) pl. 17, no. 271; in faience, see Julia Sansom, *Amarna, City of Akhenaten and Nefertiti* (London 1972) 81, fig. 47, the two left examples; for the Harpocrates gesture, see for example *von Saldern, Oppenländer* no. 41, a glass amulet; W. M. F. Petrie, *Amulets* (Warminster 1972) no. 126.

5 Inlay, Head of a Vulture

Egyptian
Late Dynasty XVIII, ca. 1400–1350 B.C.
Moore Collection, 1955.6.295
H. 1.9 cm., W. 3.6 cm.

Glass was frequently used as a substitute for semi-precious stones in the New Kingdom, even in royal jewelry and funerary equipment. Although it is impossible to determine the exact use of this fragment, the repeated occurrence of the vulture in royal iconography, the richness of the material, and the fine quality of the workmanship indicate that it must have been made for a royal patron.

DESCRIPTION: assembled from three separately carved pieces: opaque turquoise head, yellow beak, and red eye. CON-

DITION: fragment; chipped around break at neck; turquoise is weathered pale opalescent blue but red and yellow remain intact; part of the back surface is rough, probably from mounting. PROVENANCE: Sangiorgi Collection (according to Mrs. Moore but not listed in the 1914 catalogue). BIBLIOGRAPHY: C. J. Lamm, "Glass and Hard Stone Vessels," in *A Survey of Persian Art*, ed. A. U. Pope (London 1939) III, p. 2594, pl. 76; *Kouchakji* amulet no. 11.

6 Inlay, Royal Head

Egyptian
Ptolemaic Period, 332–30 B.C.
Moore Collection, 1955.6.347
H. 3.2 cm.

Imitating carnelian or red jasper, this profile head of a king faces left; a crown and body made from separate pieces of different colors originally completed the figure. Such inlay figures originated in Dynasties XVIII and XIX and were revived in the Ptolemaic period. The puffy cheeks, small features, and sagging chin of this head are typical of the later examples.

DESCRIPTION: carved; opaque red glass, highly polished. CONDITION: intact; virtually unweathered. BIBLIOGRAPHY: *Kouchakji* amulet no. 64. PARALLELS: Birgit Nolte in *von Saldern, Oppenländer* nos. 28 and 30 dates these inlays to the New Kingdom, but see Riefstahl, *Glass and Glazes* no. 76 for the more widely accepted Ptolemaic date. A characteristic New Kingdom example is published by Riefstahl, *Glass and Glazes* no. 43.

Later Sandcore Vessels

SIXTH–FIRST CENTURY B.C.

7 *Jug*

Eastern Mediterranean
Sixth–Fourth Century B.C.
Mansfield Collection, 1930.410
H. 10.5 cm.

Beginning in about the seventh century B.C., the manufacture of sandcore vessels was revived on a large scale in Egypt and the Near East. Although the use of color and technique suggests imitation of the New Kingdom vessels, new non-Egyptian forms were introduced which reflected the development of Greek pottery shapes. Amphoriskoi and trefoil-mouthed jugs were especially characteristic of the new series, replacing column flasks and other New Kingdom shapes. Vessels of this type continued to be produced into the first century B.C., but by this time the proportions had become exaggerated and the decoration often careless.

The basic shape of this trefoil-mouthed jug echoes a form found in Greek pottery jugs as early as the Protocorinthian oinochoai of the seventh century B.C., although its foot is precariously small. The body, handle, and foot of the glass vessel are dark blue, with characteristic two color zigzag decoration and a thread around the lip.

DESCRIPTION: sandcore; dark blue with light decoration.

CONDITION: part of foot and lip broken away; severely weathered; colors of decoration undeterminable. PROVENANCE: M. C. Borden sale, 1913. PARALLELS: *Fossing* 74–75 and fig. 52; *von Saldern, Oppenländer* no. 127 with other parallels.

8 *Jug*

Eastern Mediterranean
Sixth–Fourth Century B.C.
Moore Collection, 1955.6.8
H. 7.5 cm.

DESCRIPTION: sandcore; similar to cat. no. 7, narrower at shoulder; colors undeterminable. CONDITION: intact; severely weathered. BIBLIOGRAPHY: *Kouchakji* no. 8.

9 *Jug*

Eastern Mediterranean
Sixth–Fourth Century B.C.
Van Volkenburgh Bequest, 1940.265
H. 9.7 cm.

DESCRIPTION: sandcore; similar to cat. no. 7; dark blue with light blue and yellow zigzag band; yellow thread around neck and mouth. CONDITION: fragmentary and heavily restored; the few original fragments are quite weathered.

8, 7, 9

10, 11

10 *Aryballos*

Eastern Mediterranean
Sixth–Fourth Century B.C.
Moore Collection, 1955.6.237
H. 6.5 cm.

The round-bottomed shape of this aryballos is closer to one of the common New Kingdom sandcore vessels, the lentoid flask (cat. no. 2 above) than to contemporary Greek pottery forms.

DESCRIPTION: sandcore; dark blue with one yellow and one blue handle; light blue and yellow zigzag band; yellow thread encircles rim. CONDITION: intact; yellow weathered. PROVENANCE: said to have come from Egypt. BIBLIOGRAPHY: *Kouchakji* no. 7b. PARALLELS: *Fossing* 72–74, fig. 48; for examples with two color handles, see *von Saldern, Oppenländer* nos. 143 and 144, with other parallels.

11 *Aryballos*

Eastern Mediterranean
Sixth–Fourth Century B.C.
Van Volkenburgh Bequest, 1940.264
H. 7.3 cm.

DESCRIPTION: sandcore; similar to cat. no. 10; dark blue handles. CONDITION: intact; somewhat weathered, especially the decoration.

12 Cat. no. 12 has been deleted.

13 *Amphoriskos*

Eastern Mediterranean
Sixth–Fourth Century B.C.
Mansfield Collection, 1930.379
H. 9.0 cm.

This shape is a miniature version of a type of storage vessel produced by Greek potters from the sixth century B.C. onwards.

DESCRIPTION: sandcore; transparent dark blue; band of yellow and pale blue-horizontal and zigzag lines just below shoulder, at point of maximum diameter; light blue thread around mouth and knob base. CONDITION: intact; some iridescent weathering around neck and handles. PARALLELS: *Fossing* 71, note 2, for excavated examples, and fig. 47.

14 *Amphoriskos*

Eastern Mediterranean
Sixth–Fourth Century B.C.
Moore Collection, 1955.6.7
H. 7.5 cm.

DESCRIPTION: sandcore; similar to cat. no. 13; body fluted slightly at its widest point. CONDITION: intact; decoration weathered. BIBLIOGRAPHY: *Kouchakji* no. 7. PARALLELS: *von Saldern, Oppenländer* no. 146.

15 *Amphoriskos*

Eastern Mediterranean
Sixth–Fourth Century B.C.
Mansfield Collection, 1930.373
H. 8.25 cm.

DESCRIPTION: sandcore; similar to cat. no. 13; fluted body; yellow thread around the mouth and base. CONDITION: intact; slightly weathered.

16 *Amphoriskos*

Eastern Mediterranean
Possibly Sixth–Fourth Century B.C.
Moore Collection, 1955.6.3
H. 8.4 cm.

This vessel is a poorly executed and irregular example of the standard sandcore amphoriskos. The lack of zigzag decoration is unusual.

DESCRIPTION: sandcore; bubbly glass; opaque medium greenish blue; yellow thread around the mouth; uneven red thread spiralling awkwardly around body, up to and around neck. CONDITION: left handle restored; some tension cracks. BIBLIOGRAPHY: *Eisen* 122, pl. 4a; *Kouchakji* no. 3. PARALLELS: BM inv. 69.6–24.7, a turquoise trefoil oinochoe; *von Saldern, Oppenländer* no. 147, a dark green amphoriskos.

17 *Amphoriskos*

Eastern Mediterranean
Sixth–Fourth Century B.C.
Mansfield Collection, 1930.392
H. 8.75 cm.

16, 17

DESCRIPTION: sandcore; similar to cat. no. 13; fluted body; dark blue; yellow and pale blue zigzag band, yellow thread continuing around shoulder and neck; pale blue thread around mouth. CONDITION: rim and one handle chipped; surface virtually unweathered.

18 *Amphoriskos*

Eastern Mediterranean
Sixth–Fourth Century B.C.
Moore Collection, 1955.6.5.
H. 11.1 cm.

DESCRIPTION: sandcore; similar to cat. no. 13, but more elongated; dark blue body, handles, and base; body fluted

13, 14, 15

18, 19, 20, 21

at widest point; white zigzag band and horizontal threads; white thread around mouth and base. CONDITION: broken, with some restorations. BIBLIOGRAPHY: *Kouchakji* no. 5. PARALLELS: *von Saldern, Oppenländer* nos. 141, 217, and 218.

19 *Amphoriskos*

Eastern Mediterranean
Sixth–Fourth Century B.C.
Anonymous Gift, 1937. 178
H. 10.5 cm.

DESCRIPTION: sandcore; similar to cat. no. 18; body fluted; white spiral thread around the body and a yellow band, partially zigzag, at the point of maximum diameter; white thread around mouth; yellow thread around base. CONDITION: intact; yellow somewhat weathered. PROVENANCE: said to be from Capua; Mrs. R. Berens, sale Sotheby's, July 1923.

20 *Amphoriskos*

Eastern Mediterranean
Sixth–Fourth Century B.C.
Moore Collection, 1955.6.6
H. 12.0 cm.

This and the following vessel are part of a large variant group of sandcore amphoriskoi in which the characteristic light on dark form of decoration is reversed. Purple, blue, and green occur on a white ground, giving a distinctive appearance that may reflect a single workshop or geographical area.

DESCRIPTION: sandcore; white with wide purple zigzag band and a purple thread to the base of the handles; purple thread around mouth; fluted body. CONDITION: foot and mouth partially restored; some pitting. BIBLIOGRAPHY: *Kouchakji* no. 6. PARALLELS: *Fossing* 69–70, especially 69 note 2, with sixth century stratified finds.

21 *Amphoriskos*

Eastern Mediterranean
Sixth–Fourth Century B.C.
Mansfield Collection, 1930.409
H. 12.5 cm.

DESCRIPTION: sandcore; similar to cat. no. 20; white with purple decoration; purple thread around mouth and base. CONDITION: broken and repaired with some restoration; severely weathered. PROVENANCE: Khayat, 1909.

22 *Alabastron*

Eastern Mediterranean
Sixth–Fourth Century B.C.
Moore Collection, 1955.6.4
H. 8.0 cm.

This nearly cylindrical alabastron with a rounded bottom, short neck, and wide mouth represents the standard form, color scheme, and decorative format for alabastra of the sixth through the fourth century. The shape is close to that of Greek pottery alabastra of the fifth century B.C.

DESCRIPTION: sandcore; dark blue; yellow and pale blue

zigzag band around middle of body between horizontal yellow bands; yellow thread around mouth; dark blue handles applied after decoration. CONDITION: intact; virtually unweathered. BIBLIOGRAPHY: *Eisen* 122, pl. 4d; *Kouchakji* no. 4. PARALLELS: *Fossing* 63, note 1 for excavated examples, and fig. 34.

23 *Alabastron*

> Eastern Mediterranean
> Sixth–Fourth Century B.C.
> Van Volkenburgh Bequest, 1940.263
> H. 10.25 cm.

DESCRIPTION: sandcore; similar to cat. no. 22; body and handles blue green. CONDITION: part of rim restored; lower ends of handles broken away.

24 *Alabastron*

> Eastern Mediterranean
> Sixth–Fourth Century B.C.
> Mansfield Collection, 1930.378
> H. 10.0 cm.

DESCRIPTION: sandcore; similar to cat. no. 22; body and handles dark blue green. CONDITION: yellow thread around rim chipped; decoration somewhat weathered.

25 *Alabastron*

> Eastern Mediterranean
> Sixth–Fourth Century B.C.
> Mansfield Collection, 1930.375
> H. 9.5 cm.

Although the form and decoration of this vessel are basically that of a typical alabastron, the body increases in diameter from the neck towards the base, and there is no distinct shoulder. These modifications in shape point to later forms of alabastra. The decoration covers more of the surface here than in earlier examples, but the color scheme remains the same.

DESCRIPTION: sandcore; dark blue body and handles; yellow and pale blue decoration (yellow applied first); lower horizontal bands in two colors merge with zigzag band. CONDITION: rim chipped. PARALLELS: *Fossing* fig. 35; *von Saldern, Oppenländer* no. 166.

26 *Jug*

> Eastern Mediterranean
> Fourth–Third Century B.C.
> Moore Collection, 1955.6.2
> H. 11.5 cm.

More stable than the earlier forms, the body of this jug narrows only slightly at its base. The feather pattern succeeds zigzag decoration in the Hellenistic period, although the color scheme generally remains the same.

DESCRIPTION: sandcore; body, handles, and base ring dark blue; yellow feather decoration; yellow thread on mouth and neck. CONDITION: intact, quite weathered. BIBLIOGRAPHY: *Eisen*, pl. 4e; *Kouchakji* no. 2. PARALLELS: *Fossing* 94–96, fig. 65.

27 *Amphoriskos*

> Eastern Mediterranean
> Third–First Century B.C.

24, 23, 22, 25

Whiting Collection, 1912.935
H. 15.3 cm.

The form of this vessel is typical of glass amphoriskoi of the Hellenistic period. Especially characteristic are the elongated neck and the extension of the decoration to cover the entire vessel. The use of dark blue for the body and yellow and pale blue for the decoration continues from the earlier series, as does the less frequent use of white. The feather decoration relates this vessel to jugs of the fourth to the third century B.C., suggesting a position fairly early in the Hellenistic series.

DESCRIPTION: sandcore; dark blue with white decoration combining feather and dragged patterns; dark blue handles and base. CONDITION: broken and repaired with some restoration of the body; surface dull, with some white weathering. PARALLELS: *von Saldern, Oppenländer* no. 209, with additional parallels.

28 *Amphoriskos*

Eastern Mediterranean
Second–First Century B.C.
Mansfield Collection, 1930.377
H. 15.3 cm.

DESCRIPTION: sandcore; similar to cat. no. 27. CONDITION: broken and repaired with some restoration of the body; surface dull, with some white weathering. PARALLELS: *von Saldern, Oppenländer* no. 209, with additional parallels.

29 *Amphoriskos*

Eastern Mediterranean
Second–First Century B.C.

Anonymous Gift, 1937.179
Pres. H. 12.5 cm.

DESCRIPTION: sandcore; similar to cat. no. 27; dark blue green with red and white dragged decoration. CONDITION: base and one handle broken away; part of other handle restored; severely weathered; lacquered. PROVENANCE: Mrs. R. Berens, sale Sotheby's, July 1923. PARALLELS: *von Saldern, Oppenländer* no. 207.

30 *Amphoriskos*

Eastern Mediterranean
Second–First Century B.C.
Mansfield Collection, 1930.411
Pres. H. 12.5 cm.

DESCRIPTION: sandcore; similar to cat. no. 27, but with more conical profile; very dark blue, nearly black, with alternating red and pale blue decoration. CONDITION: handles and base broken away; neck and body broken and repaired; white weathering, especially of pale blue decoration. PROVENANCE: said to have been from Tyre; Khayat, 1909.

31 *Amphoriskos*

Eastern Mediterranean
Second–First Century B.C.
Yale University Art Gallery, 1955.6.369
Pres. H. 13 cm.

A slightly different color scheme and the traces of transparent green handles and base probably indicate a date a little later in the Hellenistic series.

DESCRIPTION: sandcore; similar to cat. no. 27, but with more conical profile; dark blue green with red and yellow dragged decoration. CONDITION: handles and base missing; surface excellent on one side, weathered on the other.

26, 29, 27

32 Alabastron

Eastern Mediterranean
Third–First Century B.C.
Moore Collection, 1955.6.48
Pres. H. 10 cm.

This alabastron has the thin cylindrical body, fairly distinct shoulder, vestigal handles, and feather pattern characteristic of many examples in the Hellenistic period.

DESCRIPTION: sandcore; body and handles dark blue; decoration of indeterminable color.   CONDITION: mouth broken away, neck partly restored; body broken and repaired; severely weathered.   BIBLIOGRAPHY: *Kouchakji* no. 50. PARALLELS: *von Saldern, Oppenländer* no. 182.

33 Alabastron

Eastern Mediterranean
Second–First Century B.C.
Mansfield Collection, 1930.380
H. 14.3 cm.

Typical of another large group of Hellenistic alabastra, this example has a sacklike body and small lug handles.

DESCRIPTION: sandcore; dark blue with white dragged decoration and horizontal bands. CONDITION: broken, with part of the bottom missing; severely weathered; colors visible only at breaks.

32, 33

Hellenistic and Roman Mold-Pressed Vessels

SECOND CENTURY B.C.–FIRST CENTURY A.D.

34 *Mold-Pressed Conical Bowl*

Eastern Mediterranean
Second–First Century B.C.
Mansfield Collection, 1930.381
H. 8.5 cm., D. 14.5 cm.

Although known as early as the Archaic period, mold-pressed glass vessels were primarily characteristic of the Hellenistic and early Roman periods. The manufacturing process was a slow one in which ground, broken, or molten glass was first heated in a mold until it fused, then cooled to permit removal from the mold. The final surface was usually achieved by wheel or fire-polishing after the vessel was removed from the mold, and wheel-cut grooves were often added as decoration. In the Hellenistic period most mold-pressed vessels were monochrome, but in the early Roman period the same technique was used to produce mosaic glass vessels.

This brown bowl and the following three bowls represent a group of simply shaped vessels with minimal decoration which, on the basis of recent finds in Palestine, can be placed in the Hellenistic period.

DESCRIPTION: mold-pressed; two wheel-cut grooves on the exterior, three wide grooves on the interior; interior wheel-polished, exterior fire-polished; brown. CONDITION: unbroken but with strain cracks; white weathering on interior and near rim on exterior. PARALLELS: for excavated parallels in Palestine, see Weinberg, "Tel Anafa" 19, figs. 1–5; cf. also *von Saldern, Oppenländer* no. 244.

35 *Hemispherical Bowl*

Eastern Mediterranean
Second–Early First Century B.C.
Moore Collection, 1955.6.9
H. 7.3 cm., D. 12.5 cm.

DESCRIPTION: mold-pressed; two wheel-cut grooves on the interior below rim; brown. CONDITION: broken and repaired, with some restoration; thick white weathering. PROVENANCE: Moore Collection no. 688. BIBLIOGRAPHY: *Eisen* 151, pl. 7a; *Kouchakji* no. 9. PARALLELS: Weinberg, "Tel Anafa" 20, profile 12; *Hayes, Toronto* no. 40, citing others.

36 *Cylindrical Bowl*

Eastern Mediterranean
Second–First Century B.C.
Moore Collection, 1955.6.10
H. 6.1 cm., D. 11.2 cm.

DESCRIPTION: mold-pressed; nearly vertical sides; flattened bottom; two wheel-cut grooves on the interior below the rim; yellow streaked with purple. CONDITION: intact; pitted surface, white and iridescent weathering. BIBLIOGRAPHY: *Kouchakji* no. 10. PARALLELS: Weinberg, "Notes" 40, profile 9; for a later date, see *Hayes, Toronto* no. 42.

37 *Shallow Bowl*

Eastern Mediterranean
Second–First Century B.C.

38, 39

Lehman Gift, 1953.28.34
H. 4.2 cm., D. 15.2 cm.

This and similar vessels provide early examples of the use of glass in its natural state, without the addition of intentional coloring agents.

DESCRIPTION: mold-pressed; wheel-cut lines on the interior below the rim and towards the center; pale green. CONDITION: intact; surface pitted, dull, and slightly iridescent. PROVENANCE: John D. Rockefeller, Jr. no. 69; Duveen Brothers no. 18. PARALLELS: Weinberg, "Tel Anafa" 20, profile 17; Weinberg, "Notes" 40, profile 16; for a later date see *Isings* type 18 and *Hayes, Toronto* no. 44.

34

38 *Ribbon Glass Bowl*

Eastern Mediterranean, possibly Alexandria, or Italy
First Century B.C.
Moore Collection, 1955.6.28
H. 4.0 cm., D. 9.1 cm.

This shallow bowl is an example of a type of mosaic glass in which strips of different colors were fused in a mold like that used for the mold-pressed mono-chrome bowls. This example has been compared to the glass from the Antikythera shipwreck of the first century B.C., especially to a bowl of the same shape and technique, now in Athens, and to another in the Metropolitan Museum, New York, part of the larger "Antikythera Group."

DESCRIPTION: mold-pressed; eight colored bands in this order: green, colorless, yellow, yellow bordered by red, green, yellow, colorless, and red, sometimes with narrow strips of colorless glass between them; colorless twisted strand rim and colorless base formed separately and added. CONDITION: broken and repaired; surface pitted. PROVENANCE: Moore Collection no. 727. BIBLIOGRAPHY: *Eisen* 163, pl. 35a; *Kouchakji* no. 30; Oliver, "Millefiori Glass" 56. PARALLELS: those cited by Oliver; *Smith, Corning* no. 147, now in the collection of Jerome Strauss; *von Saldern, Oppenländer* no. 310, and two *millefiori* examples, nos. 309 and 311.

35

39 *Bowl*

Eastern Mediterranean
First Century B.C.–First Century A.D.
Moore Collection, 1955.6.27
H. 3.7 cm., D. 6.8 cm.

This bowl appears to have been either wheel-cut from a molded blank, or molded and finished by wheel-polishing. In either case, the bowl and its foot were made as one piece. The form is comparable to a group of ribbon glass bowls of the first century B.C. (see cat.

36

37

no. 38), although these have trailed on or added bases. The shape is also found in Arretine ware.

DESCRIPTION: probably mold-pressed and wheel-polished; opaque red. CONDITION: intact; green and white weathering, especially on the interior. BIBLIOGRAPHY: *Kouchakji* no. 29. PARALLELS: Weinberg, "Tel Anafa" 21, profile 30, as probably cut or polished; *von Saldern, Oppenländer* nos. 288–90. For the Arretine ware vessels, see *Dragendorff* type 40.

40 *Ribbed Bowl*

Eastern Mediterranean
First Century B.C.–First Century A.D.
Moore Collection, 1955.6.238
H. 4.5 cm., D. 17.3 cm.

Molded ribbed, or "pillar molded" bowls are a later variation of the plain molded bowls of the Hellenistic period. The ribs of the earliest examples were formed by tooling; these probably date from the second century B.C. In the more common form represented by this bowl the ribs were molded with the vessel in one step. The interior and the exterior rim were wheel-polished, often slicing off the tops of the molded ribs. The ribs are evenly spaced and of uniform size. In the Syro-Palestinian area the earliest bowls are monochrome, but by the first century B.C. to the first century A.D. monochrome and mosaic glass bowls coexist in shallow and deep forms. The dark blue and white patterns of this bowl imitate the more precious agate or onyx. The wheel-cut grooves which decorate the interior are a feature continued from the plain Hellenistic bowls.

DESCRIPTION: mold-pressed; interior wheel-polished; two wheel-cut circles near the center of the interior, and two further out; exterior fire-polished, then wheel-polished above the ribs; dark blue with white spiral elements. CONDITION: broken and repaired, a small restoration towards the bottom; some iridescent weathering, especially affecting the white. BIBLIOGRAPHY: *Kouchakji* no. 24a. PARALLELS: *Isings* type 3a; Weinberg, "Tel Anafa" 24–27, 21 for profiles 31–37; Weinberg, "Notes" 36–39, 41 for profiles 39–45; a fragment from Dura-Europos, *Clairmont, Dura* no. 101.

41 *Deep Ribbed Bowl*

Eastern Mediterranean
First Century B.C.–First Century A.D.
Moore Collection, 1955.6.17
H. 5.2 cm., D. 10.3 cm.

DESCRIPTION: mold-pressed; interior and exterior above the ribs wheel-polished; dark blue with white and yellow spiral elements. CONDITION: intact; wheel-polishing lines visible. PROVENANCE: possibly Kouchakji Frères, 1922. BIBLIOGRAPHY: *Eisen* pl. 32 and IV; *Kouchakji* no. 17. PARALLELS: *Isings* type 3b.

42 *Ribbed Bowl*

Eastern Mediterranean
First Century B.C.–First Century A.D.
Gift of Henry F. Pearson, B.A. 1928, B.F.A. 1933, 1943.54
H. 4.4 cm., D. 15.3 cm.

The monochrome ribbed bowls are contemporary but less luxurious versions of the mosaic glass bowls. They generally occur in the same colors as the plain Hellenistic bowls, brown, natural pale green, and occasionally dark blue.

DESCRIPTION: mold-pressed; two wheel-cut lines on the interior below the rim; monochrome pale bluish green. CONDITION: broken and repaired with parts of the rim missing; light brown enamel weathering.

43 *Ribbed Bowl*

Eastern Mediterranean
First Century B.C.–First Century A.D.
Lehman Gift, 1953.28.35
H. 4.3 cm., D. 15.1 cm.

DESCRIPTION: mold-pressed; similar to cat. no. 42; interior wheel-polished, exterior fire-polished. CONDITION: intact; white and iridescent weathering. PROVENANCE: John D. Rockefeller, Jr. no. 59; Duveen Brothers no. 28.

44 *Ribbed Bowl*

Eastern Mediterranean
First Century B.C.–First Century A.D.
Moore Collection, 1955.6.40
H. 4.6 cm., D. 15.4 cm.

DESCRIPTION: mold-pressed; similar to cat. no. 42; interior wheel-polished, exterior fire-polished and wheel-polished above the ribs; wheel-cut circle in the center bottom of the interior, another farther out; transparent monochrome brown. CONDITION: rim chipped and repaired; surface pitted; white and iridescent weathering. PROVENANCE: said to have been found at Beit Shean, Palestine; Khayat, 1928; Moore Collection no. 838. BIBLIOGRAPHY: *Kouchakji* no. 42.

40

41

16 MOLD-PRESSED VESSELS

45 Patella Cup

Probably Eastern Mediterranean
First Century B.C.–First Century A.D.
Moore Collection, 1955.6.24
H. 4.2 cm., D. 8.8 cm.

Most monochrome examples of this shape are opaque,
although a number of transparent dark green, blue,
and golden brown bowls have survived; all are
intentionally colored. The same shape is produced in
mosaic glass with a trailed-on base ring. While the
form may ultimately derive from a metal prototype,
the closest parallels known to date are found in
Arretine ware.

DESCRIPTION: mold-pressed in one piece; wheel-polished;
opaque white. CONDITION: broken and repaired, with
some restorations. BIBLIOGRAPHY: *Eisen* 210, pl. 36a and
b; *Kouchakji* no. 26. PARALLELS: *Isings* type 2; *Smith, Corning*
nos. 179a–g, especially no. 179g (white); *von Saldern,
Oppenländer* nos. 278–85, especially no. 278 (white). For the
shape in Arretine ware, see *Dragendorff* type 27.

45

46 Patella Cup

Probably Eastern Mediterranean
First Century B.C.–First Century A.D.
Moore Collection, 1955.6.25
H. 4.2 cm., D. 8.7 cm.

DESCRIPTION: mold-pressed; similar to cat. no. 45; wheel-polished;
opaque red. CONDITION: thick crust of white
weathering with brown layer on top. BIBLIOGRAPHY:
Eisen 210, pl. 36c and d; *Kouchakji* no. 27.

46

47 Patella Cup

Eastern Mediterranean
First Century B.C.–First Century A.D.
Moore Collection, 1955.6.26
H. 4.2 cm., D. 7.2 cm.

DESCRIPTION: mold-pressed; similar to cat. no. 45; trans-parent
emerald green. CONDITION: intact; iridescent with
traces of white weathering; spherical bubbles. BIBLIOG-RAPHY:
Kouchakji no. 28.

47

48 Mosaic Glass Patella Cup

Eastern Mediterranean
Late First Century B.C.–First Century A.D.
Mansfield Collection, 1930.422
H. 4.5 cm., D. 10 cm.

Mosaic glass is a variant of the mold-pressed technique
in which the form and decoration of the vessel are

48

49

produced simultaneously through the fusion of numerous small mosaiclike elements. Each small element is a thin slice of a cane previously fused into a geometric, marbled, or floral pattern. Occasionally faces, animals, and birds were also used, generally as accents. These discs were arranged in a mold and held in place by a second mold that fitted into the first. The mold was heated until the glass elements fused, then cooled and finished in the same fashion as the monochrome vessels. A separate rim consisting of a twisted multicolored cane was often added.

Several varieties of mosaic glass were produced during the late Hellenistic and early Roman period, including marbled glass, lace glass, color-band, and gold-band glass, as well as the millefiori glass that was so widely imitated by Venetian glassmakers of the sixteenth and seventeenth centuries onwards. All were considered luxury items. After the discovery of glass blowing, mosaic glass vessels were replaced by quickly made blown imitations. The technique seems to have died out completely by the end of the first century A.D.

The form of this mosaic glass cup is the same as that of the contemporary monochrome cups except that a trailed-on base ring of a solid color replaces the molded and ground foot. Like the monochrome cups, most mosaic glass vessels were wheel-polished.

DESCRIPTION: mold-pressed, base ring trailed on; mosaic elements: red rod surrounded by white rods in a transparent emerald green matrix; base ring green with traces of red. CONDITION: broken and repaired; brown weathering

on the interior; exterior probably repolished in modern times. PROVENANCE: said to have been found near Aleppo, Syria; Khayat, 1927; Mansfield Collection no. 246. PARALLELS: for an example from Dura-Europos, tomb 24 (first half of the first century A.D.), see *Clairmont, Dura* 11, no. 15; see also *Isings* type 2; *von Saldern, Oppenländer* nos. 314–21.

49 *Millefiori Patella Cup*

Eastern Mediterranean
Late First Century B.C.–First Century A.D.
Moore Collection, 1955.6.21
H. 4.0 cm., D. 9.7 cm.

DESCRIPTION: mold-pressed; similar to cat. no. 48; transparent purple with three different elements: a compound floral element of transparent blue encircled with yellow and having a white rod center in a blue matrix; a compound floral element of transparent blue encircled with white in a purple matrix; a white rod within a white circle in a purple matrix. Opaque olive green base ring trailed on. CONDITION: intact; possibly modern repolishing. BIBLIOGRAPHY: *Kouchakji* no. 23.

50 *Mosaic Glass Patella Cup*

Eastern Mediterranean
Late First Century B.C.–First Century A.D.
Mansfield Collection, 1930.451
H. 4.0 cm., D. 8.7 cm.

DESCRIPTION: mold-pressed; similar to cat. no. 48; mosaic elements consisting of: 1) a yellow core surrounded by red within a circle of white rods set in purple; 2) groups of seven brown rods, each surrounded by yellow, fused and set in transparent brown; 3) a similar fused group of blue rods, each surrounded by white; and 4) a similar group with green rods encircled by yellow; some of the elements were set in and fused sideways creating large areas of one color; all these elements in a light green matrix. Trailed-on green and white base ring. CONDITION: broken and repaired with small restorations; interior surface dull, exterior somewhat iridescent. PROVENANCE: said to have been found near Honis (Homs?) Syria; Khayat, 1930; Mansfield Collection no. 250.

50, 51, 52

53

51 *Mosaic Glass Patella Cup*

Eastern Mediterranean
Late First Century B.C.–First Century A.D.
Moore Collection, 1955.6.22
H. 4.5 cm., D. 9.9 cm.

DESCRIPTION: mold-pressed; similar to cat. no. 48; two different elements: a blue core surrounded by white or yellow rods in a blue matrix; a red core within white or yellow rods in a green matrix. The base ring is probably green. CONDITION: broken and repaired; brown weathering; pitted surface. PROVENANCE: Kouchakji Frères, 1923. BIBLIOGRAPHY: *Eisen* 210, pls. 36g and IV; *Kouchakji* no. 24.

52 *Mosaic Glass Patella Cup*

Eastern Mediterranean
Late First Century B.C.–First Century A.D.
Moore Collection, 1955.6.23
H. 3.8 cm., D. 9.6 cm.

DESCRIPTION: mold-pressed; similar to cat. no. 48; three different elements: white spirals in a blue matrix; white spirals in a purplish brown matrix; white or yellow rods in

a dark blue matrix; dark base ring. CONDITION: piece missing from rim; white weathering, often obscuring colors and patterns. BIBLIOGRAPHY: *Eisen* 198, pl. IV; *Kouchakji* no. 25.

53 *Mosaic Glass Bowl*

Probably Eastern Mediterranean
Late Second–First Century B.C.
Moore Collection, 1955.6.20
H. 7.8 cm., D. 14.1 cm.

This vessel belongs to a group of hemispherical bowls related by their mosaic elements and opaque tesserae to a bowl with a flaring rim now in the Metropolitan Museum of Art, New York, which is dated by Andrew Oliver, Jr. on the basis of its similarity to vessels recovered from the Antikythera shipwreck. The bowls share a colorless matrix with yellow spirals having a white center in a blue ring, a twisted strand rim, and opaque tesserae of varying colors, in this case purple, green, white, and blue. The rim is blue and opaque white. All of the hemispherical bowls are wheel-polished both on the interior and the exterior.

DESCRIPTION: mold-pressed; wheel-polished; mosaic pattern as described above. CONDITION: intact; exterior slightly weathered. PROVENANCE: probably the "ancient glass 'millefiori' bowl of dominant yellow color" bought by Mrs. Moore from Harold Woodbury Parsons on 5 December 1928. According to Parsons, the bowl was found at Kertsch and was formerly in the Kanenko Collection in Kiev. BIBLIOGRAPHY: *Kouchakji* no. 21; Oliver, "Millefiori Glass" 60, fig. 19. PARALLELS: those cited by Oliver: BM inv. 73.8–20.419 and inv. 73.8–20.420 (hemispherical) and MMA inv. 91.1.1399 (outsplayed rim, ring base).

54 *Mosaic Glass Plate*

Eastern Mediterranean
First Century B.C.
Moore Collection, 1955.6.16
H. 2.1 cm., D. 15.6 cm.

The raised ring in the center of this plate suggests that it may have been lathe cut from a blank rather than mold-pressed in the manner typical of other mosaic glass vessels, a technical difference which points to an early date. The trailed-on base ring is consistent with those on the small mosaic glass bowls.

DESCRIPTION: probably lathe cut from a millefiori blank; three different elements: yellow spirals in a transparent blue matrix; a white core in red within a circle of eight yellow dots, the whole encircled by red and set in a purple matrix; at least two elements with a red core encircled by white and surrounded by white dots in a dark, probably purple, matrix. Trailed-on base ring of indeterminable color. CONDITION: broken and repaired; white weathering. PROVENANCE: Moore Collection no. 795. BIBLIOGRAPHY: *Eisen* 197, pl. 30a; *Kouchakji* no. 16; *Smith, Corning* 82–83; Amyx, *Echoes* no. 163. PARALLELS: *Smith, Corning* no. 134, now MMA, inv. 59.11.6; TMA inv. 23.1397; *Sammlung E. und M. Kofler-Truniger Luzern*, exhibition catalogue, Zürich 1974, no. 459, pl. 36.

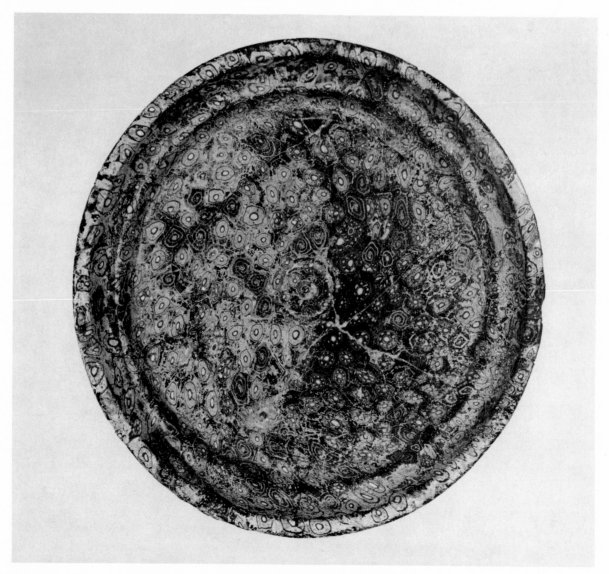

55

55 Mosaic Glass Beaker or Deep Bowl

Eastern Mediterranean or Italy
First Century B.C.–First Century A.D.
Moore Collection, 1955.6.15
H. 8.9 cm., D. 11.5 cm.

No parallel for this shape in mosaic glass has come to my attention, although shallow bowls with flaring rims and ring bases were recovered from the Antikythera shipwreck of the first century B.C. and exist elsewhere in collections. One such bowl, in the Oppenländer Collection, has white rods in a purple matrix like this cup, its shape dating this particular variety of mosaic glass to as early as the first century B.C. Shallow segmental dishes with white and yellow rods were found at Pompeii, and fragments of other vessels have turned up in numerous excavations, generally of first century A.D. date.

DESCRIPTION: mold-pressed; wheel-cut groove in the rim, two more on the exterior below the rim; purple with white rods. CONDITION: bottom broken and repaired with a few fragments missing. PROVENANCE: Kouchakji Frères, 1923; Moore Collection no. 758. BIBLIOGRAPHY: *Eisen* 197, pl. 29; *Kouchakji* no. 15. PARALLELS: for the shallow bowls with flaring rims, see Oliver, "Millefiori Glass" 56–57, figs. 10–12; *von Saldern, Oppenländer* nos. 312 and 313, the latter with white rods in a purple matrix. The shallow dishes from Pompeii are now in the Museo Nazionale Archeologico in Naples: inv. 13586 (purple with white rods); inv. 13599 (purple with white rods); inv. 109434 (green with yellow rods, a common type). There is also a bowl with no number and of uncertain provenance (blue with white and yellow rods) which is a close parallel to these three shallow dishes. Other shallow dishes include Axel von Saldern, "Ancient Glass in Split," *JGS* 6 (1964) 43–44, no. 4; and *Smith, Corning* no. 133, now CMG inv. 55.1.80. For a bottle with white rods in a green matrix, see *Smith, Corning* no. 141.

Early Roman Vessels

BLOWN, FIRST CENTURY B.C.–
FIRST CENTURY A.D.

56 *Unguentarium*

> Eastern Mediterranean
> First Century A.D.
> Moore Collection, 1955.6.62
> H. 5.7 cm.

Unguentaria, or perfume bottles, are probably the earliest blown glass vessels. In their simplest form they are merely a bubble on the end of the blow pipe, with little modification beyond a short neck and a flattened base. Vessels of this type have been found with mold-pressed bowls in late Republican and Augustan tombs at numerous Italian sites, and the earliest finds of blown glass in the eastern Mediterranean are a few small bottles from mid-first century B.C. contexts in Israel. Many of these early bottles were intentionally colored, although some forms, such as the tubular unguentarium (cat. no. 78, below) were generally natural pale green. The use of opaque glass and rich colors is a dominant feature of glass to the end of the first century A.D. The opaque green of this example, as well as its shape, place it within the first half of the first century A.D.

DESCRIPTION: free-blown; rim folded in; opaque dark green. CONDITION: intact; pale brown enamel weathering. PROVENANCE: Moore Collection no. 654. BIBLIOGRAPHY: *Eisen* 292, pl. 89; *Kouchakji* no. 65. PARALLELS: *Isings* type 26a; on the evidence for the discovery and dating of early blown glass, see Grose, "Early Blown Glass," especially p. 25–27 for small blown unguentaria.

57 *Unguentarium*

> Eastern Mediterranean or Italy
> First Century A.D.
> Moore Collection, 1955.6.45
> Pres. H. 8.6 cm.

Within the context of the first blown vessels, this small bottle represents an early attempt to alter the basic shape of the bubble. Bottles of this form occur both in the rich transparent colors characteristic of the first century A.D. and in color-band glass combining bands of blue, green, brown, and colorless glass, sometimes including a gold band. There are numerous examples of this shape from Aquileia suggesting that some vessels of this type were made there, but the variations among these Aquileia bottles indicates that they were probably free-blown rather than mold-blown as Isings believes.

DESCRIPTION: free-blown; transparent dark blue. CONDITION: rim restored; negligible weathering. PROVENANCE: Moore Collection no. 718. BIBLIOGRAPHY: *Eisen* 214, pl. 42; *Kouchakji* no. 47. PARALLELS: *Isings* type 7; *Calvi, Aquileia* pl. 3, nos. 3–4; *Auth, Newark* no. 49, with blown and color-band parallels.

58 *Bottle*

> Eastern Mediterranean
> First Century A.D.
> Lehman Gift, 1953.28.10
> Pres. H. 7.2 cm.

The globular body of this dark blue bottle was tooled while still hot to create a distinct shoulder. The form is unusual, but there are parallels, including one of the same color from Aquileia.

DESCRIPTION: free-blown; tooled line at shoulder; transparent dark blue. CONDITION: mouth and upper section of neck broken away; iridescent. PROVENANCE: John D. Rockefeller, Jr. no. 15; Duveen Brothers no. 13. PARALLELS: *Calvi, Aquileia* pl. 4, no. 2; sale Sotheby Parke Bernet, New York 8 May 1976, lot 201 (purple).

59 *Miniature Perfume Bottle*

> Eastern Mediterranean
> First Century A.D.
> Moore Collection, 1955.6.103
> H. 3.8 cm.

The sloping shoulder, rounded rim, and yellow color suggest that this bottle should be dated to the first half of the first century A.D.

DESCRIPTION: free-blown; rounded rim; transparent yellow. CONDITION: rim partially restored, iridescent. BIBLIOGRAPHY: *Eisen* 370, pl. 90e; *Kouchakji* no. 107. PARALLELS: *Calvi, Aquileia* pl. 3, nos. 1 and 2.

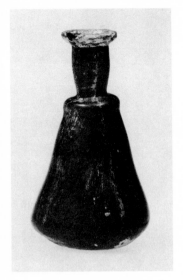

56, 57, 58, 59

60 *Flask with Two Handles*

Eastern Mediterranean
First Century A.D.
Lehman Gift, 1953.28.26
H. 7.6 cm.

DESCRIPTION: free-blown; cut-out base; rim folded out and down; ridged handles; two parallel wheel-cut lines encircle the body just below the base of the handles; transparent dark blue with white handles and rim edge. CONDITION: neck and left handle broken and repaired; right handle partially restored; rim chipped; iridescent. PROVENANCE: John D. Rockefeller, Jr. no. 57; Duveen Brothers no. 5. PARALLELS: *Smith, Corning* no. 206 (red with white handles); *Fremersdorf, Denkmäler* III, 31, pl. 31, inv. 42.185 (white) and inv. 42.186 (blue and white with blue handles) with parallels; *von Saldern, Oppenländer* no. 541 (blue) and no. 542 (blue with white handles and rim edge); *Hayes, Toronto* no. 119 (blue with brown handles), no. 120 (blue with blue handles), no. 121 (dark blue with white handles) and no. 122 (purple with white handles); *Auth, Newark* no. 93 (dark blue with white handles); *SPB, Constable-Maxwell* no. 145 (blue with yellow handles), no. 146 (blue with grayish handles), and no. 147 (blue with blue handles and white rim edge). The cut-out base on the Yale example is unusual.

61 *Bottle*

Eastern Mediterranean or Italian
First Century A.D.
Van Volkenburgh Bequest, 1940.278
H. 9.8 cm.

Although related to a class of first century piriform bottles in monochrome and splash glass, the body of this vessel has been tooled to form a cylinder that widens into a stable flattened base. This variation is rare, and a parallel from Aquileia suggests that it may have been made in Italy.

DESCRIPTION: free-blown; slightly cut-out concave base; rim folded in; body and handles pale greenish yellow. CONDITION: one handle mended; light brown weathering and iridescence. PARALLELS: *Calvi, Aquileia* pl. 1, no. 1 (dark blue with green handles). For the piriform group, see for example, *Clairmont, Dura* no. 123.

62 *Amphoriskos*

Eastern Mediterranean
First Century A.D.
Moore Collection, 1955.6.61
H. 9.5 cm.

This pale blue amphoriskos with its flat base and high shoulder is not a common shape in glass. Two examples in bronze, however, were found with bronze strigils at Pompeii. Both were equipped with knobbed lids which were attached by a woven chain to one of the two handles. Although it would be difficult to say which was the prototype, the similarity of these vessels once again demonstrates the close relationship between glass and metal vessels in the early development of glass.

DESCRIPTION: free-blown; rim folded down, up, and flattened; body and handles opaque pale blue. CONDITION: intact; brown encrustation on mouth and one handle. PROVENANCE: Moore Collection no. 828. BIBLIOGRAPHY: *Eisen* pl. 91; *Kouchakji* no. 64. PARALLELS: *Auth, Newark*

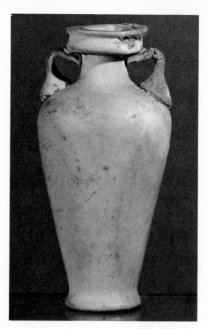

60, 61, 62

no. 352; Damascus Museum, no. unknown (Dura photo); Charles Ede, Ltd., *Roman Glass*, sale catalogue, London 1973, no. 58 illus. (royal blue); Charles Ede, Ltd., *Roman Glass*, sale catalogue, London 1976, no. 38 illus.; Vessberg, "Cyprus" pl. 6, no. 27 (pale green); *SPB, Constable-Maxwell* no. 148 (dark blue). The bronze examples are now in the Museo Nazionale Archeologico, Naples.

63 *Amphoriskos*

> Eastern Mediterranean
> First Century A.D.
> Moore Collection, 1955.6.44
> Pres. H. 8 cm.

Although found throughout the Mediterranean, amphoriskoi with pointed bases were fairly common in Italy, with finds notably at Pompeii and Aquileia. Some have distinct shoulders and short necks like this

example, while others have a more slender body that flows gradually into a long thin neck. Rims are generally rounded or folded in. Colors range from rich dark transparent hues to combinations of dark colors and white festoons. An elegant version in cameo glass from Pompeii is now in the Museo Nazionale Archeologico, Naples.

DESCRIPTION: free-blown; rim folded in and flattened; transparent dark blue. CONDITION: broken and repaired with point of base missing; surface pitted; white and iridescent weathering. PROVENANCE: Moore Collection no. 666. BIBLIOGRAPHY: *Eisen* 214, pl. 42; *Kouchakji* no. 46; *Hayes, Toronto* 52 no. 102. PARALLELS: *Isings* type 9; *Hayes, Toronto* no. 102; *Calvi, Aquileia* pl. 1, nos. 5 and 6.

64 *Amphoriskos*

> Eastern Mediterranean
> First Century A.D.
> Moore Collection, 1955.6.250
> Pres. H. 11.0 cm.

Although incomplete, this vessel represents a typical undecorated version of the tall-necked amphoriskos without a distinct shoulder.

DESCRIPTION: free-blown; brown. CONDITION: mouth and upper part of neck missing; white weathering and some surface pitting. BIBLIOGRAPHY: *Kouchakji* no. 126b.

65 *Alabastron*

> Eastern Mediterranean or Italy
> First Century A.D.
> Moore Collection, 1955.6.34
> H. 24.5 cm.

63, 64

This tall, fragile perfume container is decorated with an elegant white festoon pattern on an amber background. Its closest parallels are a group of first century vessels with festoons in the Museo Nazionale Archeologico in Naples, probably from Pompeii.

DESCRIPTION: free-blown; rim turned in; brown with white bands applied and dragged before inflation. CONDITION: broken and repaired with minor restorations; some white weathering. BIBLIOGRAPHY: *Kouchakji* no. 36. PARALLELS: Naples, Museo Nazionale Archeologico inv. 13573/325 and inv. 13571/325, probably from Pompeii; Athens, National Archaeological Museum inv. 2909, from Amorgos; Nicosia, Cyprus Museum inv. D1865-1935 and inv. D1998-1935; Munich, Antikensammlungen inv. S. H. 42, on loan from Dr. Franz Haniel; *Auth, Newark* nos. 54 and 140; E. B. Dusenbery, "Ancient Glass from the Cemeteries of Samothrace," *JGS* 9 (1967) 44, no. 32.

66 *Miniature Pseudo-Mosaic Glass Bottle*

Eastern Mediterranean
First Century A.D.
Moore Collection, 1955.6.38
H. 5.7 cm.

The multi-colored decorative banding of this small bottle is reminiscent of that used in molded gold-band bowls, pyxides, and alabastra, but the effect of the blowpipe shows clearly here in the swirling pattern of the bands. Also in contrast to the molded examples, the banding of this bottle lies solely on the exterior surface, thin bands applied before blowing that spread irregularly as the bubble expanded.

DESCRIPTION: free-blown; rounded rim; green and white bands on a brown matrix. CONDITION: mouth partially restored. PROVENANCE: possibly Kouchakji Frères, 1919; Moore Collection no. 662. BIBLIOGRAPHY: *Eisen* pl. 42; *Kouchakji* no. 40. PARALLELS: *von Saldern, Oppenländer* nos. 340, 351, and 352; *Auth, Newark* no. 53.

67 *Pseudo-Mosaic Glass Bottle*

Eastern Mediterranean
First Century A.D.
Mansfield Collection, 1930.460
Pres. H. 9.1 cm.

Another instance of the glassblower imitating an earlier technique is the irregular agatelike pattern of this brown and white bottle. The source for the visual effect is a series of mosaic glass bottles of the first century, which themselves imitated vessels carved from agate or onyx. Unlike the mosaic glass bottles, however, the decoration in this case, like that

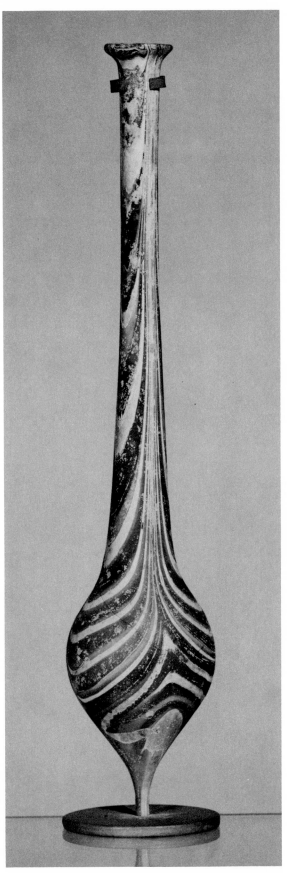

66, 67, 68

of the previous example, is only on the surface, a white thread applied to the gob of glass before the vessel was blown.

DESCRIPTION: free-blown, irregularly shaped body; dark brown with dragged white thread decoration. CONDITION: mouth broken away, with the break ground down; possibly modern repolishing. PROVENANCE: said to have been found in Jebel, Syria; Khayat, 1904; Mansfield Collection no. 151. PARALLELS: *Calvi, Aquileia* pl. 6, nos. 1–3, and pp. 36 and 38, citing Syrian parallels on p. 38, note 63.

68 *Pseudo-Mosaic Glass Bottle*

Eastern Mediterranean
First Century A.D.
Moore Collection, 1955.6.30
H. 8.6 cm.

DESCRIPTION: free-blown; similar to cat. no. 67; rim folded in; brown with white decoration. CONDITION: intact; white weathering. PROVENANCE: Moore Collection no. 658. BIBLIOGRAPHY: *Eisen* 228 pl. 42e; *Kouchakji* no. 32. PARALLELS: *von Saldern, Oppenländer* nos. 342 and 346.

69, 70, 71

69 *Pseudo-Mosaic Glass Bottle*

Eastern Mediterranean
First Century A.D.
Moore Collection, 1955.6.29
H. 8.5 cm.

Traces of two handles on the shoulder of this vessel are an unusual feature within the mosaic glass and imitation mosaic glass series. The neck and mouth are also somewhat wider than normal.

DESCRIPTION: free-blown; rim folded in and flattened; traces of handles on the shoulder only; brown with white decoration. CONDITION: broken and repaired; handles mostly broken away; white and iridescent weathering. BIBLIOGRAPHY: *Kouchakji* no. 31.

70 *Pseudo-Mosaic Glass Bottle*

Eastern Mediterranean
First Century A.D.
Moore Collection, 1955.6.36
H. 11 cm., as restored.

DESCRIPTION: free-blown; similar to cat. no. 67; translucent dark blue with white decoration. CONDITION: neck and mouth restored; lacquered. PROVENANCE: said to have been found in Syria. BIBLIOGRAPHY: *Eisen* 229, pl. 44; *Kouchakji* no. 38. PARALLELS: *von Saldern, Oppenländer* no. 350; *Fremersdorf, Denkmäler* III, pl. 19, with a rim similar to this restored rim.

71 *Bottle*

Eastern Mediterranean
First Century A.D.
Moore Collection, 1955.6.37
H. 7.3 cm., as restored.

DESCRIPTION: free-blown; similar to cat. no. 67. CONDITION: mouth restored. PROVENANCE: Moore Collection no. 721. BIBLIOGRAPHY: *Eisen* pl. 42; *Kouchakji* no. 39.

72 *Ribbed Bottle*

Eastern Mediterranean
First Century A.D.
Moore Collection, 1955.6.31
H. 4.6 cm., as restored.

The pear-shaped ribbed body with short neck seen here is characteristic of a number of small first century A.D. vessels. Monochrome and variegated examples are known. Few dated specimens survive, but among them is a colorless bottle from Dura-Europos.

DESCRIPTION: free-blown; pinched ribs; purple and white. CONDITION: lip restored; surface pitted and iridescent. PROVENANCE: Kouchakji Frères, 1919. BIBLIOGRAPHY: *Eisen* 228, pl. 42h; *Kouchakji* no. 33. PARALLELS: *Isings* type 26b. Isings' example from Dura is not ribbed, but a ribbed bottle was found at Dura in tomb 24 (see *Dura, Preliminary Report* 56, no. 11, pl. 46 and *Clairmont, Dura* 46–48, especially no. 179, pl. 23, p. 47, and note 83); *Fremersdorf, Denkmäler* III, 23, pl. 9; *Calvi, Aquileia* pl. 5, no. 5, with a larger neck.

73 *Ribbed Bottle*

Eastern Mediterranean
First Century A.D.
Moore Collection, 1955.6.32
H. 8.1 cm.

DESCRIPTION: free-blown; similar to cat. no. 72; rim folded in and flattened. CONDITION: rim and neck broken and repaired; iridescent. PROVENANCE: Kouchakji Frères, 1919. BIBLIOGRAPHY: *Eisen* 228, pl. 42g; *Kouchakji* no. 34.

72, 73

74 *Bottle*

Eastern Mediterranean
First Century A.D.
Whiting Collection, 1912.936
H. 9.5 cm.

The nearly spherical body of this bottle, its thin neck, and its everted mouth with rounded rim are characteristic of an early form also found in pseudo-mosaic glass. The spiral thread encircling the body of this example occurs most frequently on first century vessels from the eastern Mediterranean.

DESCRIPTION: free-blown; transparent yellow with a white spiral thread. CONDITION: intact; iridescent. PARALLELS: *von Saldern, Oppenländer* nos. 645, 646, 648; *Spartz, Kassel*

74, 75, 76, 77

no. 8; *Auth, Newark* no. 95. For an excavated fragment with a spiral thread from a first century context, see Grose, "Early Blown Glass" 22, fig. 6, no. 9, from the House of Livia on the Palatine, Rome, and p. 18, fig. 2, no. 8, from the Regia in the Roman Forum, with related examples cited on p. 25, note 63.

75 Bottle

Eastern Mediterranean
First Century A.D.
Moore Collection, 1955.6.70
H. 8.9 cm.

DESCRIPTION: free-blown; similar to cat. no. 74 with ovoid body; folded in rim; purple with white thread. CONDITION: intact; iridescent. PROVENANCE: Moore Collection no. 677. BIBLIOGRAPHY: *Eisen* 292, pl. 90a; *Kouchakji* no. 73. PARALLELS: *von Saldern, Oppenländer* no. 647; *Fremersdorf, Denkmäler* III, 24, pl. 12, pl. 13 right, and pl. 14 top, all from northern Italy and dated to the first century A.D.

76 Bottle

Eastern Mediterranean
First–Second Century A.D.
Moore Collection, 1955.6.217
H. 12.5 cm.

Very little of the marvered thread decoration remains on this purple flask, but from similar vessels we know that it once covered the entire surface.

The use of combed marvered thread decoration is common on Islamic glass, and its presence on this particular group of flasks has led to the suggestion that they date from the Islamic period. However, the form of these bottles, early Roman rather than Islamic, and the number of fragments of purple glass with just this sort of marvered decoration among finds from Dura-Europos, Fishbourne, and Aquileia seem to render this late date unnecessary. In addition, the purple matrix color under a decorative surface is characteristic of splash glass, another first century technique.

Blown vessels with marvered thread decoration occur again in the late Roman period, as in a fragmentary third–fourth century funnel mouthed flask from the Mithraeum at Santa Prisca in Rome, and, as stated above, experience a significant revival in the Islamic period.

DESCRIPTION: free-blown; flat base, slight neck constriction, rim folded in; purple with combed marvered thread decoration of indeterminate color. CONDITION: unbroken, but severely weathered with most of the decoration missing; white weathering and iridescence; colors of thread decoration too weathered to permit identification. PROVENANCE: Moore Collection no. 729. BIBLIOGRAPHY: *Eisen* 635, pl. 156; *Kouchakji* no. 224; *von Saldern, Oppenländer* 138, no. 384 as "possibly second century A.D." PARALLELS: *Auth, Newark* no. 237 as "early Islamic?" For the Dura fragments, see *Clairmont, Dura* 15–17, nos. 35–51, pl. XIX. For the Fishbourne bottles, see Harden and Price, "Fishbourne" 350–51, nos. 64 and 65, fig. 140. For the Aquileia bottle, see *Calvi, Aquileia* 35–36, no. 85, pl. 5, no. 4. For the shape, see *Isings* type 28, citing examples with marvered decoration. The Santa Prisca flask is discussed by Clasina Isings, "The Glass," in M. J. Vermaseren and C. C. van Essen, *The Excavations in the Mithraeum of the Church of Santa Prisca in Rome* (Leiden 1965) 518–19, no. 237, fig. 454.

77 Bottle

Eastern Mediterranean
First–Second Century A.D.
Moore Collection, 1955.6.216
H. 12.5 cm., as restored.

DESCRIPTION: free-blown; similar to cat. no. 76; purple with yellow and red combed and marvered thread decoration. CONDITION: mouth restored; broken at base of neck and repaired; fragment missing from body; iridescent. PROVENANCE: Moore Collection no. 671. BIBLIOGRAPHY: *Eisen* 635, pl. 156; *Kouchakji* no. 223; *von Saldern, Oppenländer* 138, no. 384.

78 Unguentarium

Eastern Mediterranean
First Century A.D.
Moore Collection, 1955.6.245
H. 11.4 cm.

The tubular unguentarium with a slight constriction distinguishing the body from the neck is one of the most common first century types. The body is only slightly wider than the neck, the bottom generally rounded, and the rim rounded or occasionally folded and flattened. It is usually a natural bluish green in color.

DESCRIPTION: free-blown; fire-polished rim; pale bluish green. CONDITION: intact; virtually no weathering. PROVENANCE: probably Moore Collection no. 91c. PARALLELS: *Isings* type 8.

79 Unguentarium

Eastern Mediterranean
First Century A.D.
Moore Collection, 1955.6.246
H. 10.5 cm.

DESCRIPTION: free-blown; similar to cat. no. 78. CONDITION: intact; slight iridescence. BIBLIOGRAPHY: *Kouchakji* no. 91d.

80 Bottle

Eastern Mediterranean
First–Second Century A.D.
Lehman Gift, 1953.28.22
H. 12.7 cm.

During the first and second centuries A.D. a large group of simple bottles developed from the early first century tubular and short-necked types. These vessels have the following characteristics: a body nearly one-half the total height, conical, pear-shaped,

bulbous, or close to the same diameter as the neck; a flattened base; a slight neck constriction; and a folded in and flattened rim. Most are natural pale bluish green. A few have wheel-cut lines around the shoulder, suggesting a first century A.D. date for these examples.

Terra cotta bottles of this shape with equivalent variations were common and have been found in graves at Dura-Europos among other sites. Contexts for these bottles at Dura are first century A.D. or earlier. Glass bottles appear to have gradually displaced the pottery ones after this date.

DESCRIPTION: free-blown; rim folded out, in, and flattened; pale bluish green. CONDITION: broken and repaired with a few small fragments missing; iridescent. PROVENANCE: John D. Rockefeller, Jr. no. 26; Duveen Brothers no. 33. PARALLELS: *Isings* type 28a. For the terra cotta bottles, see *Dura, Preliminary Report* 106, figs. 21–27.

81 Bottle

Eastern Mediterranean
First Century A.D.

79, 78

81, 80, 83, 82, 84

Lehman Gift, 1953.28.9
H. 9.5 cm.

The dark blue color of this bottle suggests a first century A.D. date.

DESCRIPTION: free-blown; similar to cat. no. 80; pear-shaped body; rim folded in and flattened; transparent dark blue. CONDITION: intact; iridescent. PROVENANCE: John D. Rockefeller, Jr. no. 5; Duveen Brothers no. 27.

82 *Bottle*

Eastern Mediterranean
First–Second Century A.D.
Moore Collection, 1955.6.99
H. 9.5 cm.

DESCRIPTION: free-blown; similar to cat. no. 80 with conical body; rim folded in; pale green. CONDITION: intact; surface pitted with brown weathering and iridescence. PROVENANCE: Moore Collection no. 663. BIBLIOGRAPHY: *Kouchakji* no. 103.

83 *Bottle*

Eastern Mediterranean
First–Second Century A.D.
Yale University Art Gallery, 1955.6.366
H. 11.9 cm.

DESCRIPTION: free-blown; similar to cat. no. 80 with conical

body; rim folded in; pale green. CONDITION: part of rim broken away; strain cracks on lower body; iridescent. PROVENANCE: a black number 498 on the base, possibly from Gerasa but not in the published catalogue of that site.

84 *Bottle*

Eastern Mediterranean
First–Second Century A.D.
Mansfield Collection, 1930.452
H. 16 cm.

DESCRIPTION: free-blown; similar to cat. no. 80 with pear-shaped body; rim folded in and flattened; pale green with white marvered decoration. CONDITION: broken at the neck and repaired; iridescent. PROVENANCE: Khayat, 1927; Mansfield Collection no. 248. PARALLELS: *Isings* type 28a lists some examples with marvered decoration; *Fremersdorf, Denkmäler* III, 50, pl. 106; *Fossing* 129, note 6, fig. 108.

85 *Bottle*

Eastern Mediterranean
First–Second Century A.D.
Oriental Institute, 1940.635
H. 13.2 cm.

DESCRIPTION: free-blown; similar to cat. no. 80 with pear-shaped body; rim folded in; pale green. CONDITION: intact; surface pitted and iridescent. PROVENANCE: from the Chicago excavations at Kurcoğlu, Syria.

87, 85, 86

86 *Bottle*

Eastern Mediterranean
Probably First Century A.D.
Moore Collection, 1955.6.97
H. 10.8 cm.

DESCRIPTION: free-blown; similar to cat. no. 80 with pear-shaped body; wheel-cut line around center of body; rim folded in and flattened; pale bluish green. CONDITION: intact; surface pitted and iridescent. PROVENANCE: Moore Collection no. 667. BIBLIOGRAPHY: *Eisen* 370, pl. 89b; *Kouchakji* no. 101; *Hayes, Toronto* 72, no. 242.

87 *Bottle*

Eastern Mediterranean
First–Second Century A.D.
Moore Collection, 1955.6.240
H. 11.3 cm.

DESCRIPTION: free-blown; similar to cat. no. 80 with pear-shaped body; rim folded in; pale bluish green. CONDITION: intact; surface unevenly pitted and iridescent, with some parts unweathered.

88 *Bottle*

Eastern Mediterranean
Probably First Century A.D.
Lehman Gift, 1953.28.13
H. 11.7 cm.

DESCRIPTION: free-blown; similar to cat. no. 80 with pear-shaped body; wheel-cut line around shoulder; rim folded in and flattened; pale bluish green. CONDITION: intact; one side dull and pitted, the other slightly iridescent. PROVENANCE: John D. Rockefeller, Jr. no. 21; Duveen Brothers no. 2. PARALLELS: *Spartz, Kassel* no. 59, pl. 37.

89 *Miniature Bottle*

Eastern Mediterranean
First–Third Century A.D.
Lehman Gift, 1953.28.1
H. 4.1 cm.

Although related to early bottles with a squat piriform body, the spherical-bodied type is less particularly an early shape, continuing at least into the third century.

DESCRIPTION: free-blown; flattened base; rim folded in; pale green. CONDITION: intact; surface pitted with pale brown weathering on one side. PROVENANCE: John D. Rockefeller, Jr. no. 28; Duveen Brothers no. 3. PARALLELS: *Spartz, Kassel* no. 154.

90 *Miniature Bottle*

Eastern Mediterranean
First–Third Century A.D.
Lehman Gift, 1953.28.2
H. 4.3 cm.

DESCRIPTION: free-blown; similar to cat. no. 89. CONDI-

89, 90

TION: intact; surface dull and iridescent. PROVENANCE: John D. Rockefeller, Jr. no. 20; Duveen Brothers no. 19.

91 *Aryballos with Bronze Handle*

Eastern Mediterranean
First–Second Century A.D.
Mansfield Collection, 1930.418
H. 8.1 cm., without handle

The bronze handle permitted the owner of this perfumed oil container to carry it with him to the baths, as the Greeks carried pottery aryballoi to the *gymnasion.* Two bronze rings attached the solid cast handle to the small glass handles on the vessel's shoulder.

DESCRIPTION: free-blown; concave base; rim folded down, up, and flattened; three or perhaps four groups of wheel-cut lines around the center of the body; pale green. CONDITION: intact; light brown weathering and iridescence. PROVENANCE: found by A. Khayat near Mount Carmel and sold in 1900; Mansfield Collection no. 92. PARALLELS: *Isings* type 61.

92 *Jug*

Eastern Mediterranean
First–Second Century A.D.
Lehman Gift, 1953.28.17
H. 10.6 cm.

The cut-out base of this jug is indicative of an early date, as is the handle with folded thumbrest that joins the neck below the mouth. The color range, purple to pale green, attests to the use of an intentional colorant which also points to an early date.

DESCRIPTION: free-blown; rim folded in; wheel-cut lines around shoulder; purple and pale green, with a pale green handle. CONDITION: intact; iridescent, particularly the interior. PROVENANCE: John D. Rockefeller, Jr. no. 48; Duveen Brothers no. 1. PARALLELS: *Calvi, Aquileia* pl. 7, no. 3; Vessberg, "Cyprus" pl. 6, nos. 11–15; *Berger, Vindonissa* pl. 20, no. 89; *Isings* type 52a, with ring base; *Fremersdorf, Denkmäler* IV, pl. 51, with ring base.

93 *Jug*

Eastern Mediterranean
First–Second Century A.D.
Lehman Gift, 1953.28.16
H. 11 cm.

DESCRIPTION: free-blown; similar to cat. no. 92 but with handle ending at mouth; yellowish green. CONDITION: intact; some pitting and iridescence. PROVENANCE: John D. Rockefeller, Jr. no. 40; Duveen Brothers no. 8.

94 *Square Jug*

Eastern Mediterranean
First–Second Century A.D.
Mansfield Collection, 1930.412
H. 22.6 cm.

91, 92, 93

94, 96

Square bottles were a practical solution to the problem of packing glass bottles together without breakage, and they were one of the most common forms of shipping and storage bottles throughout the Roman Empire. The addition of a handle increased the bottle's usefulness once it had reached its destination.

Two methods were used in the manufacture of these vessels. In the first, the vessel was free blown and then flattened on four sides and the base. The second method, exemplified by this jug, involved blowing into a square mold. Many of the mold-blown bottles and jugs have geometric designs on their bases, possibly the marks of individual workshops or glassmakers.

DESCRIPTION: mold-blown; wide ribbon handle; rim folded out, in, and flattened; six-pointed rosette within a circle on the base, D. of mold mark on base 6.5 cm.; pale bluish green. CONDITION: intact; brown and iridescent weathering with surface pitting. PROVENANCE: said to have been found near Taffa (probably Tafas); Khayat, 1900; Mansfield Collection no. 63. PARALLELS: for the shape, see *Isings* type 50b. For parallels to the design on the base, see J. and A. Alarcão, *Vidros Romanos de Conimbriga* (Coimbra, Portugal 1975) no. 148 and, for related motifs, *Clairmont, Dura* 123–125, no. 619, pl. 15 (with two circles) and nos. 618–22 for related motifs and other parallels.

95 *Short Square Jug*

> Eastern Mediterranean
> First–Second Century A.D.
> Stevens Gift, 1932.1173
> H. 10.9 cm.

DESCRIPTION: mold-blown; base bumpy, but no specific design is discernible; rim folded down and up, not flattened; triple ribbed handle; pale green. CONDITION: intact; dark brown weathering over white on mouth, neck, and handle; rest of surface iridescent. PARALLELS: *Isings* type 50a.

96 *Jug*

> Eastern Mediterranean
> First–Second Century A.D.
> Mansfield Collection, 1930.445
> H. 18.7 cm.

Although finds at Pompeii and elsewhere indicate that tall cylindrical jugs were manufactured in the first century, the use of wheel-cut lines as on this jug does not become popular in the eastern provinces until the second century.

DESCRIPTION: free-blown; rim folded down and up, not flattened; triple ribbed handle; wheel-cut lines in four groups around the body; pale green. CONDITION: intact;

iridescent. PROVENANCE: Khayat, 1900; Mansfield Collection no. 90. PARALLELS: *Isings* type 51b.

97 *Lid from a Pyxis*

Eastern Mediterranean
First Century A.D.
Moore Collection, 1955.6.33
H. 2.2 cm., Max. D. 7 cm.

This lid once topped a pyxis of matching blue and

white marbled glass. Unlike the more common small pointed lids which functioned as stoppers, this lid would have covered most of the top of the vessel, probably meeting an outer rim.

DESCRIPTION: free-blown; dark blue and white. CONDITION: intact; brown weathering. PROVENANCE: Moore Collection no. 776. BIBLIOGRAPHY: *Eisen* 229–30 (incorrectly as Moore Collection no. 766); *Kouchakji* no. 35. PARALLELS: *von Saldern, Oppenländer* no. 299, smaller, with a less pronounced dome. For pyxides with pointed lids, see *Auth, Newark* nos. 145 and 146, the latter of a similar blue and white marbled fabric; *von Saldern, Oppenländer* no. 298; *Hayes, Toronto* no. 129, with additional parallels; *SPB Constable-Maxwell* nos. 44 and 45 (blue and white marbled).

95

97

98 *Cup*

Eastern Mediterranean
First Century A.D.
Lehman Gift, 1953.28.32
H. 8.4 cm.

Among the earliest drinking vessels to be produced after the discovery of glass blowing was this simple ovoid type with a restrained decorative touch of wheel-cut bands.

DESCRIPTION: free-blown; ground rim; a wide band of wheel-cut lines around the center of the body, and a single line below the rim; pale green. CONDITION: broken and repaired with some chips missing; iridescent with traces of white weathering. PROVENANCE: John D. Rockefeller, Jr. no. 62; Duveen Brothers no. 20. PARALLELS: *Isings* type 12; Vessberg, "Cyprus" pl. 3, no. 21; *Calvi, Aquileia* pl. 6 no. 4; *Spartz, Kassel* no. 30; *Berger, Vindonissa* pl. 6, no. 94.

99 *Cup*

Eastern Mediterranean
Late First Century A.D.
Moore Collection, 1955.6.127
H. 9.8 cm.

Based on a simple conical shape, this beaker has a hollowed out foot for stability. Starting with a fairly thick blown "blank," the glassmaker ground and polished the surface to create the foot, to thin the walls and refine the profile, and then to add the decorative bands.

DESCRIPTION: free-blown; wheel-polished ground rim; four wide and three narrow wheel-cut lines on the exterior; pale green. CONDITION: intact; brown weathering on the interior; exterior pitted and iridescent. BIBLIOGRAPHY: *Eisen* 124, pl. 108; *Kouchakji* no. 133; *Hayes, Toronto* 56, no. 134. PARALLELS: *Isings* type 21; *Berger, Vindonissa* pl. 7, no. 105.

99, 100

100 *Facet-Cut Beaker*

> Eastern Mediterranean
> First Century A.D.
> Moore Collection, 1955.6.133
> H. 9.3 cm.

Reflecting the rise in popularity of colorless blown glass in the second half of the first century A.D., facet-cut vessels with honeycomb patterns have been found throughout the Roman Empire and beyond its boundaries. Besides beakers, for which this type of decoration is common and well suited, bowls, plates, jugs, and even a rhyton received the same treatment. The honeycomb pattern varies from rows of distinct ovals or circles with spaces between them to a closely knit and regular diamond pattern. The method of manufacture is the same, however; the compact diamond pattern is simply ovals placed closer together. The raised ridges seem to be peculiar to the group of beakers with a honeycomb band of which this is an example; bowls and other shapes have the normal wheel-cut grooves around the rim and elsewhere.

DESCRIPTION: wheel-cut from a blown blank; two rows of oval facets between ridges; another ridge below the rim; narrowing profile above a hollowed out foot; rounded rim; nearly colorless with a slight yellow tinge. CONDITION: intact; iridescent with some brown weathering. PROVENANCE: Moore Collection no. 723. BIBLIOGRAPHY: *Eisen*

425, pl. 109; *Kouchakji* no. 140; *Clairmont, Dura* 60, note 141; Andrew Oliver, Jr., *Miscellanea Wilboureana*, forthcoming. PARALLELS: *Clairmont, Dura* 60–66, especially nos. 236–47 and note 141 with other parallels and bibliography; see in particular the facet-cut beakers from Begram, Afghanistan, which are of generally high quality and show considerable variety in their shapes: Hamelin, "Bégram," (1953) 121–28, pls. 7 and 8. A beaker in Boston, *von Saldern, Boston* no. 27, shows clearly the use of oval facets to form the compact honeycomb pattern.

101 *Ribbed Bowl*

> Northern Italy or Yugoslavia
> First Century A.D.
> Moore Collection, 1955.6.41
> H. 6.1 cm., D. 7.6 cm.

Ribbed bowls of this type have been found throughout the Roman Empire, but a sufficient number of them were discovered in Northern Italy and Yugoslavia to suggest their production in these areas. The contexts of these finds indicate a date of the second half of the first century A.D. Various methods of manufacture have been proposed: mold blowing is often mentioned, but in this example at least, the ribs were clearly pinched after the vessel was blown and the thread decoration added. Most of these bowls

101

are of transparent dark colors such as blue, purple, and brown, with white thread decoration, but a small group of opaque white bowls with blue or purple thread decoration reverse the more common color scheme.

DESCRIPTION: free-blown; pinched ribs; rounded rim; opaque white with blue thread decoration. CONDITION: broken and repaired with small restorations of the rim and body; slight weathering. PROVENANCE: Kouchakji Frères, 1919. BIBLIOGRAPHY: *Eisen* 212, pl. 37a; *Kouchakji* no. 43; W. von Pfeffer and T. E. Haevernick, "Zarte Rippen-

schalen," *Saalburg Jahrbuch* 17 (1958) no. 100. PARALLELS: von Pfeffer and Haevernick, "Zarte Rippenschalen" 76–91; T. E. Haevernick, "Die Verbreitung der 'zarten Rippenschalen,'" *Jahrbuch der Römisch-germanischen Zentralmuseums Mainz* 14 (1967) 153–66; *Isings* type 17. On the technique, see most recently Price, "Glass," 122, fig. 217, "pinched ribs." For another recent find in Yugoslavia, see Susan H. Auth, "Roman Glass," in *Excavations at Salona, Yugoslavia (1969–1972)*, C. W. Clairmont, with S. H. Auth and V. von Gonzenbach (New Jersey 1975) 152, no. 23, pl. 32, no. 22 (brown with white thread).

102, 103

102 *Cup*

Eastern Mediterranean
First Century A.D.
Moore Collection, 1955.6.11
H. 3.2 cm., D. 4.2 cm.

As is often the case with early blown vessels, the shape of this small cup differs little from some of its mold-pressed antecedents.

DESCRIPTION: free-blown; rounded rim; pale green. CONDITION: intact; brown enamel weathering on the interior. PROVENANCE: Moore Collection no. 651. BIBLIOGRAPHY: *Eisen* 151, pl. 8; *Kouchakji* no. 11. PARALLELS: *Spartz, Kassel* no. 31; *Berger, Vindonissa* pl. 7, no. 100 (mold-pressed); Vessberg, "Cyprus" pl. 3, nos. 3 and 10.

103 *Cup*

Eastern Mediterranean
First Century A.D.
Moore Collection, 1955.6.42
H. 3.3 cm., D. 6.9 cm.

DESCRIPTION: free-blown; similar to cat. no. 102, but shallower; small projection on one side, probably accidental; brown. CONDITION: intact; iridescent. PROVENANCE: Moore Collection no. 688. BIBLIOGRAPHY: *Kouchakji* no. 44.

104 *Cup or Bowl*

Eastern Mediterranean
First Century A.D.
Moore Collection, 1955.6.92
H. 6 cm., D. 10.1 cm.

The shape of this vessel relates it to a common Roman pottery type produced from the first to the third century A.D.

DESCRIPTION: free-blown; rounded rim; pad base; pale green. CONDITION: intact; pitted; brown and iridescent weathering. BIBLIOGRAPHY: *Kouchakji* no. 95. PARALLELS: *Isings* type 41b; Michel Vanderhoeven, *Verres Romains (Ier–IIIme siècle) des Musées Curtius et du Verre à Liège* (Liège 1961) nos. 33–40. For the pottery form, see *Dragendorff* type 33.

105 *Cup or Bowl*

Eastern Mediterranean
Late First–Second Century A.D.
Stevens Gift, 1932.1174
H. 6 cm., D. 11.7 cm.

DESCRIPTION: free-blown; similar to cat. no. 104, with slightly convex profile and everted rim; trailed-on base

104

105

106

107

ring; pale green. CONDITION: intact; brown weathering, iridescence, and pitting. PARALLELS: *Isings* type 41b; Vessberg, "Cyprus" pl. 1, no. 30, citing parallels from Pompeii.

106 *Cup or Bowl*

Eastern Mediterranean
First–Second Century A.D.
Moore Collection, 1955.6.113
H. 4.5 cm., D. 7.5 cm.

This small bowl is a common type throughout the Roman Empire, probably the functional successor to the mold-pressed patella cup that died out towards the end of the first century A.D. The newer free-blown type sits on a folded base and has a cut-out ridge below the rim. A larger version of this shape has parallels in Roman red ware vessels, mainly of second century date. However, the use of dark blue for this particular example suggests that it should still be dated within the first century.

DESCRIPTION: free-blown; rounded rim; transparent dark blue. CONDITION: intact; pale brown enamel weathering, flaking, with iridescence underneath. PROVENANCE: Moore Collection no. 756. BIBLIOGRAPHY: *Eisen* 355, pl. 91a; *Kouchakji* no. 119; Vessberg, "Cyprus" 147, note 1; *Hayes, Toronto* 80, no. 295. PARALLELS: *Isings* type 69; Vessberg, "Cyprus" 147 classifies them as pyxides. For the larger version with pottery parallels, see *Hayes, Toronto* 80 and Vessberg, "Cyprus" 147.

107 *Cup or Bowl*

Eastern Mediterranean
First–Second Century A.D.
Lehman Gift, 1953.28.29
H. 4 cm., D. 8.3 cm.

DESCRIPTION: free-blown; similar to cat. no. 106; pad base; pale bluish green. CONDITION: ridge chipped and repaired; thick white weathering and iridescence. PROVENANCE: John D. Rockefeller, Jr. no. 66; Duveen Brothers no. 22.

108 *Shallow Dish*

Eastern Mediterranean
First Century A.D.
Lehman Gift, 1953. 28.33
H. 2.3 cm., D. 13.3 cm.

The rounded rim and cut-out ridge at the base of this shallow dish distinguish it from later versions with a folded foot or ring base. Like many early blown glass vessels, this dish imitates mold-pressed and terra sigillata prototypes.

DESCRIPTION: free-blown; sloping sides with rounded rim; raised dome in the center of the bottom; cut-out ridge around lower outer edge; transparent yellowish brown. CONDITION: intact; iridescent, with some pitting. PROVENANCE: John D. Rockefeller, Jr. no. 44; Duveen Brothers no. 10. PARALLELS: *Isings* type 49, citing an example from Pompeii; Vessberg, "Cyprus" pl. 1, no. 6. For the mold-pressed version, see *Isings* type 23. Among pottery vessels, the shape resembles *Dragendorff* type 23.

108

109

109 *Splash Glass Kantharos or Skyphos*

Italian or Eastern Mediterranean
First Century A.D.
Moore Collection, 1955.6.13
H. 9.8 cm., D. 9.5 cm.

A good illustration of the fascination with vibrant colors and surface decoration characteristic of early Roman glassmakers is the technique known as splash decoration. Peculiar to the first century A.D., the technique was apparently used in both eastern and western glass centers. Briefly, the effect is achieved by sprinkling or marvering small fragments of multi-colored glass onto the partially blown bubble on the end of the blowpipe. The further inflation of the bubble to form the vessel distends these tiny and now molten fragments into drop-shaped "splashes." The interior of the vessel remains the monochrome of the matrix color, often dark blue.

This type of decoration was particularly successful when applied to closed forms such as amphoriskoi, where the monochrome interior was not visible and thus did not detract from the overall effect; and

indeed this seems to have been the shape most commonly chosen for the technique. A splash glass askos from Pompeii is more unusual but equally effective. Open forms were also treated in this way, especially drinking cups of various first century shapes including the one-handled cup, the carchesium, and the kantharos. The cups often have an opaque white band at the rim. It would appear that all the shapes used for splash decoration have metal proto-types or parallels, but this coincidence probably results from the close relation of glass and metal shapes that generally characterizes this early phase.

DESCRIPTION: free-blown; transparent dark blue with splash decoration in yellow, red, and white on body and foot; white band encircles the rim; dark blue handles. CONDITION: broken and repaired with some restoration; much of the color of the splash decoration lost through weathering; interior iridescent, brown and white weathering on handles. PROVENANCE: Moore Collection no. 793. BIBLIOGRAPHY: *Eisen* 154, pl. 14a; *Augustan Art* 23; *Kouchakji* no. 13; *Clairmont, Dura* 12, note 23. EXHIBITED: *Bicentennial of the Discovery of Pompeii* MMA 1948. PARALLELS: on the technique and dating, see Fritz Fremersdorf, "Römische Gläser mit buntgefleckter Oberfläche," *Festschrift für August Oxé*

110

a white band around the rim. More frequently seen in monochrome colors, these vessels imitated metal-ware, both in shape and in the wheel-cut bands which encircled the body. Feet and stems varied in height, and some examples had handles which echoed those of terra cotta kalyx kraters. Probably made in large matching sets, the glass vessels must have served as drinking cups at banquets.

DESCRIPTION: free-blown body; dark blue with red, yellow, and white splash decoration; opaque white band around rim. CONDITION: stem and foot restored; body broken and repaired with minor restorations; surface worn with much of decoration lost. PROVENANCE: Fahim Kouchakji, 1940. BIBLIOGRAPHY: *Eisen* 154, pl. 14b, restored differently; *Kouchakji* no. 13a. PARALLELS: for the shape, *Isings* type 36a. Other examples in splash glass, all with a white rim, include: *von Saldern, Boston* no. 21 (light blue with green, red, and white) purchased in Athens; *JGS* 8 (1966) 129, no. 6, CMG inv. 64.1.3 (amber with white, blue, red, and yellow); Andrea Benkö, *Üvegcorpus, Régészeti Füzetek*, Ser. II–11, Szam, Magyar Nemzeti Múzeum, Történeti Múzeum (1962) 169–70, no. 15/5, pl. 39, no. 6, found in Laibach, Hungary, Weinerstrasse 138, inv. 5437; Kern, "Glaskelche in Leiden" pl. 22, no. 1, Leiden, Rijksmuseum van Oudheden inv. I 1935/11.1 (blue with white) and inv. K 1947/12.3 (amber with red, white, blue, and green), both with handles, said to have been found in South Russia. A related group of one-handled cups with splash decoration and a white rim band includes Louvre inv. MND 1178 (dark blue with yellow and white) from the region of Kertsch; and *von Saldern, Oppenländer* no. 390, citing an additional example in Leningrad.

111 *Carchesium with Painted and Splash Glass Decoration*

Probably Italian
First Century A.D.
Moore Collection, 1955.6.14
H. 13.7 cm., D. 14.3 cm.

Compared to most other forms of decoration, painted glass is rare. The combination of painting and splash glass that occurs in this vessel, however, is to the best of my knowledge unique, and it is the splash glass above all else that dictates a first century date.

Glass painting seems to have originated in the first century, when glass was still to a great extent a luxury item and glassmakers were interested in rich colors and adorned surfaces. Among these first century vessels is a group of painted cups, mostly natural pale green but elaborately covered with animal and plant motifs which sometimes suggest a land-scape. As D. B. Harden has shown, these vessels have been found at both eastern and western sites, and since they form such a distinctive group, his suggestion

(Darmstadt 1938) 116 ff.; Kern, "Glaskelche in Leiden." Other shapes commonly found with this decoration: *Isings* types 15, 36, 37, 38, 59; less common types include Harden *Masterpieces* no. 70, aryballos, and no. 71, jug, *von Saldern, Boston* no. 22, vase, and *von Saldern, Oppenländer* no. 396, bowl, and one odd irregularly shaped jar with a concave base and rounded rim in the Cyprus Museum, Nicosia, inv. D1929/1935 (dark blue with yellow and white spots). For the askos from Pompeii, see *Pompeii A.D. 79*, exhibition catalogue, BMFA, 1978, vol. II, 157, no. 101. For light colored interiors, see *Auth, Newark* no. 55, amphoriskos, with other examples. For the revival of the technique in the Islamic period, see *von Saldern, Oppenländer* no. 748. The closest parallel to the Yale kantharos is TMA inv. 23.1499 (H. 10.2 cm., D. 9.5 cm.), a virtual duplicate of the Yale example in color and technical details and probably from the same workshop. A rim fragment from an undated context at Dura-Europos is probably from a similar kantharos; see *Clairmont, Dura* 12, no. 26, pl. 18.

110 *Splash Glass Carchesium*

Probably Northern Italian
First Century A.D.
Moore Collection, 1955.6.267
H. 13 cm., as restored, D. 15 cm.

The carchesium, another typical first century shape, was occasionally adorned with splash decoration and that they represent a migration of the craftsman like that postulated for Ennion seems plausible. The second major group of painted glasses are the second century pyxis lids from Cyprus. In keeping with their function as cosmetic containers, these vessels were normally topped with lids bearing a lively figure of Aphrodite or Eros.

Later painted glass is in some instances more sophisticated, with the introduction of shading and other illusionistic features. These can be seen in such pieces as a second–third century hunting and fishing scene from Begram, Afghanistan, believed by Harden to have been made in Egypt, and a Rhenish cup with animals and their trainer from a third century grave in Nordrup, Denmark. Another fine third century piece is the so-called Daphne jug, now in the Corning Museum of Glass. Like the fragments of its companion vessel from the Dura-Europos excavations, the jug is opaque white with gilding as well as paint. The relation of the Dura fragments to a Thetis mosaic at Antioch-on-the-Orontes has been viewed as linking the Dura vessel and thus the Corning jug to that city. Landscapes with animals occur again in some fourth century painted flasks from the western empire found in Cologne and stylistically related to some of the engraved vessels from the same area. A fourth century portrait glass plate from Cologne remains an interesting rarity.

The Yale cup does not really fit into any of these groups. The dark blue glass and, as stated above, the splash glass decoration indicate that it must date from the first century. But the closest parallel to the knotted branches that encircle the body is not in glass but in silver: the olive cups from the House of Menander at Pompeii. Like those exquisite cups, this glass vessel must have been a luxurious addition to the collection of its first century owner.

DESCRIPTION: free-blown body; rim folded out, down, and up on itself; body and matrix of foot dark blue; splash decoration on foot red, yellow, and light blue; painted decoration on body in white consisting of single brush stroke rays emanating from the foot, knotted olive branches around the body, and a row of dashes between two bands below the rim; interior undecorated.   CONDITION: broken and repaired with some fragments restored (photograph includes some painted restoration); break at joint of foot and body, but a perfect join in one area includes splash decoration left on body; brown and iridescent weathering.   PROVENANCE: Kouchakji Frères, 1922.   BIBLIOGRAPHY: *Eisen* 154, color plate II; *Augustan Art* 23, fig. 52; *Kouchakji* no. 14.   PARALLELS: For glass painting, see Harden, "Roman" 50, 58–59, pls. I, F and IX, A, B, D, and E; for the first century cups, see, for example, Harden, *Masterpieces* no. 68 and *von Saldern, Oppenländer* no. 397; for the Cyprus lids, see, among others, Vessberg, "Cyprus" 150, pl. 21; the Begram

III

fragments are illustrated by Harden, "Roman" pl. IX, D as is the cup from Denmark now in the National Museum, Copenhagen, pl. IX, E; the Daphne vase is illustrated in *Smith, Corning* no. 342, as well as many other places; for the Dura-Europos fragments, now at Yale, see *Clairmont, Dura* 34–35, pl. 20, cat. 126; for the fourth century Cologne vessels, see Doppelfeld, *Köln* 67–68, pls. 163–65. One of the olive cups from the House of Menander is reproduced in D. E. Strong, *Greek and Roman Gold and Silver Plate* (Cornell 1966) pl. 33A.

112 *Cup*

Eastern Mediterranean
Late First Century A.D.
Moore Collection, 1955.6.251
H. 10.3 cm.

From the first century onward, free-blown glass cups of varying shapes replaced most other forms of drinking vessels. Among the early types of drinking cups, some imitated mold-pressed or wheel-ground beakers, while others, such as this type, had a more fluid profile which took full advantage of the freedom offered by glass blowing. Faint wheel-cut lines continue to appear on many of the first century types.

DESCRIPTION: free-blown; cut-out base; rim turned in slightly but unworked; wheel-cut lines around the body; yellow.   CONDITION: intact; surface worn and iridescent.

112, 113, 114

BIBLIOGRAPHY: *Kouchakji* no. 131a; *Hayes, Toronto* 57, no. 137. PARALLELS: *Isings* type 36b; *Fremersdorf, Denkmäler* IV, pl. 73; additional examples cited by Hayes.

113 *Cup*

Eastern Mediterranean
Late First–Second Century A.D.
Moore Collection, 1955.6.125
H. 8.5 cm.

DESCRIPTION: free-blown; similar to cat. no. 112; ground rim; wheel-cut lines around the body; pale green. CONDITION: rim chipped; pitted and iridescent. PROVENANCE: Moore Collection no. 697. BIBLIOGRAPHY: *Eisen* 359, pl. 93; *Kouchakji* no. 131; *Hayes, Toronto* 57, no. 137.

114 *Cup*

Eastern Mediterranean
Late First Century A.D.
Moore Collection, 1955.6.126
H. 10.5 cm.

The irregular profile, rounded towards the base, and the folded foot indicate that this is a free-blown imitation of similar beakers ground from a blown blank (for example cat. no. 99, above). Its wheel-cut bands also echo its prototype, but the blown version took far less time and care to produce.

DESCRIPTION: free-blown; ground rim; folded pad base; pale bluish green. CONDITION: intact; surface worn and iridescent. PROVENANCE: Moore Collection no. 704.

BIBLIOGRAPHY: *Eisen* 425, pl. 108; *Kouchakji* no. 132; *Hayes, Toronto* 56, no. 134.

115 *Cup*

Eastern Mediterranean
Late First Century A.D.
Mansfield Collection, 1930.436
H. 12.6 cm.

DESCRIPTION: free-blown; similar to cat. no. 114, but taller with an everted rim; wheel-cut bands around body; pale green. CONDITION: broken and repaired; pitted, with light brown and iridescent weathering. PROVENANCE: said to have been found at Jericho; Khayat, 1909; Mansfield Collection no. 179. BIBLIOGRAPHY: *Hayes, Toronto* 56, no. 133.

116 *Cup*

Eastern Mediterranean
First–Second Century A.D.
Moore Collection, 1955.6.117
H. 9.7 cm.

Although the want of dated parallels for this purple beaker makes confirmation difficult, the color, wheel-cut lines, rim treatment, and lack of foot or base combine to suggest an early date.

DESCRIPTION: free-blown; flattened base; unworked rim; wheel-cut lines around body; purple. CONDITION: intact; pitted and iridescent. BIBLIOGRAPHY: *Kouchakji* no. 123. PARALLELS: Vessberg, "Cyprus" pl. 3, no. 5, from an undated context at Idalion, although Vessberg states that

117, 115, 116

the horizontal lines on the Cypriote example are mold-blown.

117 *Cup*

Eastern Mediterranean
First–Second Century A.D.
Moore Collection, 1955.6.118
H. 10.5 cm.

DESCRIPTION: free-blown; similar to cat. no. 116, but taller with a slightly everted rim; concave base; ground rim; wheel-cut lines; pale green. CONDITION: intact; flaking brown weathering over iridescence.

MOLD-BLOWN, FIRST CENTURY A.D.

118 *Jar Signed by Ennion*

Eastern Mediterranean
First Century A.D.
Moore Collection, 1955.6.66
H. 6.5 cm., Max. D. 8.8 cm.

The blowing of vessels into a mold, in which the shape of the vessel and its decoration are formed simultaneously, was an early technical discovery that achieved great popularity in the first century A.D. First used to produce highly decorative objects, the technique rapidly evolved into a method of mass-producing less ornate and less sophisticated vessels and as such lasted throughout the Roman period.

The reusability of the mold was the key to this development, since although the making of the mold required considerable care and effort in the initial stages, once finished it could be used to create any number of identical vessels with little more effort than it took to make a free-blown vessel. As a result, the mold-blown vessels are the only group for which we can truly speak of exact parallels or duplicates, and, with the exception of a few groups of wheel-cut or engraved glass, the only vessels which can be separated into workshops with any confidence. The inventors of the mold-blowing technique definitely owed a conceptual debt to the mold-made pottery of the period, notably Arretine and lead-glazed wares, and certain decorative motifs clearly derive from late Hellenistic and early Roman metalwork.

The identification of glassmaking workshops is aided, though rarely, by the signature of an artist. Undoubtedly the most famous of these signatures is that of Ennion, the master craftsman of mold-blown vessels. More than twenty signed Ennion pieces are now known. It is generally accepted that he was among the first to specialize in mold-blown glass and that he worked in or near Sidon, on the Lebanese coast, where this technique is thought to have originated. It has also been suggested, on the basis of the localization of findspots of certain shapes of signed vessels, that Ennion subsequently moved to Italy and established a workshop there. Most of the Ennion cups were found in Italy and thus were probably made there, while other types of vessels come primarily from eastern Mediterranean sites. The Yale jar and its only parallel (Chrysler Museum,

118

Norfolk, Virginia) were both said to have come from Sidon, and although these provenances were provided by dealers, they at least suggest products of an eastern rather than an Italian workshop.

The shape of this jar may ultimately derive from a popular Hellenistic type in pottery and metal with a wider mouth and, in metal, often decorated with the gadroons seen here and in many other works by Ennion and his colleagues and followers. The network band around the middle seems closer to contemporary facet-cut glass vessels than to objects in any other medium. Despite such relationships and derivations, Ennion's vessels show a high degree of originality and a well-developed decorative sense. The careful execution and the complex four part mold of this jar are characteristic of the quality of his workmanship.

DESCRIPTION: mold-blown, four part mold; concave mold-blown base; unworked rim; three bands of decoration: uppermost a band of vertical ribs rounded at the bottom; a band of network pattern in the center; gadroons form the transition to the concave base, which has three concentric circular ridges and a raised central knob at center; a dovetailed rectangular panel in the upper band bears the signature

ΕΝΝΙΩΝ ΕΠΟΙΕΙ, "Ennion made it." Pale greenish blue. CONDITION: intact; interior slightly iridescent. PROVENANCE: said to have been found in Sidon; Fahim Kouchakji, 1928. BIBLIOGRAPHY: R. Dussaud, *Syria* 10 (1929) 82–83, with half-tone figure and line drawing on title page; Harden, "Mould-blown Inscriptions" 167, cat. A3, pl. 28, no. 4 (inscription). Harden identified the Yale piece as that described by Dussaud. *Augustan Art* 22; Harden, "Yahmour" 89; *Kouchakji* no. 69; Hayward, "Yale" 50, no. 1, fig. 2; von Saldern, *Oppenländer* 159, no. 447; *Auth, Newark* 65, no. 58; *Cambridge, Fitzwilliam* no. 52b; *SPB, Constable-Maxwell* no. 280. PARALLELS: from the same mold: *JGS* 10 (1968) 181, no. 6, Chrysler Museum, Norfolk, Virginia, ex coll. Mrs. E. T. Newell, New York, from Sidon via the dealer Azeez Khayat ca. 1915–18, also published by Harden, "Yahmour" 89, pl. 8, no. 2. The shape, along with a similar decorative format and the same dove-tailed rectangle for the inscription, was used by Aristeias, a Cypriote, for a signed vessel: see *SPB, Constable-Maxwell* no. 280. On

44 EARLY ROMAN VESSELS

Ennion and his migration to Italy, see Harden, "Mould-blown Inscriptions" 164 ff. and Harden, "Roman" 49–50. For the coin of Claudius, see Harden, "Mould-blown Inscriptions" 167, cat. A2 iv. Uninscribed imitations were fairly common, as for example *von Saldern, Oppenländer* no. 448. For a Hellenistic source, see, among others, Andrew Oliver, Jr., *Silver for the Gods*, exhibition catalogue, TMA 1977 no. 10.

119 *Bottle with Plant Motifs*

Eastern Mediterranean
First Century A.D.
Moore Collection, 1955.6.52
H. 8.3 cm.

A fairly large series of bottles considered Sidonian and often related to the work of Ennion is characterized by a wide band around the body divided into six panels by an architectural framework of columns or beaded lines and pediments or lunettes. A single object appears within each panel; usually these objects are all of one type, with vases, plants, fruits, birds, and items of athletic equipment occurring most frequently. Ribs or plant motifs generally decorate the shoulder, and the gadroons common to most early first century mold-blown vessels normally form the transition from the central band to the base. None of these vessels is signed.

This opaque white bottle is a typical example. Three types of stylized plants appear in the archi-

119

120

tectural panels; each type is shown twice. Faint plant motifs decorate the shoulder and gadroons appear below. The plants in the panels are particularly close to some on a cup in the British Museum signed by Ennion.

DESCRIPTION: mold-blown, four part mold; concentric mold-blown circles on the base; rim folded out, in, and up; opaque white. CONDITION: intact; virtually unweathered. PROVENANCE: Kouchakji Frères, New York; sale American Art Association, Anderson Galleries, 1927; Fahim Kouchakji, 1939. BIBLIOGRAPHY: *Eisen* 253, fig. 122, pl. 52d; sale catalogue, liquidation of Kouchakji Frères, American Art Association, Anderson Galleries, 25–26 January 1927, no. 216, illus.; *Kouchakji* no. 54; *SPB, Constable-Maxwell* no. 71. PARALLELS: from the same mold: T. S. Buechner, "Ancient Glass in the Corning Museum," *Archaeology* 5 (1952) 218, inv. 50.1.8 (opaque white); Israeli, "Museum Haaretz" 37; present location unknown, sale Parke Bernet, New York 1946, lot 256, illustrated in Israeli, "Museum Haaretz" 37; Philadelphia, University Museum, inv. MS 5014, said to be from Aleppo, Syria (amber). For a variant with two species of plants and an undecorated shoulder, see Israeli, "Museum Haaretz" 37 and *SPB, Constable-Maxwell* no. 71, with gadroons on the shoulder. For the

MOLD-BLOWN VESSELS 45

Ennion cup in the BM, see Harden, *Masterpieces* no. 58. For a similar panelled arrangement on a fragment of an Arretine vase, see Brown, *Terra-Sigillata* no. 89, pl. 21.

120 *Bottle with Plant Motifs*

Eastern Mediterranean
First Century A.D.
Mansfield Collection, 1930.423
H. 10.8 cm.

This bottle shows an unusual combination of four different plant motifs with a jug and a pair of strigils. The shoulder is exceptionally elaborate, with six different animals divided into pairs by plants. Gadroons again appear below. In view of the similarity in general design as well as in details of the beaded lines and stylized plants between this and the previous example, it is likely that these two, at least, were produced in the same workshop.

DESCRIPTION: mold-blown, four part mold; order of motifs: strigils, jug, then four plants; shoulder animals, in confronting pairs, possibly a cock and a dog, a sheep and a bull, a cat and a peafowl (Hayward, "Yale" 53); concentric circles on the base; rim folded in; virtually colorless. CONDITION: intact; blue weathering on the interior. PROVENANCE: Khayat, 1921. BIBLIOGRAPHY: Hayward, "Yale" 53, no. 7, fig. 8; Israeli, "Museum Haaretz" 37; *SPB, Constable-Maxwell* no. 175. PARALLELS: from the same mold: CMG inv. 50.1.9 (yellow green, one dark handle); *Auth, Newark* no. 324, also published in *Eisen* fig. 119; *SPB, Constable-Maxwell* no. 175 (blue, with one handle).

121 *Pyxis with Geometric and Plant Motifs*

Eastern Mediterranean
First Century A.D.
Moore Collection, 1955.6.56
H. 8.3 cm.

Related to the two previous bottles by its central band of eight architectural panels, this opaque white pyxis combines geometric and plant motifs in a group of four different items each repeated once. The alternating palmettes on the lid occur in metalwork and stone reliefs of the period.

DESCRIPTION: mold-blown, body in four part mold, lid in three part mold; band of overlapping leaves or petals around six concentric circles on base; central band of eight panels: spoked circle, plant (palmette), circle within a lozenge, plant (lotus flower?), each repeated once, in the same order; lid: concentric circles and a band of alternating palmettes; rims unworked; opaque white. CONDITION: intact; very little weathering. PROVENANCE: Hakey Bey, Director of Antiquities, Constantinople; Khayat, 1925.

BIBLIOGRAPHY: *Eisen* 272–73, pl. 58; *Kouchakji* no. 59; Israeli, "Museum Haaretz" 37. PARALLELS: from the same mold: Froehner, *Gréau* 59, pl. 43, nos. 2, 3, and 4, MMA inv. 17.194.238 (opaque white); Harden, *Masterpieces* 52, no. 59, from Sidon (opaque white) also published in E. Dillon, *Glass* (London 1907) pl. 6, no. 3; BM inv. 92.6–13.52, fragmentary, lid missing (opaque medium blue); Athens, National Archaeological Museum inv. 2779, from the Kerameikos (opaque white with blue spots), with the lid differing from other examples in that it has the same petals as the base rather than the usual palmettes; Athens, National Archaeological Museum inv. 2764, from Athens, a grave near Stadiou Street (opaque white); *JIV* 2 (1963) 6, fig. 9, Krakow, Poland, National (Czartoryski) Museum (opaque white), lid missing; CMG inv. 54.1.7, ex coll. R. W. Smith (opaque white), lid missing; present location unknown, sale Sotheby Parke Bernet, New York, 22 November 1974, lot 295, illus. (amber), lid missing, from a German private collection. See also Kisa, *Glas* I, 95.

122 *Bottle with Vases*

Eastern Mediterranean
First Century A.D.
Moore Collection, 1955.6.53
H. 7.8 cm.

Numerous parallels and variants of this vessel have survived, and it appears to have been one of the most common of the early mold-blown bottles. Variants are distinguishable by the use of different vessels in the arcade; at least three such series are known.

DESCRIPTION: mold-blown, three part mold; six jugs and footed amphorae or hydriae (all different) fill spaces between columns; grape vine encircling vessel below arcade; ring base; rim folded in; opaque grayish green. CONDITION: small hole in one of the vessels; brown and white weathering; flaking. PROVENANCE: said to have been found at Mount Carmel, Syria; Khayat, 1912. BIBLIOGRAPHY: *Eisen* 247–48, pl. 50, center; *Kouchakji* no. 55. PARALLELS: too numerous to cite individually, but see, for example, *Eisen* pls. 50–52; for an excavated example, see *Clairmont, Dura* no. 146. I can find no evidence for Eisen's suggestion that these bottles are cult vessels.

123 *Jug*

Eastern Mediterranean
First Century A.D.
Moore Collection, 1955.6.272
H. 9.9 cm.

Some uncertainty remains in the identification of the six objects in the rectangular panels of this jug. The three wine vessels and the crossed *thyrsoi* suggest Dionysiac connotations, but without a clear understanding of the round shieldlike object and the small square object next to it (a basket?) no conclusions about a general theme can be drawn. Although the decorative formula is within the scope of other panelled vessels, the attention to detail and quality of workmanship that might link them to Ennion's workshop is generally lacking here.

DESCRIPTION: mold-blown, four part mold; six panels: circular object, amphora, crossed *thyrsoi*, jug, amphora, and square (woven? checkerboard?) object; concentric circles on the base; ribs above and below the central band; pale green with dark blue handle. CONDITION: unbroken but with some strain cracks; white weathering and pitting. BIBLIOGRAPHY: *Kouchakji* no. 54a. PARALLELS: *Eisen* pl. 51; *von Saldern, Boston* no. 31; Philadelphia, University Museum inv. MS 5016; *Smith, Corning* no. 79; BM inv. 1913.5–22.10 from Syria, inv. S181, and a fragmentary example, inv. 84.12–28.21; *Hayes, Toronto* no. 84; *von Saldern, Oppenländer* no. 443.

124 *Pyxis with Ivy Garlands*

Eastern Mediterranean
First Century A.D.
Moore Collection, 1955.6.58
H. 4.5 cm. without lid, 6.1 cm. with lid

This vessel is one of a small group of pyxides that form part of a far larger family of bottles and jugs with a central band of ivy garlands, apparently from the same or closely related molds. The quality of workmanship and the gadroons on the shoulder and base relate the whole group to vessels by Ennion and his workshop.

DESCRIPTION: mold-blown, body in a four part mold; garlands of ivy leaves, buds, and berries, joined at intervals by bows, encircling the body; tongue pattern on domed lid; concentric circular ridges on base; rim ground; transparent dark blue. CONDITION: upper part of the lid original, side restored; body broken in one place and repaired, with small restoration; white weathering and pitting. PROVENANCE: said to have been found near Tyre, Syria; Khayat, 1924; Moore Collection no. 830. BIBLIOGRAPHY: *Eisen* 273, pl. 60b (old restoration); Harden, "Mould-blown Inscriptions" 185, Appendix B, III 2a; *Kouchakji* no. 61. PARALLELS: pyxides, probably from a single mold: *Smith, Corning* no. 92 (brown), now CMG inv. 55.1.70; *Smith Corning* no. 93 (manganese red); *SPB, Constable-Maxwell* nos. 153 and 154 (opaque white with alien lids of blue and brown); de Ridder, *de Clercq* no. 278 (opaque white) from Athens, Louvre inv. MNE 107. A group of jugs from related molds includes: BM inv. 1913.5–22.19, without bows (bluish green) from Syria; Naples, Museo Nazionale Archeologico, no inv., without bows (bluish green?); Nicosia, Cyprus Museum inv. 1936 II–19 12, without bows, each group of branches different (pale

121

122

123

124

125

green with dark blue handle); Nicosia, Cyprus Museum inv. D1711/1935, same mold as previous piece (pale green); TMA inv. 23.438 (dark blue) and inv. 23.482 (dark blue); *von Saldern, Oppenländer* nos. 441 (pale bluish green) and no. 442 (brown). Also included in this group of jugs are a number of pieces sold at auction at the American Art Association, Anderson Galleries, New York in the 1920s: Khayat sale, 26–27 March 1926, no. 252, without bows (light greenish); Kouchakji Frères liquidation sale, 25–26 January 1927, no. 215, without bows (blue) and possibly no. 24 (amber, not illus.); Khayat sale, 11–12 April 1928, no. 352, without bows (color not stated); Khayat sale, 18–19 April 1929, no. 245 (deep blue). A few examples have two handles: *von Saldern, Oppenländer* no. 440 (opaque white with dark blue handles); *Auth, Newark* no. 59 (purple with white handles).

125 *Pyxis with Palmettes*

Eastern Mediterranean
First Century A.D.
Moore Collection, 1955.6.57
H. 5.4 cm., as restored.

Rows of palmettes alternatingly upright and inverted are a common decorative motif on metalwork and as a border on relief sculpture during the Roman period. It is therefore not surprising that there should be at least three different molds for glass pyxides which use this pattern, as well as a number of bottles and jugs made from the same or closely related molds. A first century A.D. date for the group is confirmed by a pyxis found at Pompeii, but most vessels with known provenances come from Syria.

DESCRIPTION: mold-blown, three part mold; band of alternating palmettes; dark blue. CONDITION: lid missing; base restored from another vessel and too large; some restorations of the preserved part of the body; iridescent. PROVENANCE: said to have been found near Homs, Syria; Khayat, 1914. BIBLIOGRAPHY: *Eisen* 273, pl. 60a; Harden, "Mould-blown Inscriptions" 185, Appendix B, III 1 b; *Kouchakji* no. 60; *SPB, Constable-Maxwell* no. 155. PARALLELS: from the same or closely related molds, varying mainly in the spacing of the palmettes: Harden, "Mould-blown Inscriptions" 185, Appendix B, III 1 a–e; *Smith, Corning* nos. 90 and 91, now CMG inv. 55.1.69 and inv. 55.1.68 respectively; Toledo, *Glass* 24, inv. 67.5 A and B; TMA inv. 56.3, with three handles applied at the top of the frieze, no lid (greenish with purple streaks); *von Saldern, Oppenländer* no. 444; *Auth, Newark* no. 61; *SPB, Constable-Maxwell* no. 155; J. H. C. Kern, "A Fragmentary Mould-blown Glass Pyxis from Pompeii," *Oudheidkundige Medelingen (Leiden)* N. R. 35 (1954) 33–37, Leiden, Rijksmuseum van Oudheden inv. PP22, citing related jugs; for the Newark Museum jugs cited by Kern, see now *Auth, Newark* nos. 62 and 321.

126 *Lotus Beaker*

Eastern Mediterranean
First Century A.D.
Moore Collection, 1955.6.271
H. 11.5 cm.

A very large family of vessels found at Pompeii and other sites throughout the Roman Empire, these so-called lotus beakers were made in a variety of sizes. This example is a small version, but it does have the dots between the lotus buds that characterize the more complex molds. It is tempting to consider a luxurious glass and silver vase in the British Museum as the source for these widely produced glass vessels since the visual effect of blowing the glass into a silver vase with rows of oval holes is similar to that of these beakers. Unfortunately there is no more than a tenuous connection between the silver and glass vase, probably found at Brindisi and made in Italy, and the glass vessels from Pompeii and other Italian sites.

DESCRIPTION: mold-blown, four part mold; five rows of lotus buds with raised dots; concentric circles on base; unworked rim; pale green. CONDITION: intact; heavy encrustation on exterior; interior iridescent. PROVENANCE: Fahim Kouchakji, 1939. BIBLIOGRAPHY: *Eisen* 257; *Kouchakji* no. 52a. PARALLELS: *Isings* type 31, citing the finds from Pompeii. For the silver and glass vase in the BM, see Harden, *Masterpieces* no. 74.

126

127 *Argonaut Flask*

Eastern Mediterranean or Italian
First Century A.D.
Moore Collection, 1955.6.54
Pres. H. 8 cm.

Subjects drawn from mythology and epic poetry are rarely illustrated on glass vessels. This small bottle shows two scenes related to the story of Jason and the Argonauts and their voyage to bring back the Golden Fleece. On one side a man, seated under a tree, prepares to sacrifice an animal. This is Phrixus, who, in order to escape death at the hand of his stepmother, fled on the back of a golden-fleeced ram to Colchis, where he sacrificed the ram to Zeus, protector of fugitives. This episode is the foundation of the Argonaut saga, for the Golden Fleece remained in the sanctuary on Colchis and Jason was later sent there by his uncle Pelias to fetch it. This journey was dangerous, but after many trials the *Argo* and its crew reached their destination, and on the second side of the bottle Jason, shown as a warrior of heroic size, is about to step ashore from the bow of his ship.

The subject reflects the strong Roman interest in

Greek mythology and epic poetry which characterized the late first century B.C. and most of the following century. The familiarity of Roman authors with the Argonaut saga was based on the third century B.C. Greek epic poem the *Argonautica* of Apollonius Rhodius which, incidentally, links the two episodes illustrated on the bottle (Ap. Rhod. *Argon.* 2.1143–47 and 2.1194–95). A Latin translation or adaptation of this work, now lost but cited by Ovid (*Am.* 1.15.21) and Quintilian (*Inst.* 10.1.87), was written by Varro Atacinus, probably in the third quarter of the first century B.C. Ovid and Virgil were both influenced by it. During the reign of Vespasian (A.D. 69–79) a new epic version of the story was begun by Valerius Flaccus. Although he left the work unfinished at his death in A.D. 92 or 93, the eight books which he completed have survived; they carry the story up to Jason's departure from Colchis with Medea. That this work was known in contemporary Roman literary circles is demonstrated by Quintilian's statement of regret at the premature demise of its author

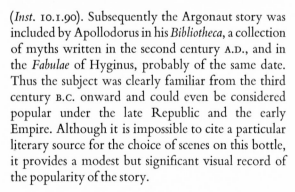

127, Sides A (Phrixus) & B (Jason)

(*Inst.* 10.1.90). Subsequently the Argonaut story was included by Apollodorus in his *Bibliotheca*, a collection of myths written in the second century A.D., and in the *Fabulae* of Hyginus, probably of the same date. Thus the subject was clearly familiar from the third century B.C. onward and could even be considered popular under the late Republic and the early Empire. Although it is impossible to cite a particular literary source for the choice of scenes on this bottle, it provides a modest but significant visual record of the popularity of the story.

DESCRIPTION: mold-blown, two part mold; flat base; opaque white. CONDITION: rim and upper part of neck broken away; no traces of handles; white weathering. PROVENANCE: Moore Collection no. 818. BIBLIOGRAPHY: *Eisen* 254, pl. 53; *Kouchakji* no. 57; Hayward, "Yale" 58–59, no. 11; Amyx, *Echoes* no. 168; *SPB, Constable-Maxwell* no. 90. PARALLELS: Giovanni Mariacher, *Il Museo Vetrario di Murano* (Milan 1970) 18, fig. 4, from the Dalmatian necropolis, formerly in the museum in Zara (apparently dark blue or purple with the base of a white handle on the neck); *JGS* 5 (1963) 141, no. 3, CMG inv. 62.1.16, no traces of handles (opaque white); *Bulletin of the Houston Texas Museum of Fine Arts* n.s. II (1972) 175, fig. 5 (opaque white), restored from the yardarm up, ex coll. R. W.

Smith; Selim and Andrée Abdul-Hak, *Catalogue Illustré du Département des Antiquités Gréco-Romaines au Musée de Damas* (Damascus 1951) 113, no. 6, inv. 12.813, two handles, described as restored (opaque white), found at Tell Nabi Mind, also published by Al°Ush et al., *Catalogue du Musée National de Damas* (Damascus 1969) 104, fig. 39, as inv. C5573; *SPB, Constable-Maxwell* no. 90, two handles (opaque white).

128 *Jug with Basket Pattern*

> Eastern Mediterranean
> First Century A.D.
> Moore Collection, 1955.6.55
> H. 9.2 cm.

The body of this small jug appears to be encased in a woven basket in imitation of a practice known from at least one surviving fourth century A.D. example which must have been common in earlier centuries as well. Numerous parallels with one and two handles remain, including a variant with the wreath reversed and another variant without the wreath, both found at Aquileia.

DESCRIPTION: mold-blown, two part mold; flat base; rim

folded in; handle and body pale green. CONDITION: unbroken but with strain cracks on one side towards the base; white and iridescent weathering. PROVENANCE: Kouchakji Frères, 1923. BIBLIOGRAPHY: *Eisen* 270–71, pl. 55 (2 views); *Kouchakji* no. 58; Israeli, "Museum Haaretz" 39; *von Saldern, Boston* 92, no. 34; *von Saldern, Oppenländer* 150, no. 431. PARALLELS: numerous examples from the same or similar molds, including *Auth, Newark* no. 63; Israeli, "Museum Haaretz" 40, nos. 8a and 8b; *von Saldern, Boston* no. 34; *von Saldern, Oppenländer* no. 431, all with additional parallels; Alexander Nesbitt, *Catalogue of the Collection of Glass formed by Felix Slade, Esq., F.S.A.* (London 1871) 31, BM inv. S184; Khayat sale, American Art Association, Anderson Galleries, New York, 26–27 March 1926, no. 418. For the Aquileia vessels, see *Calvi, Aquileia* pl. 16, nos. 3 and 4; another example without the wreath is in VAM, inv. 1033–1868. For the vessel encased in a woven basket, see *JGS* 20 (1978) 120, no. 10, CMG inv. 77.1.3.

129 *Hexagonal Bottle with Plant Motifs*

Eastern Mediterranean
First Century A.D.
Moore Collection, 1955.6.80
H. 9.2 cm.

At least three variant molds of this shape were made, and, as has often been noted, all seem to derive from a signed Ennion vessel now in the Metropolitan Museum.

DESCRIPTION: mold-blown, two part mold; each mold section has three panels with a palm frond between the two scroll patterns; above these panels, four horizontal ribs with small lunettes, each enclosing three raised dots above; base flat; rounded rim; bottle and handles dark blue. CONDITION: broken at the base and repaired; somewhat iridescent. BIBLIOGRAPHY: *Kouchakji* no. 83; *Auth, Newark* no. 60 (not *Eisen* pl. 81a). PARALLELS: from the same or related molds: *Auth, Newark* no. 60 (different mold); *von Saldern, Oppenländer* no. 439 (different mold); *Smith, Corning* no. 83, now CMG inv. 59.1.81; Athens, National Archaeological Museum inv. 2694, fragmentary; *Eisen* pl. 81a and b, 81b now MMA inv. 12.212.4; Khayat sale, American Art Association, Anderson Galleries, New York, 13–14 April 1927 no. 334.

130 *Barrel-Shaped Bottle*

Eastern Mediterranean
First Century A.D.
Moore Collection, 1955.6.60
H. 7 cm.

Breaking away from the tradition of Ennion, this glassmaker has eliminated much of the decorative surface that marked the work of the master.

DESCRIPTION: mold-blown, two part mold, poorly aligned; flat square base; rim folded in; body and handles dark blue. CONDITION: intact; slight gold iridescence on one side. BIBLIOGRAPHY: *Kouchakji* no. 63. PARALLELS: numerous examples, including: *Eisen* pl. 54; *Smith, Corning* nos. 87 and 88; VAM inv. 1012–1868; *Auth, Newark* no. 68 and Newark Museum inv. 28.263, not in the catalogue; *von Saldern, Oppenländer* no. 437.

128, 129, 130

131

131 *Jug with Palm Garlands*

> Eastern Mediterranean
> First Century A.D.
> Moore Collection, 1955.6.69
> H. 11.7 cm.

Palm fronds and ivy are both common motifs on drinking vessels and jugs, but the use of the palm fronds as garlands and the addition of the columns here are unusual. Undecorated, jugs of this type are typical of the first and second centuries.

DESCRIPTION: mold-blown, three part mold; four Doric columns connected by palm frond garlands and an ivy vine; mold-blown base ring; wide flat handle; folded rim; dark brownish green. CONDITION: unbroken, but with strain cracks at the base of the handle; some iridescent white weathering. PROVENANCE: apparently acquired from Fahim Kouchakji, 1937. BIBLIOGRAPHY: *Eisen* 275, pl. 61; *Kouchakji* no. 72; Hayward, "Yale" 52–53, no. 6, fig. 7; Dusenbery, "Wheaton College" 13; *SPB, Constable-Maxwell* no. 178. PARALLELS: from the same mold, pale green with taller necks: *JGS* 14 (1972) 153, no. 6, Pilkington Glass Museum, St. Helens, Lancashire, inv. 1970/20; *SPB, Constable-Maxwell* no. 178.

132 *Cup with Marine Motifs*

> Eastern Mediterranean or Italian
> First Century A.D.

> Moore Collection, 1955.6.59
> H. 7.3 cm., D. 7.9 cm.

The use of marine motifs, unless in a narrative context such as the fish under the *Argo* in the Yale Argonaut Flask (cat. no. 127), is unusual in glass vessels, and the unnatural combination of the sea creatures with trees

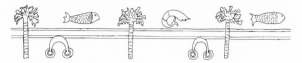

on this cup is even more extraordinary. Without the trees and marine life, the *trompe-l'œil* handles and horizontal bands would suggest an imitation of a metal vessel, but as it stands, this strange but well-executed cup is without parallel in any medium.

DESCRIPTION: mold-blown, four part mold; upper register: alternating marine animals and trees, three of each; lower register: two imitation handles; trees extending into lower register as well; rim ground; pale greenish blue. CONDITION: unbroken, but with strain cracks near the base; iridescence and white weathering. BIBLIOGRAPHY: *Kouchakji* no. 62; Hayward, "Yale" 50–51, no. 2, fig. 3; Amyx, *Echoes* no. 169.

133 *Beaker Signed by Jason*

> Eastern Mediterranean
> First Century A.D.
> Moore Collection, 1955.6.273
> H. 9.1 cm., D. 6.6. cm.

Few glassmakers signed their works. Among those who did were the early Syrian artists Jason, Meges,

132

and Neikias who produced virtually identical barrel-shaped beakers. Only the artist's name distinguishes one inscription from the next: "Let the buyer remember, *Jason* made it." Perhaps the three were rivals in the same town or workshop. These beakers differ from the works of Ennion and his group in their simplicity of form and decoration. They bear a closer resemblance to early glass beakers with wheel-cut bands than to the elaborate metalwork of which Ennion's vessels are reminiscent.

DESCRIPTION: mold-blown, three part mold; two horizontal ribs near the base, three below and two above the inscription; two raised concentric circles with a concave center on the base; unworked rim; pale bluish green. Inscribed in two parts: IACⲰN ΕΠOΗCEN, "Jason made it" on one side; MNHCOH O AΓOPACAC, "let the buyer remember"

on the other side, separated by vertical palm fronds. CONDITION: rim chipped; iridescent. PROVENANCE: probably from the J. P. Morgan Collection; purchased from Fahim Kouchakji, 1944, who probably acquired it from the Parke Bernet sale of the Morgan Collection. BIBLIOGRAPHY: *Kouchakji* no. 69a; Hayward, "Yale" 51, no. 3, fig. 4, with IACⲰN incorrectly transcribed as IACΩN. If the above provenance is correct, then the piece was also published while on loan to the MMA from the Morgan Collection: G. M. A. Richter, "The Room of Ancient Glass," Supplement to the *Bulletin of the Metropolitan Museum of Art* (New York 1930) 75, and Harden, "Mould-blown Inscriptions" 169, group B, d. PARALLELS: from the same mold: BM inv. 1913.5–22.21, Harden, "Mould-blown Inscriptions" 169, group B, a; Beirut, Lebanese National Museum inv. 1243, bought from E. Bostros, 1939, Harden, "Yahmour" 90, group B, e; MMA inv. 29.100.82, ex coll. Havemeyer, Harden, "Mould-blown Inscriptions" 169, group B, c; MMA inv. 59.11.3, ex coll. R. W. Smith, formerly ex colls. Niessen and von Gans, Harden, "Mould-blown Inscriptions" 169, group B, b, *Smith, Corning* no. 70, and, after its acquisition by the MMA, *JGS* 3 (1961) 135, fig. 4. According to D. B. Harden and Andrew Oliver, Jr., the Jason beaker reproduced in *JGS* 11 (1969) 109, fig. 3 is one of a group of forgeries taken from the beaker in Beirut, no longer on the market. For the Meges and Neikias beakers, see Harden, "Mould-blown Inscriptions" 170, groups C and D respectively.

134 *Inscribed Cup*

Eastern Mediterranean
First Century A.D.
Moore Collection, 1955.6.68
H. 6.6 cm., D. 6.9 cm.

133

A series of drinking vessels with good wish inscriptions in Greek seems to have been particularly popular in Cyprus and Syria. This cup, exhorting its user to "take the victory," ΛABE THИ NEIKHN

complements the inscription with two rows of victory wreaths. At least two molds of this type are known; their only distinguishing feature is the reversed N in the word THN, as seen here. As has been noted elsewhere, those cups with this epigraphical error must be from a single mold.

DESCRIPTION: mold-blown, three part mold; inscription bordered above and below by a thin raised line and a row of six wreaths; a vertical palm frond on each side hides the mold line; raised circle on base; rim unworked; purple. CONDITION: broken and repaired with some losses and restorations; white weathering and iridescence. PROVENANCE: said to have been excavated near Tyre, Syria; Khayat, 1928; Moore Collection no. 837. BIBLIOGRAPHY: *Kouchakji* no. 71; Hayward, "Yale" 52, no. 5, fig. 6; Amyx, *Echoes* no. 170; *Auth, Newark* no. 57; *SPB, Constable-Maxwell* no. 229. PARALLELS: those cited by Harden, "Mould-blown Inscriptions" 178–79, type Kiii, and Harden, "Yahmour" 93–94. Harden's no. Kiii e is now TMA inv. 23.411, Kiii f and g are TMA inv. 23.412, and Kiii h is TMA inv. 23.410. The provenance of the Yale cup, unknown to Harden at the time of his publications, would

134, 135

seem to preclude his suggested identification of it with his purple beaker no. Kiii d, which was known as early as 1874. *Auth, Newark* no. 57 cites some examples not mentioned by Harden. To these add MMA inv. 37.128.10 (probably pale green, severely weathered); Walters Art Gallery, Baltimore, inv. 47.55 (yellow); *SPB, Constable-Maxwell* no. 229 (yellow).

135 *Inscribed Cup*

Eastern Mediterranean
First Century A.D.
Moore Collection, 1955.6.67
H. 7.7 cm., D. 7.3 cm.

Another example of a "good wishes" cup, this beaker bears the Greek inscription KATAXAIPE KAI EYΦPAINOY, "greetings to all, and be of

good cheer." Vertical palm fronds divide the inscription after the first word, and pairs of palm fronds above the inscription give the effect of a wreath encircling the vessel. As with the ΛABE THN NEIKHN cups, there are at least two molds of this design, differing only in that one uses an erroneous spelling, KATAIXAIPE. An early date for these cups is confirmed by the discovery of an example in a grave on Siphnos datable to A.D. 50–100.

DESCRIPTION: mold-blown, three part mold; the inscription bordered by pairs of palm fronds and two narrow raised horizontal bands above, and by three horizontal bands and a herringbone pattern below; a vertical palm frond on each side at the mold line; one raised circle and a concave central dot on the base; rim unworked; yellowish green. CONDITION: small chip in rim; iridescent. PROVENANCE: said to have been found at Homs, Syria; Khayat, 1922. BIBLIOGRAPHY: *Eisen* 273–74, pl. 60c; Harden, "Mould-blown Inscriptions 172, no. Fii a; *Kouchakji* no. 70; Hayward, "Yale" 51–52, no. 4, fig. 5; *SPB, Constable-Maxwell* no. 181. PARALLELS: Harden, "Mould-blown Inscriptions" 172–74, type Fii, and Harden, "Yahmour" 82–84. Some of the following recent acquisitions may correspond to Harden's unlocated pieces: *Smith, Corning* no. 95, now CMG inv. 59.1.79 (greenish); *JGS* 10 (1968) 181, no. 7, VAM inv. 68.1967 (olive green); *von Saldern, Oppenländer* no. 453; Israeli, "Museum Haaretz" 35–36, fig. 4; *SPB, Constable-Maxwell* no. 181 (pale green). Two fragments cited by *Berger, Vindonissa* 49, nos. 117 and 118, could come from either mold. For the Siphnos vessel, see G. Mackworth Young, "Excavations in Siphnos IV," *Annual of the British School at Athens* 44 (1949) 85, grave 5, pls. 25, no. 2 and 26, nos. 2 and 3, now in the Benaki Museum, Athens.

136 *Cup with Dionysiac Revel*

Eastern Mediterranean
First Century A.D.
Moore Collection, 1955.6.50
H. 16.5 cm., D. 9.6 cm.

On this large and possibly ceremonial vessel, Pan, an hermaphrodite, and a maenad dance while Dionysos gives wine to the panther at his side. The grape vines encircling the vase above and below the scene add to its Dionysiac connotations. Dionysos generally appeared as a young effeminate figure in Roman art, an image based on a type current by the fourth century B.C. The only exception to the popularity of this type occurs in certain archaistic works in which the bearded Dionysos of the sixth and early fifth century B.C. is revived.

The poses of at least two of the figures, Dionysos and the hermaphrodite, are particularly close to the figures on Neo-Attic reliefs. The dancing pose of the maenad with the tambourine also occurs on marble reliefs and silver vases, but with frequent variations in costume. Dionysiac revels were a common subject on Roman relief pottery, Neo-Attic stone reliefs, and stone relief kraters of the first century A.D. Although stylistically different from the Neo-Attic works, this beaker is nonetheless related to them by its processional format.

DESCRIPTION: mold-blown, two part mold; concave folded foot; ground rim; four figures: Pan playing a lyre, with grapes, pipes, and a *cista* in the field; an hermaphrodite (the figure does not have a tail, and is therefore probably not a satyr as suggested by Hayward); a maenad in a long *chiton* playing a tambourine; Dionysos, crowned, half-draped, and leaning on a *thyrsos*, giving wine to a spotted panther from

a jug; grape vines encircling the vessel above and below the scene; transparent olive green. CONDITION: intact and virtually unweathered. PROVENANCE: said to have been found in the necropolis of Beroia at Aleppo, Syria; Kouchakji Frères, New York, 1911; von Gans Collection, 1912; Galerie Bachstitz, The Hague, 1921; Fahim Kouchakji, 1935. BIBLIOGRAPHY: Zahn, *Galerie Bachstitz II* 578, no. 160, pls. 64–65; *Eisen* 232, pls. 48–49; *Kouchakji* no. 52; Hayward, "Yale" 53–55, no. 8, figs. 1, 9, and 10. PARALLELS: from the same mold, but less carefully blown: de Ridder, *de Clercq*, no. 277, Louvre inv. MNE 105 (dark blue), also cited by Zahn, *Galerie Bachstitz II* 65, as a parallel, and illustrated in *La Revue du Louvre* 4–5 (1968) 31–33. For some related figures from Neo-Attic reliefs and Roman pottery, see Oswald and Pryce, *Terra Sigillata* pl. 33, nos. 22, 23, and 29. The shape, although more common in the third and fourth centuries, does exist in the first; see *Isings* type 34.

137 *Seasons Beaker*

Eastern Mediterranean
First Century A.D.
Moore Collection, 1955.6.49
H. 19.0 cm.

This vessel is part of a large family of mold-blown cups with four figures separated by columns. These beakers have been divided into four groups by Gladys Weinberg in a careful study of the figures and

136 B (hermaphrodite), 136 C (maenad), 136 D (Dionysos)

137 A (Poseidon)

137 B (Season), 137 C (Dionysos), 137 D (Season)

their attributes, and comparisons to gems, sarcophagi, terra cotta reliefs, and Arretine vases have led this scholar and others before her to identify the figures on the glass cups as gods and seasons.

Weinberg's group I beakers show Hermes, Herakles, Winter, and a fourth figure variously identified as Hymen, the god of marriage, or a season. Group II, of which the Yale cup is a part, has provoked more discussion, with agreement only on the bearded figure of Poseidon (A) and Dionysos with his panther (C). Mrs. Weinberg's suggestion that the other two figures are seasons, Autumn (B) and Summer (D), seems plausible, especially if Figure D in group I is accepted as a season since the D figures in both groups are clearly the same. It also seems worth noting that the object carried by Figure D on the Yale vase and on a fragment from another vessel of this group found at Dura-Europos is a two-handled vessel not a jug; it is less obvious in the other group II vessels.

There remains some question in my mind whether Figures B and D on the Yale beaker are necessarily male. Although the short tunic is normally masculine attire, it is also worn by maenads and *kalathiskos* dancers on Arretine vases. Further, it seems that the

hair styles and the upper body profiles of these two figures on the Yale vessel are noticeably feminine. This is not so clearly suggested by the other beakers of group II. Whatever the resolution of this question, however, it is obvious that these figures, if they are seasons, differ, with the exception of the figure of Winter in group I, in some marked way from the standard representations of seasons. It seems best to concur with Mrs. Weinberg that any definite conclusions about the identification of these figures and their significance would be untenable.

DESCRIPTION: mold-blown, five part mold; four figures standing on pedestals, facing alternately left and right, separated by fluted Ionic columns which are joined by garlands. Following the Weinberg designation: Figure A: bearded male dressed in an *himation*, holding a trident and a dolphin (Poseidon); Figure B: youthful figure, sex uncertain, dressed in a short *chlamys*, holding a bird in his outstretched hand and another object (a three part object resembling the flower often held by Aphrodite in archaistic reliefs) at his side; Figure C: youthful figure dressed in a short belted tunic, probably Dionysos with *thyrsos*, vessel(?), and panther; Figure D: youthful figure, sex uncertain, dressed in short *chiton* belted above the waist with a *chlamys* worn over it, carrying a two-handled vase in his right hand and a curved staff(?) over his left shoulder. Two sets of mold-blown concentric circles on the base, one set off center and apparently a mistake; rim ground; yellowish brown with purple streaks. CONDITION: intact; some iridescent white weathering. PROVENANCE: said to have come from Hama, Syria; Fahim Kouchakji, 1928. BIBLIOGRAPHY: *Kouchakji* no. 51; Hayward, "Yale" 55–57, figs. 11–14; Clairmont, *Dura* 13, note 26; Weinberg, "Mold-Blown Beakers" 41–42, group II, no. 8, figs. 20–21. PARALLELS: none from the same mold; for the series, see Weinberg, "Mold-Blown Beakers" 26–47. The dimensions for the fragment from Dura-Europos, Weinberg group II, no. 7, are max. H. 6.8 cm., max. W. 2.3 cm., two joining fragments, yellowish green. For a Dionysos on a pedestal, very close to this one in dress and pose but lacking the panther, see Brown, *Terra-Sigillata* pl. 10, nos. 30, 31, and 34. For short tunics worn by maenads and *kalathiskos* dancers, see Brown, *Terra-Sigillata* pl. 3, no. 2, group 1, and pl. 14, nos. 57 and 58 respectively.

138 *Head Flask*

Eastern Mediterranean
First Century A.D.
Lehman Gift, 1953.28.14
H. 10.2 cm.

Mold-blown head flasks in the shape of a human head in the round apparently originated in the first century A.D. Survivors from this early group are rare, and the only excavated examples are two negroid heads found at Pompeii. This bottle, of which eight identical examples are known, shows a female head with a very distinctive hair style. The hair is parted in the center, combed down to meet a row of curls or waves that continues to a bun at the nape of the neck. A small nodus of hair appears at the center front, and two long corkscrew curls hang down the sides of the neck from the back. The woman wears small pendant earrings and shows signs of age in the sagging wrinkles on her neck.

The hair style closely resembles that worn by Livia, the wife of Augustus, and her contemporaries, and it dates the bottle to the first century A.D. If the vessel represents a specific person, as the attention to detail suggests, it is most likely Livia herself.

The question then arises of the function of such a bottle and its place in the iconography of Livia. Dio Cassius (49.38.1 and 55.2.5) mentions official statues erected in her honor in 35 B.C. with Octavian, and in 9 B.C., after the death of Drusus Major. Most of the statues dedicated to Livia in the provinces were erected after A.D. 14, the year of her adoption into the Julian *gens* under Augustus's will and her renaming as Julia Augusta. These statues include a number of joint dedications with Tiberius, as his mother, and

this type continued to be erected until Livia's death in A.D. 29. Another group represents Livia as various goddesses; these presumably date from around the time of her deification under Claudius in A.D. 42. Many of these statues are documented from dedication inscriptions in Greece and Asia Minor, and it can be assumed that similar dedications were offered in the Syro-Palestinian area and Egypt. If this group of bottles does represent Livia, it is probable that they are contemporary with this last group of statues and have some connection, if only honorific, with her cult as the divine Augusta. Even if this identification is rejected, the presence of the distinctive Julio-Claudian hair style confirms a date in the first half of the first century A.D., making these bottles important milestones in the early development of the head flask.

DESCRIPTION: mold-blown, two part mold; rounded rim; transparent brown body and handle. CONDITION: neck of bottle broken and repaired with two restorations in the rim; hair at the center front forehead restored; small loss at the base of the handle; white weathering and iridescence.

138

139, 147, 148, 140

PROVENANCE: John D. Rockefeller, Jr. no. 1; Duveen Brothers no. 32. PARALLELS: from the same mold: *Smith, Corning* no. 281, now CMG inv. 55.1.91 (brown); *Smith, Corning* no. 282, sale Sotheby Parke Bernet, New York, 2 May 1975, lot 183 (pale bluish green); Berlin, Antiken-abteilung inv. 30219.135, ex coll. von Gans, cited by *Smith, Corning* 143, no. 281 (pale green); Hartford, Wadsworth Athenaeum inv. 1930.55 (colorless with a pale green tinge) cited by *Smith, Corning* 143; Washington, D.C. Smithsonian Institution, ex coll. Robert Guggenheim, cited by *Smith, Corning* 143; Toledo, *Glass* 24, inv. 67.8, ex coll. Sangiorgi; Stanford University inv. 17277 (light green), ex coll. Leland Stanford, Jr. said to have been found on Rhodes. For the head flasks from Pompeii, see *Isings* type 78a. For portraits of Livia, see Walter Hatto Gross, *Iulia Augusta, Untersuchungen zur Grundlegung einer Livia-Ikonographie* (Göttingen 1962), reviewed by Helga von Heintze, *AJA* 68 (1964) 318–20; Vagn Poulsen, *Les Portraits Romains* I (Copenhagen 1962) 65–75; Cornelius C. Vermeule III, *Roman Imperial Art in Greece and Asia Minor* (Cambridge, Mass. 1968) 177, and for dedications in Asia Minor pp. 214–16, 218, 220, 224, and 225. For some anonymous female portraits contemporary with Livia and showing a similar hair style, see Anton Hekler, *Greek and Roman Portraits* (New York 1972, reprint) pl. 208.

139 *Date Flask*

Eastern Mediterranean
First Century A.D.
Moore Collection, 1955.6.64
H. 7.2 cm.

The wrinkled surface texture and the color of this vessel combine to give a naturalistic representation of a dried date. Small mold-blown flasks of this type were common in the first and second centuries A.D. and have been found throughout the empire. The short-necked naturalistic examples, in brown or dark blue, are probably earlier than the long-necked and less detailed examples. The date range for the latter group can be established from a late first to second century find at Dura-Europos. An exceptional early date flask from a tomb at Aquileia has a layer of white glass blown inside the outer brown layer.

DESCRIPTION: mold-blown, two part mold; short neck with rounded rim; brown. CONDITION: intact; iridescent.
BIBLIOGRAPHY: *Kouchakji* no. 67; *Hayes, Toronto* no. 87.
PARALLELS: *Isings* type 78d; *Clairmont, Dura* 40, no. 150, pl. 21; *Calvi, Aquileia* pl. 17, no. 3.

140 *Date Flask*

Eastern Mediterranean
First Century A.D.
Lehman Gift, 1953.28.18
H. 7.3 cm.

DESCRIPTION: mold-blown, two part mold; similar to cat. no. 139; rounded rim; brown. CONDITION: small holes and a crack in the body; some iridescence. PROVENANCE: John D. Rockefeller, Jr. no. 65; Duveen Brothers no. 15.

141 *Date Flask*

Eastern Mediterranean
First Century A.D.
Mansfield Collection, 1930.395
H. 6.5 cm.

DESCRIPTION: mold-blown, two part mold; similar to cat.

141, 144, 142, 145, 146

no. 139; rim folded in; brown. CONDITION: broken at the lip; pitted with white weathering.

142 *Date Flask*

Eastern Mediterranean
First Century A.D.
Mansfield Collection, 1930.424
H. 7.7 cm., as restored

DESCRIPTION: mold-blown, two part mold; similar to cat. no. 139; brown. CONDITION: broken and repaired, mouth restored; iridescent. PROVENANCE: Khayat, 1925.

143 *Date Flask*

Eastern Mediterranean
First Century A.D.
Mansfield Collection, 1930.394
H. 7.3 cm.

DESCRIPTION: mold-blown, two part mold; similar to cat. no. 139; rim folded in; brown. CONDITION: intact; slightly weathered.

144 *Date Flask*

Eastern Mediterranean
First Century A.D.
Mansfield Collection, 1930.376
H. 7.1 cm., as restored.

DESCRIPTION: mold-blown, two part mold; similar to cat. no. 139; brown. CONDITION: neck restored; some irridesence.

145 *Date Flask*

Eastern Mediterranean
First Century A.D.
Moore Collection, 1955.6.65
H. 7.3 cm.

DESCRIPTION: mold-blown, two part mold; similar to cat. no. 139; neck pinched on both sides; rim folded in; dark blue. CONDITION: intact; some iridescence. PROVENANCE: probably found near Sidon; Khayat, 1930. BIBLIOGRAPHY: *Kouchakji* no. 68.

146 *Date Flask*

Eastern Mediterranean
First Century A.D.
Mansfield Collection, 1930.393
H. 7.1 cm.

DESCRIPTION: mold-blown, two part mold; similar to cat. no. 139; neck pinched; rim folded in; dark blue. CONDITION: a few tension cracks; one side dull.

147 *Date Flask*

Late First–Second Century A.D.
Van Volkenburgh Bequest, 1940.292
H. 6.75 cm.

DESCRIPTION: mold-blown, two part mold; similar to cat. no. 139 but less naturalistic; slightly flattened oval shape; skin texture only minimally defined; ground rim; brown. CONDITION: hole in the body below the shoulder, with cracks in the same area.

148 *Date Flask*

Eastern Mediterranean
Late First–Second Century A.D.
Mansfield Collection, 1930.396.2
H. 7.3 cm.
DESCRIPTION: mold-blown, two part mold; similar to cat.
no. 147; rim folded in; brown. CONDITION: broken and
repaired; iridescent.

BLOWN, SECOND–THIRD CENTURY A.D.

149 *Bottle*

Eastern Mediterranean
First–Second Century A.D.
Van Volkenburgh Bequest, 1940.274
H. 14 cm.

Contemporary with the early short-necked unguentaria are a series of bottles with longer necks and a
body one-third or less of the total height. These
vessels generally have a conical body and a small
mouth. Blue green and dark green are the dominant
colors. The type appears to be primarily eastern.

DESCRIPTION: free-blown; rim folded in and flattened; dark
green. CONDITION: intact; pitted with thick white
weathering. PARALLELS: *Isings* type 28b; *Dura, Preliminary
Report* pl. 44 from tomb 24, loc. IV, and pl. 52 from tomb
40, loc. VI.

150 *Bottle*

Eastern Mediterranean
First–Second Century A.D.
Moore Collection, 1955.6.98
H. 11.6 cm.

DESCRIPTION: free-blown; similar to cat. no. 149, with a
wheel-cut line around the body; rim folded in; thick blue
green glass. CONDITION: intact; thick light brown weathering over a pitted iridescent surface. BIBLIOGRAPHY: *Eisen*
371, pl. 89; *Kouchakji* no. 102. PARALLELS: *Calvi, Aquileia*
pl. 21, nos. 1, 2, and 4.

151 *Bottle*

Eastern Mediterranean
Second Century A.D.
Lehman Gift, 1953.28.11
H. 12.8 cm.

A variation of the tall-necked bottle with a globular
body appears in second century finds from Dura-
Europos and other sites. This form has a long life and
is found throughout the empire, making precise
dating for unexcavated pieces difficult.

DESCRIPTION: free-blown; rim folded in and flattened; pale
bluish green. CONDITION: intact; surface pitted and
iridescent. PROVENANCE: John D. Rockefeller, Jr. no. 67;
Duveen Brothers no. 21. PARALLELS: *Isings* type 28b;
Dura, Preliminary Report pl. 41 tomb 13 and pl. 54 tomb 40,
loc. XVI.

150, 149, 152, 151

152 *Bottle*

Eastern Mediterranean
Second Century A.D.
Stevens Gift, 1932.1177
H. 16.7 cm.

DESCRIPTION: free-blown; similar to cat. no. 151; rim folded in and flattened; pale bluish green. CONDITION: part of body broken and missing; iridescent.

153 *Bottle*

Eastern Mediterranean
Second Century A.D.
Lehman Gift, 1953.28.12
H. 11.1 cm.

DESCRIPTION: free-blown; similar to cat. no. 151, but without constriction at base of neck; rim folded in and flattened; pale greenish blue. CONDITION: intact; interior slightly iridescent. PROVENANCE: John D. Rockefeller, Jr. no. 41; Duveen Brothers no. 17.

154 *Bottle*

Eastern Mediterranean
Second Century A.D. or later
Yale University Art Gallery, 1955.6.359
H. 7 cm.

DESCRIPTION: free-blown; similar to cat. no. 151; rounded

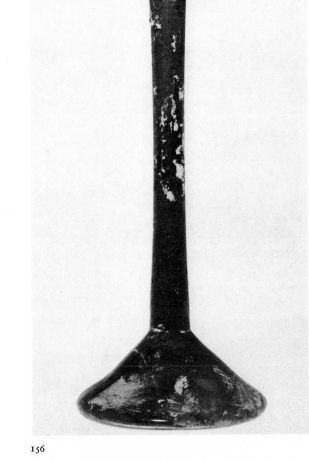

156

, 154

rim; pale green. CONDITION: rim partly broken away; brown weathering.

155 *Bell-Shaped Unguentarium*

Eastern Mediterranean
First–Second Century A.D.
Lehman Gift, 1953.28.6
H. 14.3 cm.

DESCRIPTION: free-blown; slight neck constriction; rounded rim; pale green. CONDITION: intact; faintly iridescent. PROVENANCE: John D. Rockefeller, Jr. no. 54; Duveen Brothers no. 16. PARALLELS: *Calvi, Aquileia* pl. 3, no. 5.

156 *Candlestick Unguentarium*

Eastern Mediterranean
Second–Third Century A.D.
Yale University Art Gallery, 1955.6.371
H. 22.9 cm.

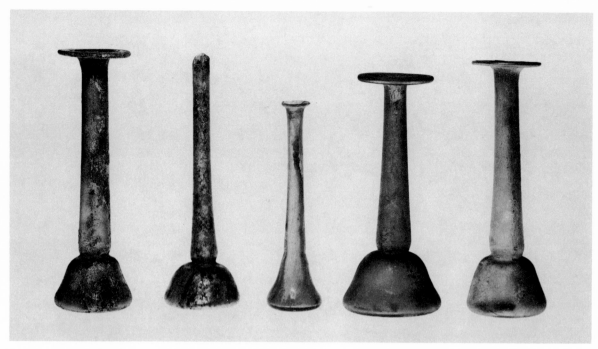

160, 159, 155, 157, 158

A common form of perfume container originating in the second century A.D. is the so-called candlestick unguentarium. Fairly large vessels, they are distinguished by a very long neck, a short body with a wide base, and a wide flattened rim. Some are constricted at the base of the neck. The shape of the body varies from conical and quite flat to bell-shaped or globular, and the majority have a concave base. Most are of natural bluish green, but dark green examples also occur. The shape seems peculiar to glass.

DESCRIPTION: free-blown; bell-shaped body with neck constriction and concave base; rim folded in and flattened; medium green. CONDITION: intact; traces of white weathering. PARALLELS: *Isings* type 82 A 2.

157 *Candlestick Unguentarium*

Eastern Mediterranean
Second–Third Century A.D.
Mansfield Collection, 1930.427
H. 16 cm.

DESCRIPTION: free-blown; similar to cat. no. 156; bell-shaped body; rim folded in and flattened; bluish green. CONDITION: intact; surface pitted and slightly iridescent. PROVENANCE: A. D. Vorce, 1898; probably Mansfield Collection no. 24. PARALLELS: *Isings* type 82 A 1.

158 *Candlestick Unguentarium*

Eastern Mediterranean
Second–Third Century A.D.
Mansfield Collection, 1930.396.1
H. 17.1 cm.

DESCRIPTION: free-blown; similar to cat. no. 156; bell-shaped body; rim folded in and flattened; pale green. CONDITION: intact; surface pitted and iridescent. PROVENANCE: said to be from Cyprus; D. Kelekian, 1898; Mansfield Collection no. 9.

159 *Candlestick Unguentarium*

Eastern Mediterranean
Second–Third Century A.D.
Yale University Art Gallery, 1955.6.361
Pres. H. 17.4 cm.

DESCRIPTION: free-blown; similar to cat. no. 156; bell-shaped body; pale green. CONDITION: mouth broken away; upper neck reconstructed; iridescent.

160 *Candlestick Unguentarium*

Eastern Mediterranean
Second–Third Century A.D.
Van Volkenburgh Bequest, 1940.273
H. 17.7 cm.

163, 161, 162, 164

DESCRIPTION: free-blown; similar to cat. no. 156; bell-shaped body; rim folded in and flattened; pale green. CONDITION: intact; surface pitted and iridescent.

161 *Candlestick Unguentarium*

Eastern Mediterranean
Second–Third Century A.D.
Lehman Gift, 1953.28.8
H. 16.9 cm.

DESCRIPTION: free-blown; similar to cat. no. 156; bell-shaped body; rim folded in and flattened; pale bluish green. CONDITION: intact; interior pitted and iridescent. PROVENANCE: John D. Rockefeller, Jr. no. 51; Duveen Brothers no. 29.

162 *Candlestick Unguentarium*

Eastern Mediterranean
Second–Third Century A.D.
Moore Collection, 1955.6.105
H. 14.8 cm.

DESCRIPTION: free-blown; similar to cat. no. 156; bell-shaped body; rim folded in and flattened; pale green. CONDITION: intact; brown weathering. PROVENANCE: Moore Collection no. 681. BIBLIOGRAPHY: *Eisen* 292; *Kouchakji* no. 109.

163 *Candlestick Unguentarium*

Eastern Mediterranean
Second–Third Century A.D.
Moore Collection, 1955.6.106
Pres. H. 14.7 cm.

DESCRIPTION: free-blown; similar to cat. no. 156; bell-shaped body; pale green. CONDITION: mouth broken away, break polished; base cracked with missing piece; surface pitted and iridescent. PROVENANCE: Moore Collection no. 680. BIBLIOGRAPHY: *Kouchakji* no. 110.

164 *Candlestick Unguentarium*

Possibly Gaulish
Second–Third Century A.D.
Gift of E. Francis Riggs, B.A. 1909 and T. Laurason Riggs, B.A. 1910, 1929.629
H. 10.1 cm.

DESCRIPTION: free-blown; similar to cat. no. 156, but more diminutive in appearance; bell-shaped body; narrow rim folded in; pale green. CONDITION: intact; iridescent. PROVENANCE: said to have been found in France.

165 *Flask*

Eastern Mediterranean
Second–Third Century A.D.

Moore Collection, 1955.6.104
H. 13.5 cm.

Although related to the bell-shaped candlestick unguentaria, this flask has a larger body which renders it more practical if visually somewhat ill-proportioned. It is not a common variant.

DESCRIPTION: free-blown; bell-shaped body; concave base; rim folded in; pale green. CONDITION: intact; one side pitted and iridescent. PROVENANCE: Moore Collection no. 693. BIBLIOGRAPHY: *Kouchakji* no. 108. PARALLELS: *Hayes, Toronto* nos. 499 and 500.

166 *Candlestick Unguentarium*

Eastern Mediterranean
Second–Third Century A.D.
Lehman Gift, 1953.28.7
H. 13.2 cm.

DESCRIPTION: free-blown; similar to cat. no. 156, but with globular body; flattened base; rim folded in; pale bluish green. CONDITION: intact; dull and iridescent. PROVENANCE: John D. Rockefeller, Jr. no. 46; Duveen Brothers no. 9. PARALLELS: *Dura, Preliminary Report* pl. 41 tomb 13.

165

167 *Unguentarium*

Eastern Mediterranean
Second–Third Century A.D.
Van Volkenburgh Bequest, 1940.276
H. 8.5 cm.

DESCRIPTION: free-blown; similar to cat. no. 156, with globular body and small irregular mouth; rim folded in; pale green. CONDITION: intact; iridescent. PARALLELS: *Hayes, Toronto* no. 571.

168 *Candlestick Unguentarium*

Eastern Mediterranean
Second–Third Century A.D.
Stevens Gift, 1932.1175
H. 17.3 cm.

DESCRIPTION: free-blown; similar to cat. no. 156, with globular body; rim folded in and flattened; pale green. CONDITION: intact; brown weathering and iridescence; surface pitted.

169 *Unguentarium*

Eastern Mediterranean
Second–Third Century A.D.
Van Volkenburgh Bequest, 1940.275
H. 13.3 cm.

DESCRIPTION: free-blown and tooled; small two part body; rim folded in and flattened; pale blue. CONDITION: intact; interior pitted and iridescent. PARALLELS: *Auth, Newark* no. 416.

170 *Unguentarium*

Eastern Mediterranean
Second–Third Century A.D.
Moore Collection, 1955.6.109
H. 6.3 cm.

Somewhat smaller than the candlestick unguentaria, this flask represents a group of less exaggerated forms which are more or less contemporary with their more flamboyant cousins. Often rather thick, the glass is generally blue green or dark green.

DESCRIPTION: free-blown; conical body; neck constricted; thick flattened base; rim folded in and flattened; pale bluish green. CONDITION: intact; pitted, with iridescent and beige weathering. BIBLIOGRAPHY: *Eisen* 370; *Kouchakji* no. 115. PARALLELS: *Dura, Preliminary Report* pl. 53 tomb 40, loc. IX, and pl. 56 tomb 46.

168, 169, 167, 166

171 *Unguentarium*

Eastern Mediterranean
Second–Third Century A.D.
Stevens Gift, 1932.1176
H. 8 cm.

DESCRIPTION: free-blown; similar to cat. no. 170; base flattened; rim folded in; green.   CONDITION: intact; pitted and iridescent.

172 *Unguentarium*

Eastern Mediterranean
Second Century A.D.
Oriental Institute, 1940.638
H. 6.6 cm.

The wide neck and thick walls and base of this unguent bottle are considered characteristic of examples manufactured in Egypt in the second and third centuries A.D. Most are dark green. Found in Syria, this bottle may well have been imported, a durable shipping container for a small and relatively inexpensive amount of perfume.

DESCRIPTION: free-blown; rim folded partially and flattened; bluish green.   CONDITION: broken and repaired, with part of the mouth, neck, and base broken away; iridescent.   PROVENANCE: Kurcoğlu, Syria.   PARALLELS: for Egyptian examples, see Harden, *Karanis* nos. 815, 817, 818, pls. 10 and 20.

173 *Unguentarium*

Eastern Mediterranean
Second Century A.D.
Oriental Institute, 1940.639
Pres. H. 5.3 cm.

DESCRIPTION: free-blown; similar to cat. no. 172; dark green.   CONDITION: rim and part of neck broken away; pitted, with black enamel weathering over iridescence.
PROVENANCE: Kurcoğlu, Syria.

174 *Unguentarium*

Eastern Mediterranean
Third Century A.D.
Van Volkenburgh Bequest, 1940.277
H. 6.5 cm.

DESCRIPTION: free-blown; similar to cat. no. 172, without neck constriction; rim folded in and flattened; dark green.
CONDITION: broken and repaired; pitted and iridescent.
PARALLELS: Harden, *Karanis* Class XIII, type E.

175 *Miniature Bottle*

Eastern Mediterranean
First–Third Century A.D.
Moore Collection, 1955.6.108
H. 2.3 cm.

This miniature bottle is opaque blue, suggesting an early date despite a shape which is generally dated to the third century. It does not seem unlikely that small, fairly carelessly made bottles such as this were made over a long period.

DESCRIPTION: free-blown; flattened base; folded in rim; opaque medium blue. CONDITION: intact and virtually unweathered. BIBLIOGRAPHY: *Kouchakji* no. 114. PARALLELS: *Hayes, Toronto* nos. 583 and 584; *Auth, Newark* nos. 511 and 512.

176 *Miniature Unguentarium*

Eastern Mediterranean
Third Century A.D.
Lehman Gift, 1953.28.3
H. 3.1 cm.

DESCRIPTION: free-blown; similar to cat. no. 175; rim folded in and flattened; pale green. CONDITION: intact; thick tan weathering, flaking away. PROVENANCE: John D. Rockefeller, Jr. no. 37; Duveen Brothers no. 7. PARALLELS: *Hayes, Toronto* nos. 583 and 584, from the Fayum; *Auth, Newark* nos. 511 and 512.

177 *Miniature Unguentarium*

Eastern Mediterranean
Third Century A.D.
Van Volkenburgh Bequest, 1940.282
H. 3.8 cm.

DESCRIPTION: free-blown; similar to cat. no. 175; rounded rim; pale green. CONDITION: intact; thick tan weathering.

178 *Miniature Bottle*

Eastern Mediterranean
First–Third Century A.D.
Van Volkenburgh Bequest, 1940.279
H. 3.8 cm.

DESCRIPTION: free-blown; similar to cat. no. 175, but with more bulbous body; flattened base; rim folded in; opaque medium blue. CONDITION: intact; brown and white weathering. PARALLELS: *Hayes, Toronto* nos. 271 and 272; *Spartz, Kassel* nos. 146–52, date third–fourth century but natural blue green.

179 *Unguentarium*

Eastern Mediterranean
Second Century A.D.
Oriental Institute, 1940.640
H. 6.8 cm.

Although part of the candlestick unguentarium family, this variety has no constriction, and the neck flows smoothly into the body. Often smaller than the constricted type, these bottles are also simpler and more restrained in form.

DESCRIPTION: free-blown; rim folded in; greenish blue. CONDITION: lower body repaired, with part of the base missing; iridescent. PROVENANCE: Kurcoğlu, Syria. PARALLELS: *Isings* type 82 B 1 or 2.

180 *Unguentarium*

Eastern Mediterranean
Second Century A.D.
Oriental Institute, 1940.637
H. 5.3 cm.

DESCRIPTION: free-blown; similar to cat. no. 179; rim folded in; dark green. CONDITION: intact; black enamel weathering. PROVENANCE: Kurcoğlu, Syria.

181 *Unguentarium*

Eastern Mediterranean
Second Century A.D.
Oriental Institute, 1940.636
H. 6.3 cm.

DESCRIPTION: free-blown; similar to cat. no. 179, with small, clublike base; rim folded in; pale bluish green. CONDITION: intact; brown and yellow enamel weathering. PROVENANCE: Kurcoğlu, Syria. PARALLELS: *Isings* type 82 B 1.

182 *Funnel-Mouthed Bottle*

Eastern Mediterranean
Second Century A.D.
Moore Collection, 1955.6.364
H. 7.9 cm.

Sack-shaped or pear-shaped flasks with a funnel mouth were found in a tomb of Antonine date at Amathus, Cyprus. Like this example, they were often carelessly made and irregular in shape.

DESCRIPTION: free-blown; concave base; rounded rim; pale green, nearly colorless. CONDITION: intact; slightly weathered. PARALLELS: Vessberg, "Cyprus" pl. 7, nos. 32 and 33; *Hayes, Toronto* no. 316, as fourth century.

183 *Bottle*

Eastern Mediterranean
Second Century A.D.
Lehman Gift, 1953.28.25
H. 5.6 cm.

171, 170, 173, 172

177, 176, 175, 178

174, 181, 180, 179

DESCRIPTION: free-blown; similar to cat. no. 182; flattened slightly on two sides; neck constricted; irregular rim; green. CONDITION: mouth chipped; slightly iridescent with some tan weathering. PROVENANCE: John D. Rockefeller, Jr. no. 24; Duveen Brothers no. 26.

184 *Bottle with Snake Thread Decoration*

Eastern Mediterranean
Late Second Century A.D.
Moore Collection, 1955.6.132
H. 15.5 cm.

Glass vessels with trailed-on thread decoration forming abstract designs on the surface were manufactured in both the eastern and western Roman Empire. Called "snake thread decoration" because of the serpentine manner in which the thread wanders over the surface, this type of decoration is one of the most original and strictly glass oriented to be produced by Roman glassmakers.

Although a certain amount of discussion has been devoted to the question of whether the technique originated in eastern or western glass factories, recent excavations would seem to bear out D. B. Harden's belief that snake thread, like so many other glass-making techniques, travelled from east to west. Eastern examples are still comparatively rare, however, and both the statistics and the virtuosity of the western products indicate that the flowering of the style took place around Cologne. Dates range from the second to the fourth century A.D.

Certain general differences can be cited between eastern and western snake thread glass, although there are, of course, exceptions to these broad characterizations. The eastern Mediterranean variety, a product of the Syro-Palestinian region, is usually monochrome, that is the snake thread is the same

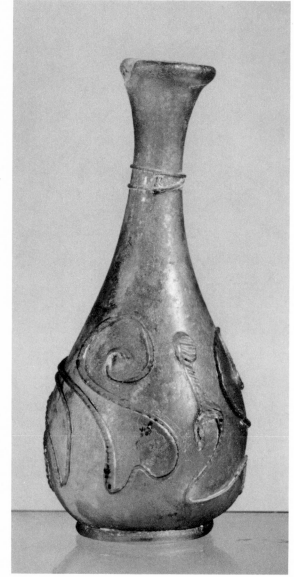

184

182, 183

color as the vessel. The snake thread itself is often flattened and ridged, as in the present example. It is differentiated in this way from the normal thread decoration which often occurs in combination with the snake thread, as can be seen from the thread that encircles the neck of this bottle. Western empire snake thread decoration is typically of a different color than the vessel. Often more than one color is used for the decoration, with yellow and dark blue being the most frequent combination. Exceptions to these patterns are not all that rare, and they include excavated examples such as a fragment of a colorless flask with deep turquoise snake thread from Dura-

Europos and a monochrome fragment found at Gulpen, The Netherlands, as well as famous pieces such as the helmeted head from Cologne in the British Museum which combines the flattened ridged snake thread normally associated with eastern vessels with the rich use of color typical of Cologne.

The present bottle has all the hallmarks of eastern snake thread with the flat ridged decoration executed in the same pale green as the vessel. It finds a close parallel in a piriform flask from Idalion, Cyprus, now in the British Museum.

DESCRIPTION: free-blown with snake thread decoration; ring base trailed on; turned in rim; pale green. CONDITION: part of the mouth and some fragments of the snake thread missing; iridescent and pitted. PROVENANCE: Kouchakji Frères, 1919; Moore Collection no. 740. BIBLIOGRAPHY: *Eisen* 378, 383, pl. 95; *Kouchakji* no. 138. PARALLELS: Harden, *Masterpieces* no. 81, inv. 71.1–23.1, from Idalion, Cyprus. For the Dura fragment, see *Clairmont, Dura* no. 175, and another example, no. 177; for the fragment from Gulpen, see Isings, *Limburg* 21, no. 58; for the helmeted head in the BM, see Harden, *Masterpieces* no. 84. On snake thread glass in general, see D. B. Harden, "Snake-thread Glasses Found in the East," *JRS* 24 (1934) 50–55; *Fremersdorf, Denkmäler* V: *Romische Gläser mit Fadenauflage in Köln;* Dan Barag, "'Flower and Bird' and Snake-thread Glass Vessels," *Annales du 4ᵉ Congrès des Journées Internationales du Verre, Ravenne-Venise, 13–20 mai 1967* (Liége, n.d.) 55–66.

185 *Miniature Bottle*

Eastern Mediterranean
Second–Third Century A.D.
Moore Collection, 1955.6.242
H. 2.6 cm.

In most respects this miniature bottle is similar to the larger flasks which it imitates, but the difficulty of working on such a small scale forced the glassmaker to substitute a rather thick pad for the usual cut-out base.

DESCRIPTION: free-blown with thick pad base; turned in rim; pale yellow. CONDITION: half of the mouth broken away; iridescent. PARALLELS: *Hayes, Toronto* no. 553, citing parallels from Karanis.

186 *Square Jug*

Eastern Mediterranean
Second–Third Century A.D.
Moore Collection, 1955.6.131
H. 10.5 cm.

A small version of the square bottle familiar from the first and second centuries A.D., this vessel has a sloping shoulder, virtually no neck, and a vestigal strap handle.

DESCRIPTION: free-blown; thick walls; rim folded in and flattened; medium green. CONDITION: part of rim restored; pitted and iridescent. PROVENANCE: Moore Collection no. 713. BIBLIOGRAPHY: *Kouchakji* no. 137.

187 *Bowl or Cup*

Eastern Mediterranean
Second–Third Century A.D.
Moore Collection, 1955.6.91
H. 6.5 cm., D. 10.1 cm.

DESCRIPTION: free-blown; cut-out foot; rounded rim; pale bluish green. CONDITION: large chip out of rim; brown weathering and iridescence. BIBLIOGRAPHY: *Eisen* 296, pl. 71 top; *Kouchakji* no. 94. PARALLELS: Vessberg, "Cyprus" 117, deep bowl type C II, pl. 2, no. 15; *Hayes, Toronto* no. 297.

185, 186, 187

MOLD-BLOWN, SECOND–THIRD
CENTURY A.D.

188 *Head Flask*

Eastern Mediterranean
Second Century A.D.
Moore Collection, 1955.6.76
H. 8 cm.

Of the fairly large series of mold-blown head flasks, by far the greatest number are double or janiform flasks. This type seems to have been a second century invention, and it continues into the third and fourth centuries, although there are few datable examples to provide a firm chronology. One excavated vessel, from a tomb at Dura-Europos, was found with a coin of Commodus, thus giving a late second century date to the vessels with stylized knobby hair. The head flasks vary widely in quality and attention to detail. The more naturalistic faces, such as this example, are less common and possibly earlier than the faces with the stylized knobby hair of the Dura bottle.

The identity of the person represented varies as well. Some vessels, including the present one, show faces of Medusa. Although these are generally the softened, benign Medusa typical of the Hellenistic period, the knotted snakes under the chin leave no doubt about the identification. Other vessels have faces of Bacchantes, with their hair wreathed in grape vines. Many vessels lack any identifying attributes; perhaps these show Eros or Cupid, a figure popular in Roman art and well suited to adorn vessels used mainly for perfume.

Exact parallels to these vessels in other media are lacking. Head flasks in bronze and terra cotta were made in the Hellenistic and Roman periods, but these are not janiform. Although the earlier bronze vessels could be regarded as prototypes for the first century glass flasks with single heads in the round, the double faced flasks seem to have been developed independently by glassmakers. The terra cotta vessels are generally later than the glass bottles. They are primarily the product of North African pottery workshops, especially that of Navigius in central Tunisia, and date from circa A.D. 280–320.

DESCRIPTION: mold-blown, two part mold with the two faces virtually identical; flat base; slight neck constriction; rim folded in; pale brown. CONDITION: intact; milky iridescent weathering. PROVENANCE: Moore Collection no. 774. BIBLIOGRAPHY: *Eisen* 330, pl. 74a; *Kouchakji* no. 79; *Hayes, Toronto* 50, no. 94. PARALLELS: apparently from the same mold: *von Saldern, Oppenländer* no. 464; probably *Vessberg, "Cyprus"* pl. 16, no. 3. On head flasks in general, see *Isings* type 78a; *Clairmont, Dura* 37–38, nos. 132–45, all janiform flasks except one, mostly fragmentary; *Vessberg, "Cyprus"* 136, flask type B VI. For the late example, see *Harden, Karanis* 214, no. 629 with a *chi-ro* monogram; *Clairmont, Dura* 37, note 36 cites other late examples. Three terra sigillata head flasks from the workshop of Navigius are now in the Louvre: inv. A06630, A06631, and A06632, all from El Aouja; see also an example from the workshop of Olitresus, *Romans and Barbarians*, exhibition catalogue, BMFA, 17 December 1976–27 February 1977, no. 133. For a bronze example, see D. G. Mitten and S. F. Doeringer, *Master Bronzes from the Classical World*, exhibition catalogue, Fogg Art Museum, Cambridge, Mass., 4 December 1967–23 January 1968, no. 310.

188, 189

189 *Head Flask*

Eastern Mediterranean
Second Century A.D.
Van Volkenburgh Bequest, 1940.270
H. 8.7 cm.

Although lacking some of the detail and expressive qualities of the previous example, this flask is not yet completely stylized. The two faces differ slightly, with one wearing a fillet.

DESCRIPTION: mold-blown, two part mold; base flattened after removal from the mold; rim folded in; pale green.
CONDITION: intact; iridescent.

190 *Head Flask with Four Faces*

Eastern Mediterranean
Second Century A.D.
Moore Collection, 1955.6.74
H. 8.5 cm.

Head flasks with four faces are rare. In this example each face is different: one wears a diadem or *stephane*, one has two curls or possibly snakes tied together on the top of the head, and the other two have curly hair but are not alike. All appear to be female, and all have the doughnut eyes that are common in the double-faced flasks. A grape vine encircles the shoulder of the flask above the faces, suggesting that they might represent maenads.

DESCRIPTION: mold-blown, two part mold; neck constricted to a sprinkler hole; rim folded in; pale bluish green.
CONDITION: unbroken, but with strain cracks in the base, a few in the body, and one in the neck; virtually unweathered.
BIBLIOGRAPHY: *Kouchakji* no. 77; Hayward, "Yale" 60, note 30; *Auth, Newark* 75, no. 76. PARALLELS: from the same mold: *Smith, Corning* no. 287, CMG inv. 59.1.151 (pale yellow). From a related mold: *Auth, Newark* no. 76, a sprinkler flask with masks. For a series of square bottles with four faces now considered to be modern, see von Saldern, "Reproductions" 309–10, and three related modern glass "weights," cat. no. A12 (Appendix).

191 *Head Flask*

Eastern Mediterranean
Late Second–Third Century A.D.
Mansfield Collection, 1930.413
H. 8.7 cm.

The stylized knobby hair of this flask would have been easy to produce in a terra cotta mold. It is characteristic of the most common type of double head flask.

DESCRIPTION: mold-blown, two part mold; base stamped with illegible inscription (maker's mark?) after removal

from mold (see drawing); rim folded in; pale green.
CONDITION: part of the mouth missing, another section repaired; iridescent with some brown weathering. PROVENANCE: said to have been found at Tel-el-Horus, Syria; Khayat, 1911; Mansfield Collection no. 198. PARALLELS: *von Saldern, Oppenländer* no. 465, with a cross on the bottom.

190, 191

Later Roman Vessels

BLOWN, THIRD–FOURTH CENTURY A.D.

192 *Flask*

> Eastern Mediterranean
> Third Century A.D.
> Mansfield Collection, 1930.404
> H. 12.8 cm.

This piriform vessel may have served as a small decanter for wine or oil. The stabilizing base ring and simple spiral thread are in keeping with a utilitarian design.

DESCRIPTION: free-blown; trailed-on thread around the neck; ring base; pale green. CONDITION: intact; pitted and iridescent. PROVENANCE: bought from Kelekian. PARALLELS: Vessberg, "Cyprus" pl. 8, no. 1; *von Saldern, Oppenländer* no. 660; *Auth, Newark* no. 154, with other parallels.

193 *Bottle*

> Eastern Mediterranean
> Late Third Century A.D.
> Gift of Shepherd Stevens, B.F.A. 1922, 1947.330
> H. 10.4 cm.

DESCRIPTION: free-blown; conical body; concave base; rim folded in; body and handles olive green. CONDITION: broken and repaired; iridescent and pitted.

194 *Jug*

> Eastern Mediterranean
> Late Third–Fouth Century A.D.
> Moore Collection, 1955.6.122
> H. 17 cm.

A tall neck and a funnel mouth encircled by a thread distinguish this cylindrical jug from first and second century examples.

192, 193

194, 196

DESCRIPTION: free-blown; concave base; trailed thread on exterior below rim; triple ribbed handle; pale green. CONDITION: intact; iridescent. BIBLIOGRAPHY: *Kouchakji* no. 128. PARALLELS: *Isings* type 126, with most datable finds coming from the Near East, although the form occurs in the western provinces as well.

DESCRIPTION: free-blown; similar to cat. no. 195 but taller, and narrow toward base; trefoil mouth; rim folded in; pale green. CONDITION: reconstructed, with losses around the middle; iridescent. PARALLELS: *Hayes, Toronto* no. 435.

195

195 *Small Jug*

Eastern Mediterranean
Third–Fourth Century A.D.
Yale University Art Gallery, 1955.6.368
H. 7.0 cm.

DESCRIPTION: free-blown; thin walls; slightly concave base; rim folded in; colorless with a greenish angular handle. CONDITION: intact; slight white weathering.

196 *Jug*

Eastern Mediterranean
Third–Fourth Century A.D.
Mansfield Collection, 1930.388
H. 15.3 cm.

197 Jug

Eastern Mediterranean
Third–Fourth Century A.D.
Moore Collection, 1955.6.219
H. 10.7 cm.

Somewhat more squat than the previous jug, this
form is more common. The combination of a purple
body and a green handle indicate a revival of the
interest in color contrast in the eastern Mediterranean
at this time which can best be seen in the trailed
thread decoration of fourth–fifth century vessels.

DESCRIPTION: free-blown; concave base; rounded rim;
purple with green handle. CONDITION: intact; virtually
unweathered. PROVENANCE: Moore Collection no. 664.
BIBLIOGRAPHY: *Eisen* pl. 157; *Kouchakji* no. 226 PARALLELS:
Isings type 88b; *Hayes, Toronto* no. 416, with round mouth,
no. 314, with trefoil mouth and neck thread; Damascus
Museum no. 81 (Dura photo) with neck thread, and no. 65,
with wide strap handle and round mouth (Dura photo). For
a mold-blown parallel with dots, see Damascus Museum
nos. 75, 78 (Dura photos), and others.

198 *Trefoil-Mouthed Jug*

Eastern Mediterranean
Late Second or Third Century A.D.
Moore Collection, 1955.6.218
H. 10 cm.

DESCRIPTION: free-blown; nearly spherical body; pontil
mark on base; rim folded in; trailed-on angular handle,
folded below rim; medium blue green. CONDITION: spout
restored; bubbly matrix; milky weathering and dull surface. PROVENANCE: Moore Collection no. 687. BIBLI-
OGRAPHY: *Eisen* pl. 157; *Kouchakji* no. 225. PARALLELS:
Isings type 88b; *Hayes, Toronto* no. 277; a single example
from Cyprus in Vessberg, "Cyprus" pl. 5, no. 13; *Fremersdorf, Denkmäler* IV pl. 62, ca. A.D. 100.

199 Jug

Eastern Mediterranean
Third Century A.D.
Gift of Edward B. Greene, B.A. 1900, 1930.44
H. 12.5 cm.

DESCRIPTION: free-blown; similar to cat. no. 198; row of
circular indentations around body below trailed-on handle,
folded slightly below the rim; bubbly pale greyish green.
CONDITION: intact; blackish weathering, now flaking off.
PROVENANCE: Alfred R. Bellinger.

200 *Jug*

Probably Western Empire, perhaps Rhineland
Third Century A.D.
Moore Collection, 1955.6.130
H. 10.1 cm.

This type of squat biconical jug with a pinched
mouth and a chain or ribbed handle seems to have
been manufactured primarily, if not exclusively, in
the western provinces. Dated finds are as early as the
second century but occur mainly in third century
contexts. The chain handles are particularly common
in the Mainz district and occur on a number of other
jug shapes in the third and fourth centuries.

DESCRIPTION: free-blown; ring base; pinched mouth with
rim folded in; chain handle; spiral thread around the body
and neck; pale green. CONDITION: small pieces of thread
decoration missing; slight iridescence. PROVENANCE:
Moore Collection no. 791; possibly the jug Mrs. Moore
bought from A. Khayat on 24 January 1925, said to have
been found in Caesarea, Palestine; if so, it was apparently
an import. BIBLIOGRAPHY: *Eisen* 446, pl. 108; *Kouchakji*
no. 136. PARALLELS: from western finds: *Isings* type 106;
W. A. van Es, *Romeinen in Nederland* (Bussum 1972) 160,
fig. 114, with globular body and a chain handle, found in
the third century cemetery of Pandhof, St. Servaas; Rhein-

197, 198, 199

isches Landesmuseum, Bonn, inv. 9198, with flat handle and no thread decoration (pale green) from Cologne, inv. 218, with round mouth and ribbed handle (greenish with a yellow gray tinge), inv. 3365, from Miesenheim, and inv. 15499, from Andernach; MMA inv. 81.10.168 and inv. 81.10.169, with round mouths (both pale green), found in a tomb at Beauvais in 1863 with other glass and a bronze coin of M.C.L. Postumus struck between A.D. 260 and 268, ex colls. Charvet and Marquand.

200

201 *Ovoid Jug*

Eastern Mediterranean
Third–Fourth Century A.D.
Moore Collection, 1955.6.123
H. 5 cm.

DESCRIPTION: free-blown; rim folded in; pad base; body, handle, and neck thread pale yellowish green. CONDITION: thread broken away near handle; pitted, with pale brown enamel weathering and iridescence. PROVENANCE: Moore Collection no. 676. BIBLIOGRAPHY: *Eisen* 361, pl. 94; *Kouchakji* no. 129. PARALLELS: *Isings* type 57; Isings, *Limburg* nos. 210 and 211; *Spartz, Kassel* no. 41; *Eisen* pl. 88, lower right.

202 *Ovoid Jug*

Eastern Mediterranean
Third–Fourth Century A.D.
Moore Collection, 1955.6.124
H. 6.7 cm.

DESCRIPTION: free-blown; similar to cat. no. 201; cut-out base; rim folded in; body and handle pale green. CONDITION: intact; pitted and iridescent. PROVENANCE: Moore Collection no. 743. BIBLIOGRAPHY: *Eisen* 361, pl. 94; *Kouchakji* no. 130. PARALLELS: Isings, *Limburg* no. 211, without base as is normal for this type; *Berger, Vindonissa* pl. 20, no. 77(14), without base; *Fremersdorf, Denkmäler* IV pl. 14, with vertical ribs and no base.

201, 202

203 *Wheel-Engraved Flask*

Eastern Mediterranean
Third–Fourth Century A.D.
Mansfield Collection, 1930.425
H. 14 cm.

Undecorated flasks of this shape occur in both eastern and western provinces of the Roman Empire, distinguishable from other globular flasks by their neck constriction and unworked rim. Decorated examples are mostly wheel-engraved. These include the well-known bottles with views of Puteoli and Baiae, two ancient harbors on the Bay of Naples, which were undoubtedly made in Italy. A second group, characterized by intersecting circles and bands, includes the Yale flask. Finds of the circle and band type have come from both eastern and western sites, Dura-Europos and Cologne among them, and it seems safe to assume that they were made in both areas.

DESCRIPTION: free-blown with neck constriction and unworked rim; wheel-engraved bands around the neck and body with a wide band of concentric circles emphasizing the point of maximum diameter; pale yellow. CONDITION: broken and repaired; tan and white weathering, pitted and iridescent underneath. PROVENANCE: found in 1902 at Tel-el-Hoson, Syria; Khayat, 1903; Mansfield Collection

203, 204

no. 138. PARALLELS: for the shape, see *Isings* type 103; a painted example with a lion hunt from Cologne is reproduced by Doppelfeld, *Köln* pl. 165; for a recent and thorough discussion of the widely published Puteoli bottles, see K. S. Painter, "Roman Flasks with Scenes of Baiae and Puteoli," *JGS* 17 (1975) 54–67, with bibliography; for the circle and band type, see, for example, *Fremersdorf, Denkmäler* III 109 ff., pls. 110 and 112, from Cologne, *Clairmont, Dura* 111–12, nos. 540 and 541, and *Smith, Corning* nos. 373 and 374.

204 *Large Bottle*

> Eastern Mediterranean
> Third–Fourth Century A.D.
> Stevens Gift, 1932.1178
> H. 21.8 cm.

DESCRIPTION: free-blown, with thin walls and a concave base; rim folded in; pale bluish green. CONDITION: lower body broken on one side with many pieces missing; dull and iridescent. PARALLELS: *Isings* type 101, a common fourth century type which originated in the third century.

205

205 Tall-Necked Bottle

Eastern Mediterranean
Third–Fourth Century A.D.
Moore Collection, 1955.6.101
H. 16.2 cm.

DESCRIPTION: free-blown; slightly concave base; rim folded
in; bubbly matrix; pale yellow with tinges of purple.
CONDITION: intact; surface severely pitted, with traces of
brown and black weathering; iridescent. PROVENANCE:
Moore Collection no. 716. BIBLIOGRAPHY: *Eisen* 370, pl.
90; *Kouchakji* no. 105. PARALLELS: Crowfoot, *Samaria-
Sebaste* fig. 94, no. 8 from a third century A.D. tomb.

206 Bottle

Eastern Mediterranean
Third–Fourth Century A.D.
Yale University Art Gallery, 1955.6.367
H. 7.2 cm.

DESCRIPTION: free-blown; rim folded in; slightly concave
base; pale green. CONDITION: intact; white weathering.
PARALLELS: *Spartz, Kassel* nos. 109, 145, and 154; *Hayes,
Toronto* no. 266.

207 Flask

Eastern Mediterranean
Third–Fourth Century A.D.
Whiting Collection, 1912.932
H. 9 cm.

DESCRIPTION: free-blown; similar to cat. no. 206; rim
folded in; pale green. CONDITION: intact; weathered.

208 Bottle

Eastern Mediterranean
Third–Fourth Century A.D.
Moore Collection, 1955.6.197
H. 6.1 cm.

DESCRIPTION: free-blown; similar to cat. no. 206; slightly
concave base; rim folded in; thick bluish green glass.
CONDITION: intact; brown and iridescent weathering.
BIBLIOGRAPHY: *Kouchakji* no. 204.

209 Indented Bottle

Eastern Mediterranean
Third–Fourth Century A.D.
Yale University Art Gallery, 1947.253
H. 5.9 cm.

DESCRIPTION: free-blown; indented body; concave base;

206, 207

208, 209

rim folded out and down; pale bluish green. CONDITION:
part of rim missing; strain cracks in the body; surface
slightly dulled.

210 Indented Bottle

Eastern Mediterranean
Third-Fourth Century A.D.
Moore Collection, 1955.6.83
H. 5.3 cm.

DESCRIPTION: free-blown, indented; concave base; rim
folded in; bottle and neck coil pale green. CONDITION:
intact; thick white weathering, flaking off, leaving an

210, 211, 212

iridescent surface underneath. PROVENANCE: Moore Collection no. 705. BIBLIOGRAPHY: *Kouchakji* no. 86.

211 *Bottle*

Eastern Mediterranean
Third–Fourth Century A.D.
Moore Collection, 1955.6.140
H. 12.5 cm.

Although close in shape to the common globular flasks of the third and fourth century, this bottle is distinguished from them by the glassblower's use of a constriction to form a decorative band around the center of the body.

DESCRIPTION: free-blown; constriction probably made with a wire; concave base; rim folded in; pale green. CONDITION: intact; iridescent. PROVENANCE: Moore Collection no. 668. BIBLIOGRAPHY: *Kouchakji* no. 147. PARALLELS: *Isings* type 101, without the constriction, for which I know no parallel.

212 *Bottle*

Eastern Mediterranean
Third–Fourth Century A.D.
Yale University Art Gallery, 1955.6.365
H. 11.7 cm.

DESCRIPTION: free-blown; irregular globular body; rim folded in; slightly concave base; pale green. CONDITION:

214, 213, 215, 216

intact; interior iridescent. PARALLELS: *Spartz, Kassel* no. III.

213 *Funnel-Mouthed Flask*

> Eastern Mediterranean
> Third–Fourth Century A.D.
> Gift of Edward B. Greene, B.A. 1900, 1930.46
> H. 10.1 cm.

The funnel mouth of this pear-shaped flask is typical of bottles of the third and fourth centuries.

DESCRIPTION: free-blown; rim folded in; medium blue green. CONDITION: part of mouth missing; traces of light brown weathering and slight iridescence. PROVENANCE: Alfred R. Bellinger.

214 *Indented Flask*

> Eastern Mediterranean
> Third–Fourth Century A.D.
> Moore Collection, 1955.6.85
> H. 12.6 cm.

DESCRIPTION: free-blown; indented; concave base; rim folded in; colorless. CONDITION: intact; iridescent and flaking. PROVENANCE: Moore Collection no. 682. BIBLIOGRAPHY: *Eisen* 295, pl. 69b; *Kouchakji* no. 88. PARALLELS: for indentations, a fairly common form of decoration, see for example *von Saldern, Oppenländer* nos. 632–38; for the shape, see Crowfoot, *Samaria-Sebaste* fig. 94, no. 10 from a third century A.D. tomb.

215 *Bell-Shaped Flask*

> Eastern Mediterranean
> Third–Fourth Century A.D.
> Van Volkenburgh Bequest, 1940.271
> H. 10.1 cm.

This flask with a bell-shaped body and funnel mouth is a later, less exaggerated, and possibly more practical form of the bell-shaped candlestick unguentarium. Like most glass of this period, it is pale green.

DESCRIPTION: free-blown; flat base; rim folded in; bubbly; pale green. CONDITION: intact; pitted and iridescent. PARALLELS: *Isings* type 133.

216 *Indented Flask*

> Eastern Mediterranean
> Fourth Century A.D.
> Moore Collection, 1955.6.84
> H. 10.9 cm.

218

DESCRIPTION: free-blown; indented; flattened base; rim folded in; pale green. CONDITION: intact; iridescent interior. BIBLIOGRAPHY: *Eisen* 295, pl. 69; *Kouchakji* no. 87. PARALLELS: Barag, *Beth She\u02bbarim* 151, nos. 1–6.

217 *Ribbed Bottle*

> Eastern Mediterranean
> Fourth Century A.D.
> Moore Collection, 1955.6.204
> Pres. H. 6.4 cm.

The faint ribs on the shoulder of this flask suggest that it is a later version of the funnel-mouthed flask. Most of the mouth is missing, destroying the proportions of the original form.

DESCRIPTION: "optic blown" or molded and blown; concave base; pale bluish green. CONDITION: most of mouth missing; iridescent. BIBLIOGRAPHY: *Kouchakji* no. 211. PARALLELS: *Hayes, Toronto* nos. 316–18; for optic blowing, see *von Saldern, Oppenländer* no. 491 with other references, and for some excavated examples with fourth century contexts see Waldemar Haberey, "Spätantike Gläser aus Gräbern von Mayen," *Bonner Jahrbücher* 147 (1942) 253, pl. 35, no. 2.

218 *Funnel-Mouthed Bottle*

> Eastern Mediterranean
> Fourth Century A.D.

217, 219, 220

Yale University Art Gallery, 1947.252
Pres. H. 10.4 cm.

DESCRIPTION: free-blown; concave base; pale green. CONDITION: mouth broken away; tan weathering. PARALLELS: *Hayes, Toronto* no. 314.

219 *Square Bottle*

Eastern Mediterranean
Third–Fourth Century A.D.
Whiting Collection, 1912.944
H. 13.3 cm.

Although the small square body is a fairly common shape among bottles in the western empire, it is less frequently found in the east. A few examples from Cyprus provide an approximate date for this Syro-Palestinian example. The molded bottoms of the so-called Mercury bottles of the western empire seem to be peculiar to that area.

DESCRIPTION: free-blown and marvered, with pontil mark on the base; rim folded in; pale green. CONDITION: intact; traces of white and iridescent weathering; exposed surface dull. PARALLELS: *Isings* type 84, mainly western examples; Vessberg, "Cyprus" 139, pl. 9, no. 13.

220 *Square Bottle*

Eastern Mediterranean
Third–Fourth Century A.D.
Moore Collection, 1955.6.162
Pres. H. 5.3 cm.

DESCRIPTION: free-blown; similar to cat. no. 219, but narrowing towards the base; plain base with pontil mark; green. CONDITION: neck and mouth missing; iridescent. BIBLIOGRAPHY: *Kouchakji* no. 169.

221 *Cylindrical Bottle*

Eastern Mediterranean
Third–Fourth Century A.D.
Mansfield Collection, 1930.433
H. 13 cm.

Cylindrical bottles of the third and fourth centuries are characterized by two types of mouth: one folded in and flattened as in this example, and the other, the more common funnel mouth with a trailed-on ring underneath. Both types are consistently pale green.

DESCRIPTION: free-blown, marvered to shape; concave base; rim folded in and flattened; pale green. CONDITION: intact; interior iridescent. PROVENANCE: acquired from A. D. Vorce in 1898; Mansfield Collection no. 32. PARALLELS: *Isings* type 102a; Damascus Museum nos. 185, 187, and 189 (Dura photos); *Hayes, Toronto* no. 433, mold-blown with vertical ribs.

222 *Cylindrical Bottle*

Eastern Mediterranean
Third–Fourth Century A.D.
Moore Collection, 1955.6.96
H. 8.3 cm.

DESCRIPTION: free-blown, marvered to shape; similar to

221, 222, 223

cat. no. 221; concave base; rim folded in and flattened; pale green. CONDITION: intact; iridescent with white weathering on the mouth. BIBLIOGRAPHY: *Kouchakji* no. 100.

223 *Cylindrical Bottle*

Eastern Mediterranean
Third–Fourth Century A.D.
Whiting Collection, 1912.937
H. 10.2 cm.

DESCRIPTION: free-blown, marvered to shape; similar to cat. no. 221; concave base; rim folded in and flattened; pale green. CONDITION: intact; iridescent.

224 *Ribbed Bottle*

Eastern Mediterranean
Third–Fourth Century A.D.
Gift of Henry F. Pearson, B.A. 1928, B.F.A. 1933, 1943.53
H. 7.6 cm.

Part of a series of vessels with mold-blown ribs, this globular flask has the funnel mouth with trailed-on ring often found on third and fourth century vessels. It is purple, a color that reappears in bottles and jars of this period, and continues, especially in combination with white, into the Islamic period.

DESCRIPTION: mold-blown; diagonal ribs; rim folded in; purple. CONDITION: broken at the neck and repaired; some iridescence. PARALLELS: *Hayes, Toronto* no. 282; *von Saldern, Oppenländer* no. 493; *Cambridge, Fitzwilliam* no. 105c; without ribs: cat. no. 207, above.

225 *Sprinkler Flask*

Eastern Mediterranean
Third–Fourth Century A.D.
Gift of Henry F. Pearson, B.A. 1928, B.F.A. 1933, 1943.51
H. 12.8 cm.

The small hole created by the neck constriction in this vessel permits only a drop or two of liquid to

224

pass through at a time, suggesting the designation "sprinkler" or "dropper" flask. Large sprinkler flasks such as this one often have pinched vertical ribs on the body, a small circle of "toes" that forms an unstable base, and a funnel mouth with a coil around the rim. The sprinkler form also occurs in contemporary mold-blown vessels, including head flasks and bottles with mold-blown or optic blown ribs.

DESCRIPTION: free-blown with pinched ribs and toes; rounded rim; pale green with a dark green coil around the mouth. CONDITION: two toes missing; white weathering. PARALLELS: *von Saldern, Oppenländer* nos. 691–94.

226 *Sprinkler Flask*

Eastern Mediterranean
Third–Fourth Century A.D.
Gift of Henry F. Pearson, B.A. 1928, B.F.A. 1933, 1943.50
H. 15.2 cm.

DESCRIPTION: free-blown with pinched ribs; similar to cat. no. 225; rounded rim; pale green. CONDITION: most of the toes missing; brown enamel and iridescent weathering.

227 *Sprinkler Flask*

Eastern Mediterranean
Third–Fourth Century A.D.
Moore Collection, 1955.6.128
H. 11 cm.

DESCRIPTION: free-blown with pinched ribs; similar to cat. no. 225, with small loops or stringholes pulled from the pinched ribs with a sharp tool; rounded rim with cut-out

ridge below; pale green. CONDITION: broken at the neck and repaired; hole in body; pitted and iridescent. PROVENANCE: Moore Collection no. 702. BIBLIOGRAPHY: *Eisen* 334, pl. 85; *Kouchakji* no. 134. PARALLELS: *Smith, Corning* 159, no. 322.

228 *Miniature Sprinkler Flask*

Eastern Mediterranean
Third–Fourth Century A.D.
Lehman Gift, 1953.28.24
H. 4.1 cm.

DESCRIPTION: free-blown with pinched ribs; flat base; rim folded in; bubbly; very pale green. CONDITION: two holes in the body, possibly broken bubbles; part of rim missing; pitted, with white weathering. PROVENANCE: John D. Rockefeller, Jr. no. 30; Duveen Brothers no. 11.

229 *Sprinkler Flask*

Eastern Mediterranean
Third–Fourth Century A.D.
Mansfield Collection, 1930.438
H. 9.6 cm.

A pear-shaped body and more fluid profile distinguish this flask from others in its family, although its basic form is consistent with the preceding examples. The dark purple glass is nearly opaque.

DESCRIPTION: free-blown with pinched ribs; cut-out ridge below the rim; flat base; purple. CONDITION: intact; weathering flaked or cleaned off, leaving a waxy surface. PROVENANCE: de Morgan sale, 1901; Mansfield Collection

225, 226, 227

228

229

no. 121. PARALLELS: without ribs, Crowfoot, *Samaria-Sebaste* fig. 95, no. 12 citing parallels from Karanis (Class IX, A).

230 *Storage or Serving Flask*

Eastern Mediterranean
Third–Fourth Century A.D.
Mansfield Collection, 1930.454
H. 15.3 cm.

DESCRIPTION: free-blown; folded base; rim folded in; trailed-on handles and body both pale green. CONDITION: intact; iridescent with traces of light brown weathering. PROVENANCE: Mansfield Collection no. 33. PARALLELS: *Hayes, Toronto* no. 411, citing others; *Auth, Newark* no. 452.

231 *Indented Bottle*

Eastern Mediterranean
Fourth–Fifth Century A.D.
Van Volkenburgh Bequest, 1940.290
H. 7.9 cm.

DESCRIPTION: free-blown; indented; flat base; rim folded in; body and neck thread pale green, nearly colorless. CONDITION: intact; brown enamel weathering and iridescence. PARALLELS: *Hayes, Toronto* no. 351, with a slightly later funnel mouth; Crowfoot, *Samaria-Sebaste* fig. 95, no. 14 without neck ring, from the North Cemetery; base treatment unusual.

232 *Flask*

Eastern Mediterranean
Fourth–Fifth Century A.D.
Mansfield Collection, 1930.399
H. 11.8 cm.

DESCRIPTION: free-blown; indented; folded foot; rim folded in; pale green with contrasting dark green handles and trailed thread decoration. CONDITION: hole in body; pale brown and iridescent weathering. PROVENANCE: Khayat, 1900; Mansfield Collection no. 84.

230

231, 232, 233

233 *Flask*

Eastern Mediterranean
Fourth–Fifth Century A.D.
Van Volkenburgh Bequest, 1940.286
H. 12.4 cm.

Despite a similarity to the preceding example, the elaboration of the thread decoration, the change in proportion, and the carelessness of the execution visible in the pushed in body, lumpy handles, and vestigal thumbrests combine to make this a less pleasing container than its simpler cousin.

DESCRIPTION: free-blown; folded foot; folded in rim; body, handles, and zigzag thread decoration yellowish green. CONDITION: some thread decoration missing; pale brown, white, and iridescent weathering, with considerable loss of surface at the foot and neck. PARALLELS: *Hayes, Toronto* no. 349.

234 *Flask*

Eastern Mediterranean
Third–Fourth Century A.D.
Moore Collection, 1955.6.121
H. 18.5 cm.

DESCRIPTION: free-blown; rim folded in; handles and body bluish green. CONDITION: cracked at the shoulder; iridescent with traces of light brown weathering. BIBLIOGRAPHY: *Eisen* 361, pl. 94a; *Kouchakji* no. 127; *Hayes, Toronto* no. 411. PARALLELS: *Hayes, Toronto* no. 411, citing others; *von Saldern, Oppenländer* no. 666, smaller and less well-proportioned, with simpler handles and a neck ring of a contrasting color; Vessberg, "Cyprus" no. 793.

235 *Flask*

Eastern Mediterranean, probably Syrian or Egyptian
First Half of the Fourth Century A.D.
Mansfield Collection, 1930.384
H. 19.4 cm.

This flask, related in shape to large terra cotta amphorae used for shipping wine, represents a distinctive group of olive green flasks and jugs with virtually identical wheel-cut decoration carelessly executed and barely penetrating the surface. The color and the shallow abrasion suggest manufacture in Egypt, but examples found in Germany may have been a local imitation.

DESCRIPTION: free-blown; knob base; wide folded handles; thick coil below the rim; olive green. Wheel-cut decoration: central band of vertical strokes between two bands of ovals within rectangular panels. CONDITION: broken and repaired, with losses at the shoulder. BIBLIOGRAPHY: presumably the vessel cited by *Hayes, Toronto* 102, no. 365 as Yale acc. no. 1930.455. PARALLELS: *Hayes, Toronto* nos. 365 and 366; Abdul-Rahim Masri, "Collection de Verres du Musée de Hama," *JIV* 3 (1964) 74, no. 12, fig. 73, from Homs; *Auth, Newark* no. 162, an unusual variant with turquoise handles and rim thread; Harden, *Karanis* 246 ff.

236 *Large Flagon*

Eastern Mediterranean
Third–Fourth Century A.D.
Mansfield Collection, 1930.386
H. 40.4 cm.

Although no provenance is known for either this

distinctive vessel or its very close parallel from the same collection (cat. no. 237), it is not unlikely that they came from the same tomb group.

DESCRIPTION: free-blown; rim folded in; rounded base with pontil mark; elongated body, indented below base of handles; body and handles pale green. CONDITION: intact; brown and iridescent weathering. PARALLELS: Neuburg, *Glas* pl. 24 top, from a tomb group in Palestine; *Hayes, Toronto* no. 339, with one handle, citing other parallels.

237 *Large Flagon*

Eastern Mediterranean
Third–Fourth Century A.D.
Mansfield Collection, 1930.387
H. 37.7 cm.

DESCRIPTION: free-blown with pontil mark on base; similar to cat. no. 236, without body indentations; rim folded in; body and handles pale green. CONDITION: one handle repaired, with a loss at its base; brown and iridescent weathering.

238 *Flask*

Eastern Mediterranean
Fourth Century A.D.
Moore Collection, 1955.6.111
H. 12.7 cm.

Tube-shaped toilet flasks with a bulge in the center were a common fourth century type, joining the candlestick form and the simpler test tube shape unguentaria which survive in smaller numbers in the late Roman period.

DESCRIPTION: free-blown; rounded rim; streaked and bubbly matrix; pale bluish green. CONDITION: strain cracks in rim; slightly iridescent. BIBLIOGRAPHY: *Eisen* 60; *Kouchakji* no. 117.

239 *Vessel in the Shape of a Fish*

Eastern Mediterranean
Third Century A.D.
Moore Collection, 1955.6.178
Pres. L. 13.5 cm., H. of body 5.2 cm.

Blown vessels in the shape of a fish were produced both in the Cologne area and the eastern part of the Roman Empire, and finds in both locations point to a third century date for their manufacture. The eastern examples are distinguished mainly by the use of hot trailed-on threads for the eyes and fins, and they are thus well within the mainstream of Syrian

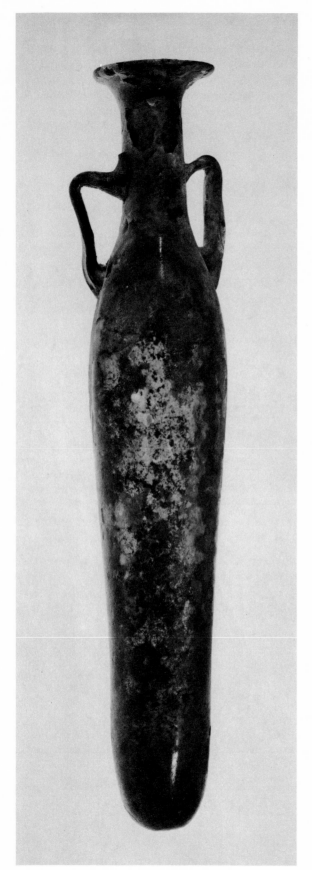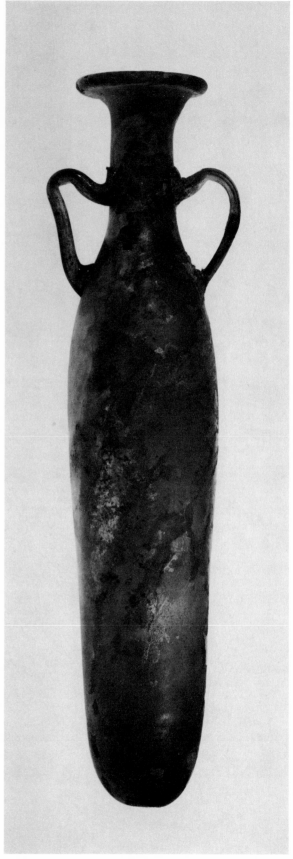

236, 237

glass of the period. The only examples from known eastern contexts to date are those excavated at Begram, Afghanistan, in a third century context, and it is among these that the Yale fish finds its closest parallels. The gold chain on the Yale vessel appears to be unique among glass vessels, although a similar chain occurs on a bronze fish in the Metropolitan Museum, dated to the fourth to fifth century A.D. A separate stopper, also on a chain, closes the mouth of this bronze fish, and one can easily see the practical need for a similar stopper in the glass vessel. The gold chain, of a common Roman type made of folded links, is joined at the bottom by a circular ornament of gold wire.

DESCRIPTION: free-blown in the shape of a fish with an open mouth; yellow body with trailed-on dark purple eyes, mouth, dorsal and side fins; gold chain attached through loops in the glass side fins, loop-in-loop chain of twisted figure eight links; two short chains joined by a circular gold wire wheel with three cross bars. CONDITION: tail missing; only trace of one eye remains; iridescent, with traces of white weathering. PROVENANCE: Galerie Bachstitz, The Hague; P. Jackson Higgs, New York 1923. BIBLIOGRAPHY: *Eisen* 531, pl. 130 (with restored tail); *Kouchakji* no. 185; von Saldern, "Reproductions" 314, note 75; Hamelin, "Bégram," 4 (1954) 180, illustrated (drawing) pl. 39. PARALLELS: J. Hackin, *Recherches Archéologiques à Bégram, Mémoires de la Délégation Archéologique Française en Afghanistan* 9 (Paris 1939) pl. 10, fig. 26, nos. 193[46] and 184[37], pl. 19, fig. 43, no. 218[72], fig. 44, no. 210 (*in situ*), and fig. 45, no. 210[64], especially nos. 193 and 210. On fish vessels in general, with a third century find from Cologne, see *Isings* type 95a. For a similar gold chain with circular wire clasp, see Wolf and Evelyne Rudolph, *Ancient Jewelry from the Collection of Burton Y. Berry* (Bloomington, Indiana 1973) no. 80a. The loop-in-loop chain is known at least as early as the Hellenistic period and seems to have been taken over by Roman craftsmen from the Greeks. The bronze fish vessel in the MMA inv. 62.10.4 is said to come from Istanbul.

240 *Vessel in the Shape of a Fish*

Eastern Mediterranean
Third Century A.D.
Moore Collection, 1955.6.179
Pres. L. 13.5 cm.

This less elaborate fish has pinched ridges suggestive of reasonably naturalistic dorsal fins.

DESCRIPTION: free-blown in the shape of a fish with an open mouth; pinched fins; trailed-on mouth coil and side loop; pale green. CONDITION: part of tail and much of the mouth missing; pitted; brown enamel weathering. PROVENANCE: Moore Collection no. 866. BIBLIOGRAPHY: *Kouchakji* no. 186.

238

241 *Funnel-Mouthed Jug*

Eastern Mediterranean
Fourth–Fifth Century A.D.
Mansfield Collection, 1930.414
H. 8.1 cm.

DESCRIPTION: free-blown; concave base; rim folded in; pale green body and thread decoration. CONDITION: intact; thick brown and iridescent weathering, flaking and pitted. PROVENANCE: Khayat, 1900; Mansfield Collection no. 61. BIBLIOGRAPHY: *Hayes, Toronto* 98, no. 344, with other parallels. PARALLELS: Crowfoot, *Samaria-Sebaste* fig. 96, no. 9; the form seems to be typically Syrian.

242 *Funnel-Mouthed Jug*

Eastern Mediterranean
Fourth–Fifth Century A.D.
Van Volkenburgh Bequest, 1940.268
H. 8.6 cm.

DESCRIPTION: free-blown; indented; similar in shape to cat. no. 241; concave base; rim folded in; body and handle pale green. CONDITION: intact; light brown weathering, flaking, over iridescence. PARALLELS: *Hayes, Toronto* no. 437, with a thread around the neck.

243 *Ovoid Jug*

Eastern Mediterranean
Fourth–Fifth Century A.D.
Van Volkenburgh Bequest, 1940.266
H. 13.75 cm.

This yellow jug represents a group with ovoid bodies and strap handles whose sole decoration is a thread around the neck and the funnel mouth. A subgroup, elegantly shaped, carefully made, and often with contrasting threads, was produced in Cologne.

DESCRIPTION: free-blown; cut-out foot; pontil mark; wide flanged strap handle; rounded rim with thread around exterior; yellow body, handle, and thread decoration. CONDITION: intact; brown and iridescent weathering. PARALLELS: *Isings* type 120; Vessberg, "Cyprus" pl. 6, no. 19; Kisa, *Glas* C186–88, D189, figs. 39–40, as cited by Vessberg; Harden, *Karanis* pl. 19, no. 712, Class XI; Damascus Museum no. 822 (Dura photo). For the Cologne series, see *Fremersdorf, Denkmäler* III 47 ff., pls. 93 ff.

244 *Jug*

Eastern Mediterranean
Fourth–Fifth Century A.D.
Whiting Collection, 1912.931
H. 10.9 cm.

DESCRIPTION: free-blown; similar to cat. no. 243, with a rounder body; cut-out foot; rim folded in; medium blue green.

245 *Jug*

Eastern Mediterranean
Fourth–Fifth Century A.D.
Whiting Collection, 1912.934
H. 17.7 cm.

A taller form in the same family of jugs, this vessel has a distinct shoulder and narrows towards its base. It is yellow, a fairly common color for these jugs.

DESCRIPTION: free-blown; cut-out base; rim folded in; yellow. CONDITION: intact; severely weathered with a white layer flaking off. PARALLELS: Damascus Museum no. unknown (Dura photo); *von Saldern, Oppenländer* no. 682.

239

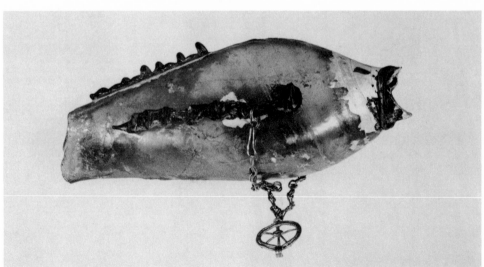

240

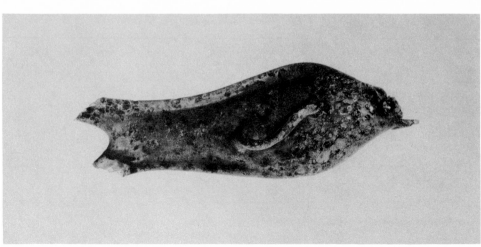

241, 243, 242

246, 245, 244

246 Indented Jug

Eastern Mediterranean
Fourth–Fifth Century A.D.
Van Volkenburgh Bequest, 1940.267
H. 14.5 cm.

Lacking a foot, this jug has an indented body in addition to the thread decoration of the main group.

DESCRIPTION: free-blown; flat base with pontil mark; rim folded in; handle and threads pale green; body yellow. CONDITION: intact; white and iridescent weathering. PARALLELS: *Hayes, Toronto* no. 439.

247 Jug

Eastern Mediterranean
Fourth Century A.D.
Moore Collection, 1955.6.86
H. 10.9 cm.

DESCRIPTION: free-blown; vertical indentations; flat base; rim folded in; pale yellowish green. CONDITION: intact; pitted and iridescent. BIBLIOGRAPHY: *Eisen* 428, pl. 107; *Kouchakji* no. 89. PARALLELS: closely related to small bottles such as cat. no. 231 above.

248

248 *Cup or Bowl*

Eastern Mediterranean
Third–Fourth Century A.D.
Yale University Art Gallery, 1955.6.360
H. 6.5 cm.

This simple shape is distinguished from earlier forms by its rounded profile and turned out rim.

DESCRIPTION: free-blown; base slightly concave; rounded rim; pale greenish blue. CONDITION: reconstructed from fragments with a few losses; some iridescence. PARALLELS: *Isings* type 96.

249 *Cup*

Eastern Mediterranean
Third–Fourth Century A.D.
Mansfield Collection, 1930.402
H. 9.1 cm.

Many indented cups were based on this form with its slightly convex profile and no base. The form originated in the first century but most examples seem to be second century or later. A taller and thinner fourth century type without indentations is probably a continuation of the form.

DESCRIPTION: free-blown; concave base; convex profile; unworked rim; yellow. CONDITION: intact; pitted and iridescent. PROVENANCE: Khayat, 1900; Mansfield Collection no. 67. PARALLELS: *Isings* types 32, originating in the first century but with later examples from Karanis, 110 (indented) and 109 (footed), both fourth century; Vessberg, "Cyprus" pl. 3, nos. 27 and 40, and pl. 4, no. 7 (footed); *Auth, Newark* no. 376; Damascus Museum no. unknown (Dura photo); Crowfoot, *Samaria-Sebaste* fig. 95, no. 21 (indented).

250 *Indented Cup*

Eastern Mediterranean
Third–Fourth Century A.D.
Moore Collection, 1955.6.87
H. 8.9 cm.

A common variety of the indented beaker, this type has a cut-out base. Like other forms, the footed type originates in the first century and continues into the late Roman period. Most early examples are taller than this one.

DESCRIPTION: free-blown; indented; cut-out base; unworked rim; pale green. CONDITION: very thin and severely weathered, with two large holes in the body; dark and light brown enamel weathering. PROVENANCE: Moore Collection no. 700. BIBLIOGRAPHY: *Eisen* 295, pl. 69a; *Kouchakji* no. 90. PARALLELS: Vessberg, "Cyprus" beaker

249, 251, 250

type B IV a, especially pl. 4, no. 13; *Isings* type 35; Grose, *Toledo* fig. 16.

251 *Indented Cup*

> Eastern Mediterranean
> Third–Fourth Century A.D.
> Mansfield Collection, 1930.449
> H. 8.6 cm.

A wider version of the previous beaker, this vessel represents the late Roman form. Certain details, notably the rounded rim, the thread trailed on around the neck, and the ring base, are also typical of the later versions.

DESCRIPTION: free-blown and indented; ring base; rounded rim; pale green. CONDITION: intact; iridescent, pitted, and flaking. PROVENANCE: Khayat, 1900; said to have been found at Harran; Mansfield Collection no. 93.

252 *Shallow Footed Bowl or Dish*

> Eastern Mediterranean
> Third–Fourth Century A.D.
> Moore Collection, 1955.6.114
> H. 4.5 cm., D. 12.6 cm.

This shallow bowl or dish has a flaring mouth and stands on a cut-out base. It is a form which originated in the late second or early third century, but it continued to be made into the fourth century.

DESCRIPTION: free-blown; cut-out base; rim folded out; colorless. CONDITION: intact; pitted, with dark brown and iridescent weathering. PROVENANCE: Moore Collection no. 679. BIBLIOGRAPHY: *Eisen* 355, pl. 92; *Kouchakji* no. 120. PARALLELS: *Isings* type 97a; *Hayes, Toronto* no. 463.

253 *Serving Bowl*

> Eastern Mediterranean
> Third–Fourth Century A.D.
> Mansfield Collection, 1930.391
> H. 9.0 cm., D. 23 cm., irregular

DESCRIPTION: free-blown; similar to cat. no. 252, but larger; cut-out base; rim folded out; colorless. CONDITION: reconstructed, with considerable restoration of the body; iridescent, with some dark brown weathering at the foot.

254 *Basket*

> Eastern Mediterranean
> Third–Fourth Century A.D.
> Moore Collection, 1955.6.214
> H. 6.1 cm., including handles

Made in imitation of a woven straw basket, this vessel is decorated on the sides with vertical zigzags which vaguely suggest the patterns of weaving. The decoration is opaque white, on a brown body.

DESCRIPTION: free-blown; concave, domelike base; rim folded out and down. CONDITION: broken and repaired with some restoration; brown enamel weathering. PROV-

253

252, 254

255, 256

ENANCE: Moore Collection no. 713. BIBLIOGRAPHY: *Eisen* 636, pl. 155; *Kouchakji* no. 221. PARALLELS: *Smith, Corning* no. 238, with other examples; *von Saldern, Oppenländer* no. 597, with four feet and a basket handle over the top.

255 *Bowl*

Eastern Mediterranean
Fourth–Fifth Century A.D.
Moore Collection, 1955.6.157
H. 8.8 cm., D. 11.6 cm.

DESCRIPTION: free-blown; cut-out foot; coil rim; pale green body, zigzag, and spiral thread. CONDITION: intact; brown weathering flaking at the top, with iridescence underneath; some spiral thread missing. BIBLIOGRAPHY: *Eisen* 429; *Kouchakji* no. 164. PARALLELS: Harden, *Karanis* pl. 14, nos. 260 and 274 (undecorated).

256 *Miniature Bowl*

Eastern Mediterranean
Third–Fourth Century A.D.
Moore Collection, 1955.6.259
H. 3.3 cm., D. 4.5 cm.

DESCRIPTION: free-blown; pad base; rim turned in; thick, very pale green glass. CONDITION: intact; brown and iridescent weathering. BIBLIOGRAPHY: *Kouchakji* no. 243. PARALLELS: *von Saldern, Oppenländer* no. 709.

257 *Gilded Beaker with Inscription*

Syrian or Egyptian
Third–Fourth Century A.D.
Moore Collection, 1955.6.205
H. 15 cm., D. mouth 4.8 cm.

The gilded decoration on this beaker consists of bands of thin gold leaf which are incised and scraped away to create the designs. This technique links the beaker with the limited number of gilded vessels from the late Roman period, such as those with Egyptian subjects from the Meroitic necropolis of Sedeinga (Sudanese Nubia), rather than to the more numerous gilded vessels of the Islamic and Mediaeval eras, when the gold was applied in suspension in a medium and fixed by firing. Similarly, incised gold leaf was used in the well-known early Christian gold glasses found in the Roman catacombs, although the second layer of glass which encases and protects the gold in the catacomb glasses was not used for the vessel.

The Greek inscription is yet another variant of the convivial exhortation ΠΙΕ ΖΗϹΗϹ, "drink and

257

may you live," which appeared first in pagan contexts (see cat. no. 280 below) and was later adopted by the Christians and given a eucharistic meaning. Both the wreath and the rosettes are common decorative motifs throughout the eastern Mediterranean in the Roman period.

DESCRIPTION: free-blown; ring base; wheel-polished rim; transparent deep purple; three bands of incised gold leaf decoration: top—Greek inscription ΠΙΕ ΖΗΣΗΣ ΑΕΙ between thin gold bands; middle—three rows of rosettes in a gold field, each rosette encircled by a gold and a purple band, some with projecting purple arrows, thin purple band and purple arrows at edges of field; bottom—wreath. CONDITION: unbroken; surface losses, especially to lower section; losses iridescent and pitted. PROVENANCE: said to be from Damascus; von Gans Collection; Galerie Bachstitz, The Hague; Fahim Kouchakji. BIBLIOGRAPHY: Zahn, *Galerie Bachstitz II* 59–61; *Eisen* 570, pl. V, frontispiece to vol. II; *Kouchakji* no. 212. PARALLELS: for the gold glasses from the catacombs, see Morey, *Gold Glass*; for the glasses from Sedeinga, with another variant of the ΠΙΕ ΖΗΣΗΣ inscription, see J. Leclant, "Glass from the Meroitic Necropolis of Sedeinga (Sudanese Nubia)," *JGS* 15 (1973) 52–68, especially 56–66, and, on the inscription, note 22.

258 Cup with Wheel-Cut Decoration

Probably Cologne
Fourth Century A.D.
Moore Collection, 1955.6.182
H. 11.2 cm., D. 11.8 cm.

With the widespread introduction of colorless glass for blown vessels, wheel-cut figural scenes replaced mold-blown relief decoration early in the second century A.D. Colorless vessels with mythological scenes inscribed in Greek were made in Egypt in the second and third centuries and exported to cities around the eastern Mediterranean (a fragment with a scene of Artemis and Actaeon was found at Dura-Europos) and in the western provinces (Harden cites four found at Cologne, for example). Local glass makers adopted the technique with their own variations in style and subject matter.

One such regional variant appears to be a family of vessels based on parallel wheel-cut lines grouped together to create solid areas. These striped solids, applied in different directions to create drapery, hair, architecture, and trees, result in blocky figures and skeletal landscapes with far less detail, sculptural quality, and movement than is seen in the Egyptian vessels. The subject matter is different as well, with Biblical scenes replacing those of Greek mythology. Moses striking the rock and the raising of Lazarus are the most common, but Adam and Eve, Abraham and Isaac, and Christ raising the daughter of Jairus are also recognizable. In some cases these scenes appear in combination, using both Old and New Testament subjects. Other examples, like the Yale beaker with the raising of Lazarus, feature just one scene, filling in the remaining space with unidentified onlookers. Dancers, busts in medallions, and even swimming dolphins occur in this style, but they seem to have no mythological significance. Bowls and beakers were the shapes used by this group of artists, and only the exterior was decorated. Fremersdorf considers them to have been made in Cologne, and their findspots would appear to confirm his suggestion.

DESCRIPTION: free-blown conical beaker with heavy rounded bottom; exterior wheel-cut decoration of the raising of Lazarus in a landscape with four onlookers (see drawing); wheel-cut line below the rim; very pale green, nearly colorless. CONDITION: broken and repaired with rim fragment near the head of Lazarus restored; virtually unweathered. PROVENANCE: found at Boulogne-sur-Mer; ex coll. Engel Gross; Fahim Kouchakji, 1925. BIBLIOGRAPHY: *Eisen* 547, fig. 234, pl. 134; *Kouchakji* no. 189; *Fremersdorf, Denkmäler* VIII, 187, pl. 267. PARALLELS: *Fremersdorf, Denkmäler* VIII type D-5, nos. 179–88, pls. 246–269. See also Harden, "Roman" 54–57, and for the Dura Actaeon fragment, *Clairmont, Dura* 57, no. 235, fig. 1, pl. 24.

259 Cup

Eastern Mediterranean
Fourth Century A.D.
Mansfield Collection, 1930.426
H. 8.2 cm.

Applied dots of blue glass decorate a large series of lamps and cups produced in the eastern Mediterranean. The vessels are colorless or a natural pale green. The blue dots which encircle the body occur singly or in groups, the latter often forming geometric shapes such as triangles or diamonds. The lamps are conical and the cups generally ovoid. Wheel-cut lines above and below the blue dots of this example define the area to be decorated.

DESCRIPTION: free-blown; flattened base; unworked rim; two single blue dots and two triangles composed of six dots each; pale green. CONDITION: intact; extremely thin due to losses from flaking of the interior, leaving iridescent weathering. PROVENANCE: T. B. Clark, 1898; Mansfield Collection no. 27. PARALLELS: *Isings* type 96; *von Saldern, Oppenländer* no. 727; *Fremersdorf, Denkmäler* VII, pls. 93, 110, and 112, which Fremersdorf considers of eastern manufacture despite western contexts. For the lamps, see Crowfoot and Harden, "Glass Lamps." Despite general acceptance of any vessel with blue dots as a lamp (*Auth, Newark* nos. 500 and 501 for example), the evidence seems insufficient to preclude the use of some as cups. Certainly the following example would have been difficult to suspend in the traditional manner.

260 *Cup or Bowl*

Eastern Mediterranean
Fourth Century A.D. or later
Mansfield Collection, 1930.428
H. 7.6 cm.

Obviously differing in some respects from the preceding more typical example, this cup is close to a small group which Fremersdorf considers to have been made in Cologne in the second half of the third century, characterized by a squat shape, the greater protrusion of blue glass blobs, and their arrangement in irregular rows. As Isings points out, however, this type of blue dot decoration survives throughout the Arabian period in the eastern Mediterranean, and projecting blobs in irregular rows occur on eastern vessels from the third century through the Mediaeval period. Lacking a western provenance, an eastern Mediterranean source and a later date for this vessel are thus more likely.

DESCRIPTION: free-blown; thick, slightly flattened base; unworked rim; two irregular rows of protruding blue blobs; very pale green. CONDITION: intact; white and iridescent weathering; pitted. PROVENANCE: D. G. Kelekian, 1898; Mansfield Collection no. 8. PARALLELS: *Fremersdorf, Denkmäler* VII, 7–8 and 31, pls. 34 and 35; *Isings* type 96; for the protruding blobs, see *von Saldern, Oppenländer* no. 694 (third–fourth century) and *Davidson, Corinth* 87–88, nos. 742–744, pls. 57 and 58.

261 *Stemmed Cup*

Eastern Mediterranean
Fourth Century A.D.
Moore Collection, 1955.6.115
H. 7.6 cm., D. 11.5 cm.

DESCRIPTION: free-blown in two parts and joined; wide, flaring mouth; rim folded in; folded domelike foot; pale brown (body) and blue green (foot). CONDITION: intact; pitted and iridescent. BIBLIOGRAPHY: *Eisen* 356, pl. 92a; *Kouchakji* no. 121. PARALLELS: *Isings* type 111, some with separately made stems; primarily an eastern Mediterranean type.

262 *Stemmed Cup or Bowl*

Eastern Mediterranean
Fourth Century A.D.
Moore Collection, 1955.6.116
H. 10.7 cm., D. 14.5 cm.

A development of the preceding type, this cup has a cut-out ridge at the lower turning point of the body and a double beaded stem.

DESCRIPTION: free-blown in two parts and joined; rim folded out; pale yellowish brown. CONDITION: intact; pale brown enamel weathering, flaking, over iridescence; iridescent areas pitted. PROVENANCE: Moore Collection no. 711. BIBLIOGRAPHY: *Eisen* 356, pl. 92b; *Kouchakji* no. 122.

263 *Conical Lamp*

Eastern Mediterranean
Fourth Century A.D.
Mansfield Collection, 1930.453
H. 17.5 cm.

Conical vessels such as this one were set into horizontal metal rings suspended on chains for use as lamps. Many were decorated with the wheel-cut lines that appear on this colorless example, while another large group featured dots of blue glass in a row around the body.

DESCRIPTION: free-blown; unworked rim; five bands of wheel-cut lines; colorless. CONDITION: intact; brown and white weathering. PROVENANCE: Khayat, 1903; said to have been found at Fik Houran; Mansfield Collection no. 144. PARALLELS: *Isings* type 106d; *Harden, Karanis* 155 ff., type A 1 b; for use as lamps, see *Crowfoot and Harden,* "Glass Lamps."

264 *Jar*

Eastern Mediterranean
Third Century A.D.
Mansfield Collection, 1930.401
H. 8.0 cm.

259, 260

I, 262

63, 264, 266, 265

Jars of this shape, with or without ring bases, often had slightly concave lids whose edges covered the rim of the vessel. The finest of these lids were painted on the underside, and the frequency of Eros as the subject suggests these were jars for cosmetics. The thread decoration around the neck is common.

DESCRIPTION: free-blown; ring base; rounded rim; trailed-on neck thread; pale green. CONDITION: intact; pitted and iridescent. PROVENANCE: said to be from Haifa; Khayat, 1899; Mansfield Collection no. 57. PARALLELS: a common type among Cypriote finds: see Vessberg, "Cyprus" pls. 4, nos. 24–27 and 33–35, and 14, nos. 3 and 5 (painted lids); also a fine painted lid with Eros in the Newark Museum, inv. 73.132, *JGS* 16 (1974) 125, no. 6.

265 *Ribbed Jar*

Eastern Mediterranean
Third Century A.D.
Moore Collection, 1955.6.93
H. 9.1 cm.

DESCRIPTION: free-blown; a variant of cat. no. 264; trailed-on threads forming vertical ribs; wheel-cut circle just below the mouth; rounded rim; base slightly concave; colorless. CONDITION: intact, but thin; flaking pale brown weathering and iridescence: PROVENANCE: Moore Collection no. 661. BIBLIOGRAPHY: *Eisen* 336, pl. 88a; *Kouchakji* no. 96. PARALLELS: Vessberg, "Cyprus" pl. 4, no. 27; *von Saldern, Oppenländer* no. 659, with honeycomb thread decoration.

266 *Jar*

Eastern Mediterranean
Third–Fourth Century A.D.
Whiting Collection, 1912.928
H. 15.1 cm.

This elongated form with a cut-out foot is far less common than the preceding type.

DESCRIPTION: free-blown; elongated; cut-out foot; rounded rim; pale bluish green. CONDITION: intact; iridescent. PARALLELS: Crowfoot, *Samaria-Sebaste* fig. 94, no. 13, from a third century A.D. tomb.

267 *Miniature Jar*

Eastern Mediterranean
Third–Fourth Century A.D.
Moore Collection, 1955.6.90
H. 4.5 cm.

Although diminutive in size, this jar shows the basic form of a common third to fourth century vessel which was decorated in a variety of ways including tooling and trailed-on threads. A globular body and funnel mouth are the main characteristics of the type.

DESCRIPTION: free-blown; rounded rim; pale green. CONDITION: intact; brown enamel weathering with iridescence underneath. PROVENANCE: Moore Collection no. 733. BIBLIOGRAPHY: *Eisen* 315; *Kouchakji* no. 90.

268 *Jar*

Eastern Mediterranean
Third–Fourth Century A.D.

Mansfield Collection, 1930.406
H. 7.6 cm.

DESCRIPTION: free-blown; similar to cat. no. 267; large funnel mouth; slightly indented body; rim folded in; pale green. CONDITION: intact; surface pitted and iridescent. PROVENANCE: said to have been found at Birsan, Syria; Khayat, 1909; Mansfield Collection no. 183.

269 *Jar*

Eastern Mediterranean
Third–Fourth Century A.D.
Yale University Art Gallery, 1947.251
H. 8.4 cm.

DESCRIPTION: free-blown; similar to cat. no. 267; indented; concave base; rim folded in; pale green. CONDITION: hole in mouth; heavy brown weathering and iridescence. BIBLIOGRAPHY: *Hayes, Toronto* 79, no. 291, with its former Yale acc. no. 1947.181. PARALLELS: Crowfoot, *Samaria-Sebaste* fig. 94, no. 5, from a third century A.D. tomb.

270 *Jar*

Eastern Mediterranean
Third–Fourth Century A.D.
Moore Collection, 1955.6.89
H. 8.3 cm.

DESCRIPTION: free-blown; similar to cat. no. 267; indented; rim folded in; pale purple. CONDITION: intact; brown weathering over iridescence. PROVENANCE: Moore Collection no. 696. BIBLIOGRAPHY: *Eisen* 295, pl. 69 bottom left; *Kouchakji* no. 92; *Hayes, Toronto* 80, no. 294, with parallels.

271 *Jar*

Eastern Mediterranean
Third–Fourth Century A.D.
Mansfield Collection, 1930.447
H. 7.5 cm.

DESCRIPTION: free-blown; similar to cat. no. 267; indented; rim folded in; yellowish green. CONDITION: part of rim broken away; iridescent. PROVENANCE: said to be from Bana, Syria; Khayat, 1900; Mansfield Collection no. 96.

272 *Jar*

Eastern Mediterranean
Late Third–Fourth Century A.D.
Van Volkenburgh Bequest, 1940.818
H. 6.2 cm.

268, 270, 269, 271

273, 275, 274, 272

DESCRIPTION: free-blown; similar to cat. no. 267; concave base; rim folded in; trailed-on handles, zigzag band, and mouth ring blue green, on a pale green body. CONDITION: intact; white weathering, some iridescence and pitting. PARALLELS: *Hayes, Toronto* nos. 387–88 and 418; handle treatment similar to examples with cut-out ridge below the mouth, as for example Neuburg, *Glas* fig. 59.

DESCRIPTION: free-blown; similar to cat. no. 267; concave base; rim folded in; pale bluish green with somewhat darker blue green trailed-on handles and zigzag thread decoration. CONDITION: intact; surface pitted, body iridescent, decoration weathered white. PROVENANCE: said to be from Syria. BIBLIOGRAPHY: *Kouchakji* no. 143B. PARALLELS: *Hayes, Toronto* nos. 387–88 and 418.

273 *Jar*

Eastern Mediterranean
Late Third–Fourth Century A.D.
Moore Collection, 1955.6.254
H. 7.0 cm.

274 *Jar*

Eastern Mediterranean
Fourth Century A.D.
Moore Collection, 1955.6.136.
H. 11.5 cm., including handle

276

DESCRIPTION: free-blown; similar to cat. no. 267; concave base; rim folded in; pale green with dark green side and top handles and zigzag thread decoration. CONDITION: hole in body near one handle due to weathering; brown and iridescent weathering. BIBLIOGRAPHY: *Eisen* 430, fig. 177, II e; *Kouchakji* no. 143. PARALLELS: for the basket handle on jars, see *Hayes, Toronto* nos. 155 and 356; *Auth, Newark* no. 176; Damascus Museum, two examples, nos. unknown (Dura photos); this type of handle is more commonly found on multiple cosmetic tubes, as cat. nos. 327–29 below.

275 *Jar*

> Eastern Mediterranean
> Fourth Century A.D.
> Mansfield Collection, 1930.450
> H. 9.3 cm.

DESCRIPTION: free-blown; a fairly unusual footed variant of the common jar type; rim folded in; mouth ring; pale purple with purple handles and thread. CONDITION: one side broken and repaired, with painted gold iridescence; pitted and iridescent where original surface is evident. PROVENANCE: ex coll. Adjamian, formerly the Persian Consul General at Aleppo; Khayat, 1930; Mansfield Collection no. 252. PARALLELS: *Auth, Newark* no. 473, with foot, but with zigzag thread around the neck instead of handles; Barag, *Beth She^carim* fig. 97:27, with base ring; Damascus Museum, no. unknown, footed with basket handle and zigzag around the neck (Dura photo).

MOLD-BLOWN AND PATTERN MOLDED, THIRD–FOURTH CENTURY A.D.

276 *Tyche Bottle*

> Eastern Mediterranean
> Second–Third Century A.D.
> Moore Collection. 1955.6.81
> H. 15.6 cm.

The figure represented by this flask is clearly related to the famous monumental statue of the Tyche of Antioch by Eutychides executed around 296 B.C. Although lacking the dynamic tension of the original Hellenistic sculpture, the pose of this seated figure, her legs crossed and her foot resting on the head of the river god Orontes, reproduces the salient visual features of an image that was reproduced in various media for at least four centuries. The Antioch Tyche is known today only through coins, small scale copies in marble and bronze, and a few ancient references. Pausanias mentions it (6.2.6–7) and Pliny provides the date for the sculptor's activity in the one hundred twenty–first Olympiad (*N.H.*34.51). The sixth century A.D. chronographer Johannes Malalas (*Chronogr.* 11.276) gives a detailed description of the figure crowned by Antiochos and Seleukos and standing in a four columned shrine, both possibly Trajanic additions to the original figure. Coins of the Antioch mint from Tigranes I, King of Syria from 83–69 B.C., onward show Tyche seated with her legs crossed and the river god Orontes at her feet. Only a few third century coins show the crowning of Tyche and the four columned shrine; earlier coins show her alone without an architectural setting.

This famous image was equally popular outside Antioch and was adapted by many other cities to represent their own Tyches. Different attributes were sometimes added to distinguish local Tyches, as, for example, a lion for the Tyche of Palmyra, and the sex of the river god varied from city to city. It is likely that the small Eros with a torch on the side of the Tyche bottle is such a local symbol. Although no exact parallel exists which would indicate a particular city for this Tyche, the two most closely related Tyches are those of Midaeum in Phrygia, whose Tyche appears between two torch-bearing Erotes on a coin of Caracalla, and Dura-Europos, whose Tyche is shown on one occasion, in a wall painting of the sacrifice of Julius Terentius from the Temple of Bel, seated with the figure of a small boy at her side. She is identified by an inscription and appears next to the Tyche of Palmyra, shown with a lion and a female river goddess.

DESCRIPTION: mold-blown, two part mold; flat base; vertical neck replacing the mural crown of the sculpture; rounded rim; light purple streaked with yellow. CONDITION: broken and repaired; front leg and foot and proper right arm restored, also some restoration along break lines; iridescent with some brown enamel weathering and pitting. PROVENANCE: Kouchakji Frères, New York, June 1925. BIBLIOGRAPHY: *Eisen* 333, pl. 82; *Kouchakji* no. 84. PARALLELS: from the same mold: Yale University Art Gallery acc. no. 1955.6.274, cat. no. 277, below; Berlin, Staatliche Museen, Antikenabteilung, inv. 30219.238 (purple streaked with yellow) von Gans Collection, A. Greifenhagen, "Ancient Glass in the Berlin-West Museum," *JGS* 4 (1962) 63–64, fig. 8; CMG inv. 66.1.209 (pale green streaked with purple) Sangiorgi Collection, Sangiorgi, *Vetri Antichi* no. 99, pl. 15; MMA inv. 44.11.6 (purple) von Gans and Baurat Schiller Collections, Tobias Dohrn, *Die Tyche von Antiochia* (Berlin 1960) 26, no. 21, pl. 25; Neuburg Collection, Tel Aviv, F. Neuburg, *Glass in Antiquity* (London 1929) 79, pl. 16, fig. 55.

For a thorough study of the Antioch Tyche, see Dohrn, *Tyche*. For the coins, see Dohrn, *Tyche* pls. 30 and 31. Tyche crowned appears on a coin of Elagabalus (A.D. 218–222; Dohrn, *Tyche* pl. 31, no. 2); Tyche in a four columned

shrine (*tetrakionion*) on coins of Trajanus Decius (A.D. 249–251) and Volusianus, son of the Emperor Trebonianus Gallus (A.D. 251–253; Dohrn, *Tyche* pl. 3, nos. 4 and 5 respectively). The coin with Erotes from Midaeum is cited by Dohrn, *Tyche* 54, and a drawing of the Dura and Palmyra Tyches from the Terentius fresco is reproduced by Dohrn, *Tyche* pl. 7, no. 1, to show the relation of the Palmyra Tyche to the eastern goddess Cybele. For a fragment of a glass bowl with wheel-cut decoration showing a city goddess labelled "Tyros" but modelled after the Tyche of Eutychides, see C. W. Clairmont, "Some Glass Vessels in the Benaki Museum, Athens," *Annales du 3e Congrès des Journées Internationales du Verre* (Damascus 1964) 133, no. 2. Clairmont dates the fragment stylistically to the fourth century.

277 *Tyche Bottle*

Eastern Mediterranean
Second–Third Century A.D.
Moore Collection, 1955.6.274
Restored H. 13.5 cm., Max. Pres. H. 12.2 cm.

Although blown in the same mold as the preceding Tyche bottle, improper restoration of the head has given this flask the appearance of a small sculpture.

DESCRIPTION: mold-blown, two part mold; pale amber.

277

278

CONDITION: head largely restored, including eyes, nose, and hair except for bun in back; pieces also missing from right shoulder and upper foot; pitted and iridescent. PROVENANCE: said to have been found near Homs, Syria; Khayat, 1912. BIBLIOGRAPHY: *Kouchakji* no. 84a.

278 Grape Flask

Possibly Rhenish
Late Second–Third Century A.D.
Moore Collection, 1955.6.78
H. 18.5 cm.

Flasks in the form of a bunch of grapes were a fairly common descendant of the date flask throughout the empire. Among the more naturalistic examples such as this flask, the dominant colors are the purple and green of real grapes; this brown example is unusual. Handles seem to be primarily a Rhenish addition after the late second century A.D.; therefore, a western origin for the Yale flask is proposed.

DESCRIPTION: mold-blown, two part mold; rim folded in; vase and handles brown. CONDITION: strain crack in body; slight iridescence and some white weathering. PROVENANCE: Fahim Kouchakji, 1938. BIBLIOGRAPHY: *Kouchakji* no. 81. PARALLELS: *Isings* type 91a, without handles: in Pompeii by the first century, with handles in the Rhenish provinces at the end of the second century. Three examples with handles apparently from one mold are close to the Yale flask but not mold-mates: Kisa, *Glas* III, 773–77, fig. 309, a purple flask in the Musée du Cinquantenaire, Brussels, more recently illustrated in *JIV* 5 (1967–70) 36, fig. 19; and two in the Rijksmuseum van Oudheden, Leiden, inv. 1930/3.3 and 1930/3.2, both pale green, found together in a cremation burial at Heerlen, published by J. H. Holwerda, *Oudheidkundige Medelingen Leiden* N. T. 11 (1930) 2–6, pls. 3–4. Some naturalistic examples without handles probably of eastern origin include *von Saldern, Oppenländer* nos. 472 and 473; *Auth, Newark* no. 71, with other parallels; and two fragments from Dura-Europos, *Clairmont, Dura* 39–40, nos. 148–49, pl. 21.

279 Grape Flask

Eastern Mediterranean
Third Century A.D. or later
Moore Collection, 1955.6.79
H. 13.5 cm.

This highly stylized vessel also appears to represent a bunch of grapes: only vestigal grape leaves at the shoulder identify the geometric pattern as a fruit. The distinctive collar which characterizes this family of flasks is unusual.

DESCRIPTION: mold-blown, two part mold; cut-out base;

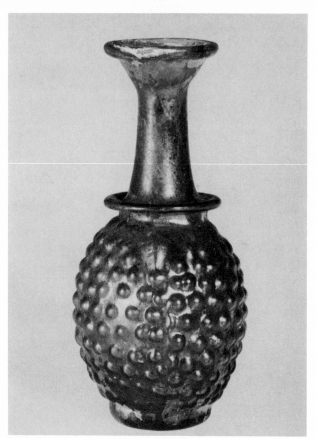

279

cut-out ridge at base of neck forming a collar; neck slightly constricted; sloping rim folded in; pontil mark; colorless or pale pinkish purple.   CONDITION: intact; rosy iridescence. PROVENANCE: Moore Collection no. 717.   BIBLIOGRAPHY: *Eisen* 331, pl. 79a; *Kouchakji* no. 82; *Hayes, Toronto* 49, no. 91; *von Saldern, Oppenländer* 172, no. 470.   PARALLELS: numerous, with the most recent publications containing lists of parallels: *Hayes, Toronto* no. 91; *Auth, Newark* no. 72; *von Saldern, Oppenländer* no. 470.

280 *Bottle with Mythological Figures*

Eastern Mediterranean
Early Third Century A.D.
Moore Collection, 1955.6.51
H. 20.9 cm.

The three figures on this vessel are readily identifiable despite the poor quality of the relief: Dionysos stands in a frontal pose, his left arm raised holding his thyrsos, his right arm lowered holding a vessel from which he feeds a panther at his feet; goat-legged Pan strides vigorously forward, his leg raised with the knee bent; Silenus, wearing a short kilt, moves to the right, carrying a wineskin on his shoulder. Similar figures occur on other glass vessels, as for example the Pan and Dionysos figures on a pair of first century Dionysiac beakers (cat. no. 136 above) and the Dionysos on a first century series of beakers with mythological figures (cat. no. 137 above). The use of columns to separate the figures also relates this bottle to the mythological beaker series.

Two complete bottles, one in the Oppenländer Collection and the other at the Corning Museum of Glass, and a set of fragments excavated at Dura-Europos (fig. 1) have been associated with the Yale flask. All show the same three figures, but with certain variations. Christopher Clairmont, in his discussion of the Dura fragments, outlines the similarities and differences among these and the Yale and Corning bottles and correctly concludes that the Dura fragments and the Corning bottle are from the same mold. As Clairmont pointed out, the Yale bottle shows distinct differences when compared to the Corning bottle; a first hand examination of the Corning flask confirms the conclusions Clairmont drew solely from the photographs of it published in the catalogue of the Sangiorgi Collection. Although the poses of the three figures are basically the same in all vessels, the poses of those on the Yale bottle are more exaggerated. Pan's knee is raised; Dionysos stands with his weight on his left leg in a slight contraposto; and Silenus holds the wineskin with his arm kept close to his chest. On the other hand, the

280 A (Dionysos)

Dura fragments and the Corning bottle show Pan with both feet on the ground, Dionysos firmly planted on both feet with his weight evenly distributed, and Silenus with his left arm somewhat more extended as he holds the wineskin. The third complete bottle, now in the Oppenländer Collection and unknown to Clairmont, appears to coincide in these

280 B (Pan), 280 C (Silenus)

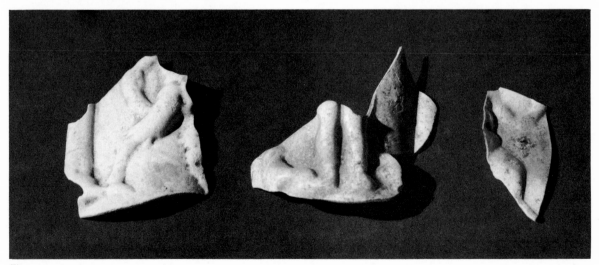

Fig. 1

details with the Yale flask, although it is known to me only from photographs.

Although Clairmont was correct in noting these differences, I cannot agree with his suggestion that they result from changes made by reworking the mold between the execution of the Yale bottle and the Dura and Corning bottles. The existence of more than one version of what must have been a prized object even in its own time has been clearly demonstrated by Gladys Weinberg for the beakers with mythological figures. With this precedent in mind it seems far more probable that two separate molds are represented here than that one was so reworked as to eliminate all the vigor of the figures while increasing the depth of the relief in the final state.

The inscription on the base was first noted by D. B. Harden and identified by him as an incomplete version of the standard drinking inscription ΠΙΕ ΖΗCHC, "drink and may you live." Another variant spelling, ΠΙΕ ΖΗCAIC, occurs inside a wreath on three base fragments from Dura, the most complete of which probably belongs with the three figured fragments discussed above. Neither the Corning nor the Oppenländer flasks has an inscription.

The date of these bottles remains uncertain. While the finds from Dura and the form of the necks of the three complete bottles point to a date in the first half of the third century, the obvious relation of the figures separated by columns to the first century mythological beakers makes it impossible to ignore the possibility of an early date.

DESCRIPTION: mold-blown, four part mold; on the base, within a wreath of palm leaves, the Greek inscription ΠΙΕ HCHC; three figures separated by columns, as described above; vertical neck constricted at its base; ground rim; pale bluish green. CONDITION: intact; white weathering and iridescence. PROVENANCE: said to have been found in Syria, near Aleppo; Kouchakji Frères, 1919. BIBLIOGRAPHY: *Eisen* 232, pls. 46–47; *Kouchakji* no. 53; Hayward, "Yale" 57–58, no. 10, figs. 15–17, noting Harden's discovery of the inscription; *Clairmont, Dura* 35–36; Weinberg, "Mold-Blown Beakers" 26, note 2; *von Saldern, Oppenländer* 167. PARALLELS: from the same mold: *von Saldern, Oppenländer* 167, no. 459, fig. 459 and color plate on p. 157. From a variant mold: CMG inv. 66.1.39, Sangiorgi Collection, Sangiorgi, *Vetri Antichi* no. 100, pl. 16; Yale University Art Gallery acc. nos. 1933.570 a–c with base fragment 1933.570d, from Dura-Europos, *Clairmont, Dura* 35–37, no. 127 a–d, pl. 21; probably also the base fragments Yale acc. nos. 1934.557a and 1933.578c, from Dura, *Clairmont, Dura* nos. 128 and 129 respectively.

281, 282

281 *Mold-Blown or Pattern Molded Jug*

Eastern Mediterranean
Third Century A.D.
Van Volkenburgh Bequest, 1940.269
H. 9.2 cm.

Faint mold-blown dots in irregular rows cover most of the body of this jug. Although a number of vessels have this decoration, duplication of shapes is rare. It may be that the shapes were formed by further inflation and tooling after removal from the mold causing faintness of decoration and an absence of clear mold seams on many of these vessels.

DESCRIPTION: mold-blown or pattern molded; no clear mold seams; concave base; trefoil mouth with rounded rim; yellow with yellowish brown handle. CONDITION: mouth broken and repaired; iridescent. PARALLELS: no exact parallels of this shape, but for the pattern on similar vessels, see *Hayes, Toronto* no. 425, with related vessels.

282 *Double Head Flask*

Eastern Mediterranean
Third–Fourth Century A.D.
Mansfield Collection, 1930.420
H. 13.2 cm.

The trefoil mouth and fragmentary handle that transform this flask into a jug relate it chronologically to third century terra cotta head flasks with trefoil mouths from the Athenian Agora. The top of the

283, Front & Back

head lost considerable detail when the vessel was reheated to form the mouth.

DESCRIPTION: mold-blown, two part mold; two faces, virtually identical; trefoil mouth with trailed thread below the rim; upper fragment of trailed-on side handle; pale green. CONDITION: handle missing except for fragment attached to rim; small fragment of nose restored; iridescent, with white weathering towards the bottom, brown near the mouth. PROVENANCE: ex coll. Adjamian, formerly the Persian Consul General at Aleppo; Khayat, 1930. PARALLELS: for the terra cotta head vases, see E. B. Harrison, *The Athenian Agora, vol. I: Portrait Sculpture* (Princeton 1953) 67, note 4, pl. 47, fig. d.

283 *Head Flask*

Eastern Mediterranean
Third–Fourth Century A.D.
Moore Collection, 1955.6.77
H. 22.5 cm.

The almond-shaped eyes, flat face, and swept back hair of this head flask recall features characteristic of Palmyrene funerary portraits and religious sculpture of the third century. The hair style makes little sense from the back, however, and the central back part has no parallels among imperial portraits or their descendants. If it is a peculiarly eastern coiffure it would be difficult to prove it, given the paucity of sculpture in the round from the Palmyra area. The tall vertical neck with a slight constriction at its base also points to a date of the third century or later.

DESCRIPTION: mold-blown, two part mold; flat bottom with added pad base; irregular rounded rim; pale green. CONDITION: alien foot removed leaving a hole in center bottom; crack across bottom and up left side; slightly iridescent. PROVENANCE: Fahim Kouchakji, 1938. BIBLIOGRAPHY: Kouchakji Frères Collection, sale catalogue, Kouchakji Frères Gallery, New York 19–20 March 1926, no. 216, as cited by *Hayes, Toronto* 50, no. 93; *Eisen* 330, pl. 77; *Kouchakji* no. 80; *Hayes, Toronto* 50, no. 93. PARALLELS: from the same mold: *Hayes, Toronto* no. 93, on a stemmed foot. The Yale flask was originally restored to correspond with this footed example despite its obvious pad base. For parallels for the frontal view of the hair style, see Malcolm Colledge, *The Art of Palmyra* (London 1976) pl. 44 (male guardian figures) and, e.g., pls. 86 and 94 (female funerary portraits).

284 *Honeycomb Beaker*

Eastern Mediterranean
Fourth Century A.D.
Moore Collection, 1955.6.71
H. 11.7 cm., D. 12.1 cm.

This vessel is visually akin to mold-blown vessels, but represents a variant technique in which the glass was first molded and then blown. In this case the glass was first pressed or blown into a honeycomb-shaped mold with ribs on its vertical sides and a circular flat base with a honeycomb pattern. The vessel was then removed from the mold and further inflated, producing the hemispherical shape and the distension of the pattern towards the bottom of the vessel. The method of manufacture of these vessels was determined by Waldemar Haberey on the basis of two surviving vessels which were allowed to cool without further inflation after removal from the mold.

284

286, 285

The technique continued into the Islamic period, but a date for this piece as early as the fourth century is suggested by a grave find at Cologne dated circa A.D. 350. The suggestion that these beakers served as lamps has often been made.

DESCRIPTION: blown, pattern molded glass; rim ground; yellow green. CONDITION: one area broken and repaired, with strain cracks; weathering generally negligible except for traces of white weathering near the rim. PROVENANCE: said to have been found near Tyre and Sidon; Fahim Kouchakji, 1925; Moore Collection no. 814. BIBLIOGRAPHY: *Eisen* 319, pl. 72b; *Kouchakji* no. 74. PARALLELS: numerous, including those cited by *Fremersdorf, Denkmäler* VI 58, and Dusenbery, "Wheaton College" 15, and others. For the technique, see Waldemar Haberey, "Zur Herstellung der römischen Wabenbecher," *Bonner Jahrbücher* 166 (1966) 208–12, citing the two uninflated examples, a conical example, and Islamic parallels. *Smith, Corning* 239 cites other Islamic parallels for his no. 476, including some eleventh and twelfth century vessels from Gurgan, Iran. The fourth century Cologne find is cited by *Isings* type 107a. For the use of the vessels as lamps, see Crowfoot and Harden, "Glass Lamps." A variant with a dot in each cell of the honeycomb pattern is in the Louvre, inv. MNE 142, from Porphyrion.

285 *Honeycomb Beaker*

Eastern Mediterranean
Fourth Century A.D.
Lehman Gift, 1953.28.31
H. 7 cm.

This vessel lacks the vertical ribs of the preceding beaker, but the manufacturing process used was undoubtedly the same. An irregular row of dots pressed in just below the rim may come from a device used to hold the vessel while it was inflated or may simply be decoration impressed with a sharp instrument. A similar row of dots appears on a facet-cut honeycomb beaker of slightly earlier date. The pattern molded honeycomb beakers are certainly related visually to these facet-cut vessels and may indeed derive from or imitate them.

DESCRIPTION: blown, pattern molded; rim irregular, ground; light purple with yellow streaks. CONDITION: intact; iridescent. PROVENANCE: John D. Rockefeller, Jr. no. 17; Duveen Brothers no. 25. PARALLELS: another without ribs: *von Saldern, Oppenländer* no. 487; for the facet-cut beaker with a row of dots below the rim, see *von Saldern, Oppenländer* no. 512.

286 *Pattern Molded Beaker*

Eastern Mediterranean
Fourth Century A.D.
Moore Collection, 1955.6.72.
H. 8.8 cm., D. 11.1 cm.

This beaker was produced by the same process used to make the honeycomb beakers but introduces a variant pattern of intersecting arcs.

DESCRIPTION: blown, pattern molded; rim ground; pale green. CONDITION: intact; iridescent. PROVENANCE: Kouchakji Frères, 1923. BIBLIOGRAPHY: *Eisen* 319, pl. 72a; *Kouchakji* no. 75; *von Saldern, Boston* 92; Dusenbery, "Wheaton College" 15, note 50. PARALLELS: BMFA inv. 50.2272, *von Saldern, Boston* no. 41; BM inv. 79.11–8.11, Dusenbery, "Wheaton College" 15; Harden, *Karanis* no. 216, pl. B (fragment). A fragment of this pattern that was molded but not inflated is cited by Harden, *Karanis* 93, note 1, fig. 1f, Berlin, Antiquarium inv. 30638. Related vessels with variant patterns include *von Saldern, Boston* no. 42, with round bosses in a network of arcs, and a similar beaker in the Louvre, inv. MNE 143, from Porphyrion.

BLOWN, FOURTH–FIFTH CENTURY A.D.

287 *Bottle with Wheel-Cut Decoration*

Eastern Mediterranean
Fourth–Fifth Century A.D.
Moore Collection, 1955.6.278
H. 8 cm.

DESCRIPTION: free-blown; concave base; rounded rim with thread around exterior below edge; pale green; shallow wheel-cut decoration consisting of a connected frieze of six circular medallions formed by branches (probably palm), each encircling an animal protome (probably six different dogs). CONDITION: unbroken with a few strain cracks; virtually no weathering. PROVENANCE: Fahim Kouchakji, 1940. BIBLIOGRAPHY: *Eisen* 547; *Kouchakji* no. 189a. PARALLELS: for the shape, *Isings* type 104b, mainly fourth century; for the engraved medallions with animal protomes, see Jorge Alarcão, "Abraded and Engraved Late Roman Glass from Portugal," *JGS* 12 (1970) 28–34, especially 30–31, no. 2, figs. 5–7.

288 *Miniature Flask*

Eastern Mediterranean
Fourth–Fifth Century A.D.
Van Volkenburgh Bequest, 1940.281
H. 4 cm.

A virtual replica in miniature of a common fourth–fifth century funnel-mouthed wine flask, this example has a neck constriction that suggests it might have been used for perfume.

287

288, 289

DESCRIPTION: free-blown; rounded rim; concave base; very pale green, nearly colorless. CONDITION: intact; thick white weathering, partially flaked off.

289 *Jar*

Eastern Mediterranean
Fourth–Fifth Century A.D.
Moore Collection, 1955.6.196
H. 6.5 cm.

Although related to third and fourth century jar shapes, the nearly vertical neck and the crimped decoration of this example suggest a Byzantine date.

DESCRIPTION: free-blown; rim folded in; concave base; single row of pinched projections around the center of the body; pale green. CONDITION: intact; iridescent. PROVENANCE: Moore Collection no. 736. BIBLIOGRAPHY: *Eisen* 616, pl. 151; *Kouchakji* no. 203. PARALLELS: Harden, "Amman" fig. 10, from a fourth–fifth century A.D. tomb at Beit Ras, Jordan; Baur, *Gerasa* fig. 18, no. 67 (244) with a different neck.

290 *Bottle with Mold-Blown Ribs*

Eastern Mediterranean
Fourth–Fifth Century A.D.
Moore Collection, 1955.6.112
H. 12.4 cm.

Mold-blown diagonal ribs encircle the conical body of this bottle. The wide cylindrical neck is constricted to a small sprinkler hole and the mouth widens above a cut-out ridge. Diagonal and vertical ribs occur as mold-blown or optic blown decorative motifs on vessels of the third to the fifth century. The reintroduction of the rich transparent colors last popular in the first century occurs at about this time.

BLOWN VESSELS III

290, 291

DESCRIPTION: mold-blown and tooled; concave base; transparent dark blue. CONDITION: broken and repaired, pitted and iridescent. PROVENANCE: Moore Collection no. 715. BIBLIOGRAPHY: *Eisen* 334, pl. 85; *Kouchakji* no. 118. PARALLELS: for mold-blown ribs, see *von Saldern, Oppenländer* nos. 491–95 and 498–99; *Hayes, Toronto* no. 428–32; Harden, *Karanis* 225, nos. 600–703 (fourth century); *Clairmont, Dura* 40 (third century); Damascus Museum, two vessels with vertical ribs (nos. unknown) and six with diagonal ribs, nos. 182, 373, 380, 385, 448, and 473 (Dura photos).

291 *Bottle*

> Eastern Mediterranean
> Fourth–Fifth Century A.D.
> Van Volkenburgh Bequest, 1940.272
> H. 11.7 cm.

DESCRIPTION: free-blown; body narrows towards base; funnel mouth with cut-out ridge below rim; base slightly concave; pale green. CONDITION: broken and repaired with some losses; surface pitted and iridescent. PARALLELS: *Isings* type 102b; *Hayes, Toronto* no. 419.

292 *Inscribed Beaker*

> Eastern Mediterranean, possibly Egyptian
> Fourth–Fifth Century A.D.
> Moore Collection, 1955.6.191
> H. 7 cm., D. 7.2 cm.

Inscribed drinking vessels with toasts, good wishes, and exhortations to victory are familiar from mold-blown examples of the first century A.D. Similar inscriptions continued to appear on the wheel-cut vessels that gradually replaced mold-blown cups.

Frequent inconsistencies and inaccuracies of spelling occur on both types.

This cup bears a variant of a common good wish inscription, ΠΙΕ ΖΗCΗC, "drink and may you live." The vessel is also decorated with a wave pattern, garlands, circles, and vertical rows of short oblique strokes. These motifs and the style of their execution relate the Yale cup to a small group of inscribed wheel-cut vessels including a tall cup in the Metropolitan Museum and a number of footed flasks. In publishing the most elaborate of these footed flasks, the Highdown Hill Goblet, D. B. Harden concluded that it was made in Egypt and offered the late fourth to fifth century A.D. date cited above.

DESCRIPTION: free-blown hemispherical cup on pad base; wheel-polished rim; pale green; wheel-cut decoration: inscription, ΔΕΖ[Ε] ΠΙ[Ε] ΖΗCΗC, with two garlands between a running wave pattern and two wheel-cut lines; below, vertical rows of short oblique lines alternating with circles with central dots. CONDITION: unbroken; pale brown enamel weathering, flaking severely, with iridescence underneath. BIBLIOGRAPHY: *Eisen* 410, pl. 101; *Kouchakji* no. 198; Harden, "Highdown Hill" 14, pl. VI, a. PARALLELS: Harden, "Highdown Hill"; G. D. Weinberg, "A Parallel to the Highdown Hill Glass," *JGS* 5 (1963) 25–28, also illustrating the MMA cup inv. 13.198.5; sale catalogue, Sotheby's, 3–4 July 1978, lot 58, pl. 10 (probably from Maaret-el Nuaman, Syria), especially close to the Missouri flask, and lot 57, with variant decoration; *SPB, Constable-Maxwell* nos. 264 and 266 (uninscribed) and no. 265 (inscribed), with variant decoration.

292

293, 294, 295, 296

293 *Footed Beaker*

Eastern Mediterranean
Fourth–Fifth Century A.D.
Whiting Collection, 1912.929
H. 11.9 cm.

A fairly common type with either straight or convex sides, this cup narrows to a large folded foot.

DESCRIPTION: free-blown; folded foot; rounded rim; pale green. CONDITION: intact; light brown and iridescent weathering. PARALLELS: *Hayes, Toronto* no. 379; *von Saldern, Oppenländer* no. 757; Vessberg, "Cyprus" pl. 4, no. 9; Neuburg, *Glas* fig. 61; Crowfoot, *Samaria-Sebaste* fig. 96, no. 10.

294 *Footed Beaker*

Eastern Mediterranean
Fourth–Fifth Century A.D.
Gift of E. Francis Riggs, B.A. 1909, and T. Laurason Riggs, B.A. 1910, 1929.630
H. 6.7 cm.

DESCRIPTION: free-blown; similar to cat. no. 293; spiral thread around rim; rim folded in; pontil mark; body and thread decoration medium green. CONDITION: intact; virtually no weathering.

295 *Stemmed Cup*

Eastern Mediterranean
Fourth–Fifth Century A.D.
Whiting Collection, 1912.933
H. 8.6 cm.

Stemmed goblets, usually natural pale green like this one, are a later addition to the repertory of drinking cups. They seem to have been primarily eastern Mediterranean products. A simple design with straight sides and a continuous profile, this glass has a large capacity for its height.

DESCRIPTION: free-blown; folded foot, kicked in; rim turned in; pale green. CONDITION: intact; flaking black weathering over iridescence. PARALLELS: Vessberg, "Cyprus" pl. 4, no. 18; *Isings* type 111; Damascus Museum nos. 220, 818, and 819 (Dura photos); Crowfoot, *Samaria-Sebaste* fig. 96, no. 7.

296 *Stemmed Cup*

Eastern Mediterranean
Fourth–Fifth Century A.D.
Moore Collection, 1955.6.270
H. 8 cm.

DESCRIPTION: free-blown; rounded profile; beaded stem; folded foot, kicked in; rim turned in; pale green; blowing spirals evident near the rim. CONDITION: cracked; beige, white, and iridescent weathering. BIBLIOGRAPHY: *Eisen* 289, fig. 62; *Kouchakji* no. 44a. PARALLELS: Crowfoot, *Samaria-Sebaste* fig. 96, no. 11, with solid beaded stem; Baur, *Gerasa* fig. 20, no. 20 (870) with solid beaded stem and a wider bowl.

297 *Jar*

Eastern Mediterranean
Fourth Century A.D.
Gift of Edward B. Greene, B.A. 1900, 1930.47
H. 7.3 cm.

Continuing a type which first appeared in the third century, the short-necked jar with a funnel mouth is a common fourth–fifth century shape. The body is

298, 299, 297

globular, the bottom generally slightly concave. Common decorations include pinched ribs, indentations, and a tooled or cut-out ridge below the rim. A large group with a trailed-on zigzag thread joining the mouth to the shoulder, or two or more "handles" performing the same function, are particularly characteristic of the Syro-Palestinian area in the late Roman and Byzantine periods. The class as a whole is primarily found in the eastern Mediterranean. Purple, brown, and yellow are typical colors, although natural pale green still occurs.

DESCRIPTION: free-blown; base slightly concave; rim folded out; purple. CONDITION: intact; iridescent. PARALLELS: *Hayes, Toronto* nos. 291–92 and 474; Crowfoot, *Samaria-Sebaste* fig. 95, nos. 15–17.

298 *Jar*

Eastern Mediterranean
Fourth Century A.D.
Moore Collection, 1955.6.202
H. 7.2 cm.

DESCRIPTION: free-blown; similar to cat. no. 297; rim folded in; base slightly concave; purple. CONDITION: intact; pitted and iridescent. PROVENANCE: Moore Collection no. 694. BIBLIOGRAPHY: *Eisen* 615, pl. 152b; *Kouchakji* no. 209; *Hayes, Toronto* 79, no. 291.

299 *Jar*

Eastern Mediterranean
Fourth–Fifth Century A.D.
Moore Collection, 1955.6.203
H. 7.6 cm.

DESCRIPTION: free-blown; similar to cat. no. 297; ring of pinched projections around center of body; rim folded in; yellowish brown. CONDITION: intact; light brown enamel weathering and iridescence. PROVENANCE: Moore Collection no. 629. BIBLIOGRAPHY: *Eisen* 616, text fig. 259j, pl. 152, bottom; *Spartz, Kassel* no. 149. PARALLELS: for the pinched decoration, see *von Saldern, Oppenländer* nos. 713–14; *Spartz, Kassel* no. 149; Damascus Museum no. 328 (Dura photo).

300 *Jar*

Eastern Mediterranean
Fourth Century A.D.
Gift of Edward B. Greene, B.A. 1900, 1930.45
Pres. H. 5.1 cm.

DESCRIPTION: free-blown; similar to cat. no. 297; concave base; brown. CONDITION: fragmentary, mouth ground down; iridescent. PROVENANCE: Alfred R. Bellinger.

300

302, 301

301 *Jar*

Possibly Western Empire
Fourth–Fifth Century A.D.
Mansfield Collection, 1930.440
H. 12.1 cm.

DESCRIPTION: free-blown; similar to cat. no. 297; pinched vertical ribs; the color and bubbly fabric differ from eastern examples; rim folded in; dark blue. CONDITION: intact; iridescent with traces of light brown weathering. PROVENANCE: M.C. Borden sale, 1913; said to have been found in France; Mansfield Collection no. 216. PARALLELS: *Auth, Newark* no. 461.

302 *Jar*

Eastern Mediterranean
Fourth–Fifth Century A.D.
Mansfield Collection, 1930.446
H. 11.1 cm.

The addition of a cut-out ridge below the rim is the distinguishing characteristic of a large group of jars otherwise similar to the plain funnel-mouthed type in form and decoration.

DESCRIPTION: free-blown; vertical pinched ribs; cut-out ridge below folded in rim; pinkish purple. CONDITION: intact; iridescent with traces of light brown weathering. PROVENANCE: D. Kelekian, 1898; Mansfield Collection no. 6. PARALLELS: *Hayes, Toronto* no. 658.

303 *Jar*

Eastern Mediterranean
Fourth–Fifth Century A.D.

Mansfield Collection, 1930.456
H. 8.9 cm.

A zigzag thread joining the rim and the shoulder is another common form of decoration, often combined, as here, with an indented body.

DESCRIPTION: free-blown; indented; concave base; rim folded in; pale green body and decoration. CONDITION: broken and repaired with some thread decoration missing; iridescent. PROVENANCE: said to be from a tomb on Mount Carmel; George F. Laimne, 1900; Mansfield Collection no. 77. PARALLELS: Barag, *Beth She^{c}arim* fig. 97:30 (before A.D. 352); Crowfoot, *Samaria-Sebaste* fig. 95, no. 17 from the North Cemetery (fourth–fifth century A.D.); *Hayes, Toronto* nos. 471, 442, and 443; numerous others from the Syro-Palestinian area. For a slightly later and less refined group from Egypt, see Harden, *Karanis* 175–76 and 179, Class VIII, A 1, pls. 6 and 17.

304 *Jar*

Eastern Mediterranean
Fourth–Fifth Century A.D.
Mansfield Collection, 1930.416
H. 7.2 cm.

DESCRIPTION: free-blown; similar to cat. no. 297; indented body; double zigzag around neck; concave base; rim folded in; body and decoration brown. CONDITION: intact; thin layer of whitish weathering. PROVENANCE: found at Gor Busan by A. Khayat in 1900 and bought from him the same year. PARALLELS: with a double zigzag, *Auth, Newark* no. 178.

304, 303, 305, 306

305 *Jar*

Eastern Mediterranean
Fourth–Fifth Century A.D.
Van Volkenburgh Bequest, 1940.293
H. 7.3 cm.

DESCRIPTION: free-blown; similar to cat. no. 297; cut-out ridge; spiral thread around body; zigzag thread around neck; concave base; rounded rim; body and decoration pale green. CONDITION: some thread decoration missing; unbroken; brown weathering. PARALLELS: *Auth, Newark* no. 178, with a double zigzag thread.

306 *Jar*

Eastern Mediterranean
Fourth–Fifth Century A.D.
Moore Collection, 1955.6.253
H. 7.2. cm.

DESCRIPTION: free-blown; similar to cat. no. 297; cut-out ridge; blue zigzag around neck; flattened base; rim folded

in; pale green. CONDITION: unbroken; part of zigzag thread missing; pitted and iridescent.

307 *Jar*

Eastern Mediterranean
Fourth–Fifth Century A.D.
Yale University Art Gallery, 1955.6.357
H. 11.4 cm.

DESCRIPTION: free-blown; similar to cat. no. 297; cut-out ridge; rounded rim; concave base; purple. CONDITION: intact; some iridescence and white weathering on one side. PARALLELS: Neuburg, *Glas* fig. 59; Harden, "Amman" fig. 8, from an early fourth century tomb at Beit Fajjar, Palestine.

308 *Jar*

Eastern Mediterranean
Fourth–Fifth Century A.D.

307, 308

309, 310, 311

Yale University Art Gallery, 1955.6.358
H. 12.2 cm.

DESCRIPTION: free-blown; virtually identical to cat. no. 307 in form, color, fabric, and weathering; possibly a pair from one tomb group; cut-out ridge below a rounded rim; concave base; purple. CONDITION: intact; iridescence and white weathering on one side.

309 *Jar*

Eastern Mediterranean
Fourth–Fifth Century A.D.
Mansfield Collection, 1930.417
H. 8.5 cm.

Two or more handles were often added to the jars with cut-out ridges below the rim. These jars may be plain or decorated with combinations of indentations, spiral and zigzag threads. Often the thread decoration is in a contrasting color.

DESCRIPTION: free-blown; two handles; indented; cut-out ridge; rounded rim; spiral thread; pale green with dark green handles and thread decoration. CONDITION: unbroken; thread decoration mostly missing; flaking white weathering and iridescence. PROVENANCE: Khayat, 1908; said to have been found at Birsan; Mansfield Collection no. 165. PARALLELS: Harden, "Amman" fig. 11, from a tomb at Talluza, Jordan.

310 *Jar*

Eastern Mediterranean
Fourth–Fifth Century A.D.
Moore Collection, 1955.6.137
H. 9.8 cm.

DESCRIPTION: free-blown; similar to cat. no. 309; cut-out ridge; indented; concave base; rounded rim; two handles; spiral thread around the body; pale green body and handles,

darker green thread decoration. CONDITION: intact; iridescent. PROVENANCE: Moore Collection no. 688. BIBLIOGRAPHY: *Eisen* 443, pl. 110; *Kouchakji* no. 144; *Hayes, Toronto* 95, no. 326 and 96, no. 332. PARALLELS: Damascus Museum no. 161 (not indented) and nos. 165 and 194 (without spiral thread, Dura photos).

311 *Jar*

Eastern Mediterranean
Fourth–Fifth Century A.D.
Mansfield Collection, 1930.398
H. 8.6 cm.

DESCRIPTION: free-blown; similar to cat. no. 309; not indented; cut-out ridge; concave base; rim rounded; two handles; zigzag thread around the neck; body, handles, and zigzag thread yellow. CONDITION: intact; white weathering and iridescence, with some pitting. PROVENANCE: said to have been found at Dirka in 1904, "in the interior of Hauran, Syria." PARALLELS: Neuburg, *Glas* fig. 59, from a tomb at Ashkalon, Palestine; *Hayes, Toronto* nos. 331 (with three handles) and 332.

312 *Jar*

Eastern Mediterranean
Fourth–Fifth Century A.D.
Moore Collection, 1955.6.135
H. 8.0 cm., 13.1 cm. with handle

The four handles of this jar have become purely decorative with the addition of a functional basket handle over the top.

DESCRIPTION: free-blown; cut-out ridge; concave base; rounded rim; thread decoration and handles dark green, contrasting with pale green jar. CONDITION: intact; pitted and iridescent. PROVENANCE: Moore Collection no. 679. BIBLIOGRAPHY: *Eisen* 430, pl. 111; *Kouchakji* no. 142. PARALLELS: *Auth, Newark* no. 176.

313 *Jar*

Eastern Mediterranean
Fourth–Fifth Century A.D.
Van Volkenburgh Bequest, 1940.294
H. 6.6 cm.

DESCRIPTION: free-blown; similar to cat. no. 309; indented body; four handles; concave base; rim folded in; pale green with darker green handles. CONDITION: intact; iridescent with white weathering.

314 *Jar*

Eastern Mediterranean
Fourth–Fifth Century A.D.
Mansfield Collection, 1930.441
H. 10.4 cm.

Differing from the general class of globular jars, this vessel has straight sides narrowing towards a flattened base.

DESCRIPTION: free-blown; cut-out ridge; rim folded in; purple with three green handles. CONDITION: part of one handle broken away; light brown and iridescent weathering. PROVENANCE: A. D. Vorce, 1898; Mansfield Collection no. 29.

315 *Jar*

Eastern Mediterranean
Fourth–Sixth Century A.D.
Moore Collection, 1955.6.134
H. 7.5 cm.

Thirteen small handles, decorative rather than functional, join the rim to the shoulder of this vessel.

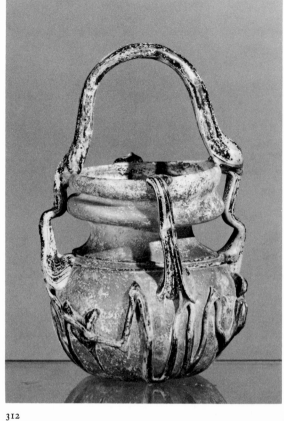

312

The addition of a base and the multiplication of the handles seem to be later Byzantine features.

DESCRIPTION: free-blown; ring base; rounded rim; body and handles purple. CONDITION: three handles missing, mouth repaired; flaking brown weathering. PROVENANCE: Moore Collection no. 714. BIBLIOGRAPHY: *Eisen* 430, pl. 110; *Kouchakji* no. 141.

313, 314, 315

316 *Jar*

Eastern Mediterranean
Fifth–Sixth Century A.D.
Mansfield Collection, 1930.429
H. 16.8 cm.

DESCRIPTION: free-blown; conical foot; cut-out ridge; rounded rim; sixteen handles; body and handles pale green. CONDITION: some breaks repaired, uppermost part of one handle restored; iridescent. PROVENANCE: from the de Morgan sale, 1901. PARALLELS: *Auth, Newark* no. 177, without foot; Grose, *Toledo* fig. 28, a smaller version with fewer handles and decoration in a contrasting color.

317 *Cosmetic Flask*

Eastern Mediterranean
Third–Fourth Century A.D.
Moore Collection, 1955.6.120
H. 11.4 cm.

A large group of single compartment cosmetic flasks are stabilized by a folded conical foot. Most have two handles and a wide funnel mouth, and many have a

316

spiral thread around the body, a zigzag thread, or applied vertical ribs. Dated finds indicate a third to fourth century date for the group.

DESCRIPTION: free-blown; bulbous lower body; conical foot; rim folded in; two handles, folded at the top to form a thumbrest; pale green. CONDITION: one thumbrest missing; dark brown weathering and iridescence. BIBLIOGRAPHY: *Kouchakji* no. 126. PARALLELS: Barag, *Beth She^carim* fig. 97:26; Neuburg, *Glas*, fig. 58, from a grave in Beit Fajjar, Palestine; *Hayes, Toronto* nos. 352, 353, 393–95, 447–55, with varying decoration, especially nos. 352 and 451 for undecorated examples; for a variant with three feet, see *Cambridge, Fitzwilliam* no. 107.

318 *Cosmetic Flask*

Eastern Mediterranean
Third–Fourth Century A.D.
Moore Collection, 1955.6.247
H. 12.2 cm.

DESCRIPTION: free-blown; similar to cat. no. 317; spiral thread around middle of body and zigzag coil around neck; folded foot; rim folded in; pale bluish green. CONDITION: most of thread decoration missing; light brown weathering and iridescence. PARALLELS: *Hayes, Toronto* nos. 452 and 455, with other parallels.

319 *Cosmetic Flask*

Eastern Mediterranean
Third–Fourth Century A.D.
Van Volkenburgh Bequest, 1940.287
H. 10.4 cm.

DESCRIPTION: free-blown; similar to cat. no. 317; smaller mouth; large angular handles; spiral thread around body; folded foot; rim folded in; body, handles, and decoration pale green. CONDITION: some thread decoration missing; iridescent and flaking. PARALLELS: *Hayes, Toronto* no. 395; Harden, "Amman" fig. 8, from a fourth century tomb at Beit Fajjar, Palestine.

320 *Cosmetic Flask*

Eastern Mediterranean
Third–Fourth Century A.D.
Mansfield Collection, 1930.405
H. 14.1 cm.

DESCRIPTION: free-blown; similar to cat. no. 317; vertical ribs; single thread below the handles; folded foot; rim folded in; purple. CONDITION: intact; iridescent. PROVENANCE: Khayat, 1908; said to have been found at Birsan; Mansfield Collection no. 167. PARALLELS: *Hayes, Toronto* no. 455, with zigzag instead of handles.

321 *Double Cosmetic Tube*

Eastern Mediterranean
Fourth Century A.D.
Lehman Gift, 1953.28.28
H. 11.1 cm.

This two-compartment cosmetic container, formed by pinching one glass bubble at the center, is the simplest variety of numerous eastern Mediterranean cosmetic tubes produced in the late Roman Empire and into the Byzantine period. Many have trailed thread decoration, and the most elaborate examples have multiple tubes and compound basket handles, sometimes in a contrasting color. The cosmetics were extracted from the tubes with thin rods of bronze, glass, and probably bone.

DESCRIPTION: free-blown; rim folded in; pale yellowish green with medium green handles. CONDITION: intact; iridescent and flaking, with some pitting. PROVENANCE: John D. Rockefeller, Jr. no. 10; Duveen Brothers no. 35. PARALLELS: *Hayes, Toronto* no. 359; Neuburg, *Glas* fig. 59, with top handle, spiral thread, and bronze cosmetic rod, from a grave at Ashkalon, Palestine; *Auth, Newark* nos. 482 and 483; Crowfoot, *Samaria-Sebaste* fig. 95, no. 24 from the North Cemetery (fourth–fifth century A.D.).

322 *Double Cosmetic Tube*

Eastern Mediterranean
Fourth Century A.D.
Moore Collection, 1955.6.185
H. 9.6 cm.

DESCRIPTION: free-blown; similar to cat. no. 321; rim folded in; body and handles pale green. CONDITION: a few chips; light brown enamel weathering. PROVENANCE: Moore Collection no. 724. BIBLIOGRAPHY: *Eisen* 587, fig. 239; *Kouchakji* no. 192; *Hayes, Toronto* 101, no. 359.

323 *Double Cosmetic Tube*

Eastern Mediterranean
Fourth Century A.D.
Lehman Gift, 1953.28.27
H. 16.8 cm., including handle

DESCRIPTION: free-blown; similar to cat. no. 321, with top handle; rim folded in; body and handles pale green. CONDITION: reconstructed with some restoration of the body; iridescent with traces of brown weathering. PROVENANCE: John D. Rockefeller, Jr. no. 32; Duveen Brothers no. 24. BIBLIOGRAPHY: *Hayes, Toronto* 101, no. 359.

324 *Double Cosmetic Tube*

Eastern Mediterranean
Fourth Century A.D.
Whiting Collection, 1912.945
H. 13.3 cm., including handle.

DESCRIPTION: free-blown; similar to cat. no. 321; top handle; rim folded in; body, handles, and spiral thread pale bluish green. CONDITION: most of spiral thread missing; iridescent and pitted. PARALLELS: Neuburg, *Glas* fig. 59; Barag, *Beth She'arim* fig. 97, nos. 22 and 23.

325 *Double Cosmetic Tube*

Eastern Mediterranean
Fourth Century A.D.
Mansfield Collection, 1930.383
Pres. H. 10.9 cm., including handle

DESCRIPTION: free-blown; similar to cat. no. 321; top handle; rim folded in; body, handles, and spiral thread pale green. CONDITION: part of top handle missing; spiral thread marvered into surface, probably applied while vessel was still hot; some pale brown weathering but surface generally good. PARALLELS: Harden, "Amman" fig. 12, with an elaborate basket handle, from a fourth–sixth century tomb at Ajlun, Jordan.

326 *Double Cosmetic Tube*

Eastern Mediterranean
Fourth Century A.D.
Mansfield Collection, 1930.390
H. 15.5 cm., including handle

DESCRIPTION: free-blown; similar to cat. no. 321; top handle; two trailed loops on each side; rim folded in; body, handles, and thread pale green. CONDITION: intact; light brown weathering over iridescence. PARALLELS: *von Saldern, Oppenländer* no. 681a without top handle; *Hayes, Toronto* no. 456; Harden, "Amman" fig. 12, with side loops, from a fourth–sixth century tomb at Ajlun, Jordan.

327 *Four-Compartment Cosmetic Container*

Eastern Mediterranean
Fourth–Fifth Century A.D.
Mansfield Collection, 1930.385
Restored H. 17.7 cm.

The increase in thread decoration and the multiplication of handles and compartments indicate a later date than that accepted for the simpler examples shown above. Like most of the later examples, the body and decoration of this vessel are the same natural pale green.

317, 320, 318, 319

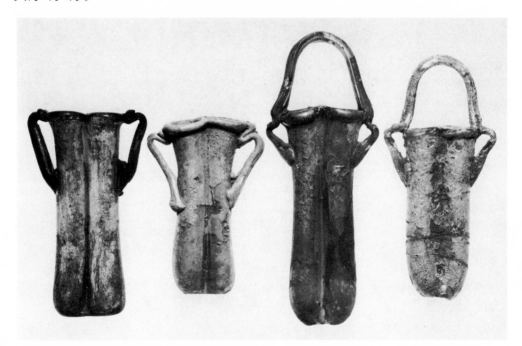

321, 322, 323, 324

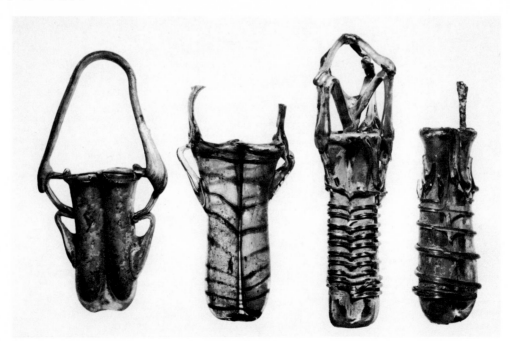

326, 325, 327, 328

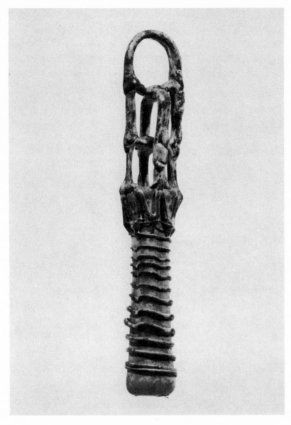

329

DESCRIPTION: free-blown; rim folded in; zigzag and spiral thread decoration and body pale green. CONDITION: upper part of handle reconstructed, probably incorrectly; some thread decoration missing; iridescent. BIBLIOGRAPHY: *Hayes, Toronto* 102, no. 362.

328 *Four-Compartment Cosmetic Tube*

Eastern Mediterranean
Fourth–Fifth Century A.D.
Moore Collection, 1955.6.186
Pres. H. 11.5 cm., L. of Bronze Rod 11.5 cm.

A bronze rod in one of the compartments of this four part vessel is perhaps that used to remove the cosmetic. The original appearance of this container must have resembled closely that of the preceding example.

DESCRIPTION: free-blown; rim folded in; thread decoration and body pale green. CONDITION: handles and parts of the thread decoration missing; pale brown weathering and iridescence. PROVENANCE: Moore Collection no. 672. BIBLIOGRAPHY: *Eisen* 587, fig. 239, pl. 143; *Kouchakji* no. 193. PARALLELS: *Hayes, Toronto* no. 362, showing a possible handle arrangement for the Yale example; *Auth, Newark* no. 183 for excavated examples with the bronze rods in place.

330

329 *Four-Compartment Cosmetic Container*

Eastern Mediterranean
Fourth–Fifth Century A.D.
Mansfield Collection, 1930.408
H. 15.5 cm.

The emphasis in this example is clearly on decoration rather than function. The very small cosmetic compartments and complex handle system, virtually equal in height to the body of the vessel, make it difficult to insert a rod to retrieve the cosmetic.

DESCRIPTION: free-blown; rim folded in; multiple handles; zigzag and spiral thread decoration and body pale green. CONDITION: a few fragments of thread decoration missing; pale brown weathering. PROVENANCE: de Morgan sale, 1901; Mansfield Collection no. 119.

330 *Double Cosmetic Tube*

Eastern Mediterranean
Fifth–Sixth Century A.D.
Mansfield Collection, 1930.389
H. 17.1 cm.

The elaboration of the thread decoration on this two compartment vessel indicates an even later date than the preceding examples. Vessels with this particular

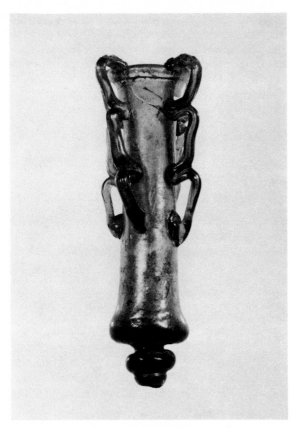

331

MOLD-BLOWN, FOURTH–FIFTH CENTURY A.D.

332 *Double Head Flask*

Eastern Mediterranean
Fourth–Fifth Century A.D.
Moore Collection, 1955.6.75
H. 9 cm.

The funnel mouth, pinched handle, and deep purple color indicate a late Roman date, despite the knobby hair of numerous earlier head flasks.

DESCRIPTION: mold-blown, two part mold; funnel mouth with unworked rim; trailed-on neck ring and pinched side handle; deep purple. CONDITION: intact; iridescent with brown enamel weathering on one side. PROVENANCE: Moore Collection no. 716. BIBLIOGRAPHY: *Eisen* 329, pl. 74b; *Kouchakji* no. 78. PARALLELS: *Auth, Newark* no. 342.

332

combination of a thin spiral thread and four heavy folded threads at the corners frequently have four compartments and an elaborate compound handle. The decoration is distinctive and of exceptional quality, and this group may be the product of a single workshop or glassmaker.

DESCRIPTION: free-blown; rim folded in; body, handle, and thread decoration pale green. CONDITION: handle repaired at its base, but it appears to belong; some fragments of the spiral thread missing; some pale brown weathering. PARALLELS: *von Saldern, Oppenländer* no. 681b (four compartments); *Toledo, Glass* 30, inv. 23.1302; *Hayes, Toronto* no. 457 (four compartments), with four part and two part parallels.

331 *Cosmetic Tube*

Eastern Mediterranean
Fifth–Sixth Century A.D.
Mansfield Collection, 1930.415
H. 12.2 cm.

The thick folded thread on four sides of this vessel relates it to the late multiple compartment group with spiral threads and elaborate handles. The addition of the knob at the base is also a late feature.

333

The funnel mouth and pinched handle occur on a group of dark blue jugs with heavy feet. One of this group, in Berlin, is a head flask, but it is a single head rather than a double faced flask. For these jugs, see *Spartz, Kassel* no. 98 and *Auth, Newark* no. 127, with parallels.

333 *Jar with Four Faces*

Eastern Mediterranean
Fourth–Fifth Century A.D.
Moore Collection, 1955.6.73.
H. 12.6 cm.

This purple jar of characteristic fourth century shape is embellished with four identical mold-blown faces. The faces have been described as masks and the hair as ritual headdresses tied under the chin. Although the loop under the chin looks more like a metal handle than strings or ribbons tied in a knot, the faces are undeniably masklike. The closest parallel for these masks seems to be a single molded mask in high relief applied to the front of a dark blue jug in Boston. But the Yale jar, with its masks flattened and enclosed in medallions, presents a more decorative appearance than the openly apotropaic quality of the mask on the jug.

DESCRIPTION: mold-blown, two part mold; four masks in medallions with small circles at their conjunctions; diagonal ribs fill the space between the medallions and the mold-blown ring on the bottom; purple with white threads on mouth and neck. CONDITION: intact; brown enamel weathering. PROVENANCE: Moore Collection no. 820. BIBLIOGRAPHY: *Eisen* 319, pl. 73; *Kouchakji* no. 76; Hayward, "Yale" 59–60, no. 12, fig. 20. PARALLELS: for the Boston jug, see *von Saldern, Boston* no. 55.

Post-Roman Vessels

BLOWN, FIFTH–SIXTH CENTURY A.D.

334 *Jug*

Eastern Mediterranean
Fourth–Sixth Century A.D.
Gift of Elmer D. Keith, B.A. 1910, 1960.2
H. 13.2 cm.

A late mold-blown series of bottles and jugs with vertical ribs is common in the eastern Mediterranean. The bottles have funnel mouths with trailed-on coils; the jugs simply add a handle to this form, or, as with this example, pinch the mouth to a trefoil shape.

DESCRIPTION: mold-blown; concave base; rounded rim; body and trailed-on handle yellowish green. CONDITION: part of mouth broken away; surface excellent. PARALLELS: Damascus Museum, no. unknown (Dura photo); *Hayes, Toronto* nos. 428–31, with round mouths; Harden, *Karanis*, Class X, nos. 700–703.

335 *Large Flask*

Eastern Mediterranean
Fourth–Fifth Century A.D.
Mansfield Collection, 1930.382
H. 26.9 cm.

This large flask is well suited for serving wine or other liquids. It represents a common fourth century shape throughout the empire.

DESCRIPTION: free-blown; concave base; rounded rim; pale green. CONDITION: several large holes in the body; crack through the bottom repaired; iridescent. PARALLELS: *Isings* type 104b; Harden, "Amman," from a fourth–fifth century A.D. tomb at Beit Ras, Jordan; Crowfoot, *Samaria-Sebaste* fig. 95, no. 10.

336 *Flask*

Eastern Mediterranean
Fifth–Sixth Century A.D.
Mansfield Collection, 1930.435
H. 16.7 cm.

The tall neck of this vessel widening into a funnel mouth is characteristic of early Byzantine flasks.

DESCRIPTION: free-blown; base slightly concave; wheel-polished rim; pale yellowish green. CONDITION: intact; pitted and iridescent, with some light brown enamel weathering. PROVENANCE: found at Beisan, Syria; Khayat, 1904; Mansfield Collection no. 154. PARALLELS: *Auth, Newark* nos. 158–61; Neuburg, *Glas* pl. 61, a tomb group from El-Ish, Palestine; Baur, *Gerasa* fragments nos. 59–62; Crowfoot, *Samaria-Sebaste* fig. 95, no. 9.

337 *Bottle*

Eastern Mediterranean
Fifth–Sixth Century A.D.
Moore Collection, 1955.6.189
H. 13.7 cm.

Two characteristically Byzantine features are combined in this flask: the tall cylindrical neck with a

334

337

wide band of spiral thread decoration and the row of crimped or pinched projections that encircles the body. A variant with a taller neck is also common.

DESCRIPTION: free-blown; concave base; rounded rim; body and thread decoration pale green. CONDITION: intact; light brown enamel weathering. BIBLIOGRAPHY: *Eisen* 615; *Kouchakji* no. 196. PARALLELS: Delougaz and Haines, *Khirbat al-Karak* pl. 59, nos. 1–2 (tomb 4), pl. 59, nos. 3 and

6 (church) for the neck shape and thread decoration, and pl. 50, no. 9 (tomb 4) for the crimped decoration; a close parallel plus a number of tall necked examples from a tomb at El-Ish, Palestine, some with piriform bodies, Neuburg, *Glas* fig. 61; *Auth, Newark* nos. 158–61; Baur, *Gerasa* fig. 31, no. 69 (28).

338 *Miniature Bottle*

Eastern Mediterranean
Fifth Century A.D.
Van Volkenburgh Bequest, 1940.285
H. 6.4 cm.

The vertical neck with rounded rim is a late characteristic; the general shape of the bottle is a precursor of the slender necked sprinkler flasks of the Islamic period.

DESCRIPTION: free-blown; body, handles, and zigzag thread pale green. CONDITION: intact; flaking white weathering and iridescence. PARALLELS: for an undecorated example, see Baur, *Gerasa* fig. 30, no. 89, from tomb 6.

339 *Bottle*

Eastern Mediterranean
Fifth Century A.D.
Moore Collection, 1955.6.201
H. 16.3 cm.

Flasks of this shape first appear in the third century, frequently decorated with wheel-cut bands, patterns, or occasionally scenes, as on the famous Puteoli bottles. However, the tall neck and crimped decoration of this example point to a Byzantine date.

DESCRIPTION: free-blown; base slightly concave; rim folded in; small pinched projections distributed irregularly over the body; pale green. CONDITION: intact; iridescent.

335, 336, 338, 339

340, 341, 342

PROVENANCE: Moore Collection no. 719. BIBLIOGRAPHY: *Eisen* 633, pl. 151; *Kouchakji* no. 208; *Hayes, Toronto* 79, no. 288. PARALLELS: *Isings* type 103; *Auth, Newark* no. 155; for crimped decoration, see *Auth, Newark* no. 160 and *Spartz, Kassel* no. 149; Delougaz and Haines, *Khirbat al-Karak* pl. 59, no. 22.

340 *Flask*

Eastern Mediterranean
Fifth–Sixth Century A.D.
Mansfield Collection, 1930.432
H. 16.9 cm.

The large funnel mouth with an uneven fire-polished rim is a common variant among late Roman and Byzantine bottles.

DESCRIPTION: free-blown; base slightly concave; pinched decoration; pale green. CONDITION: intact; iridescent. PROVENANCE: Carl Edelheim sale, 1900; Mansfield Collection no. 65. PARALLELS: *Hayes, Toronto* no. 316 (undecorated); Harden, "Amman" fig. 11, from a fifth-sixth century tomb at Bethany, Jordan.

341 *Small Flask*

Eastern Mediterranean
Fifth–Sixth Century A.D. or Later
Mansfield Collection, 1930.442
H. 6.8 cm

Although this form is sometimes dated to the second or third century A.D., the short funnel neck of this example suggests a later date.

DESCRIPTION: free-blown; concave base; rounded rim; pinched decoration; pale green. CONDITION: intact; brown weathering and iridescence. PROVENANCE: from Syria; Folsom Galleries, 1911; Mansfield Collection no. 191. PARALLELS: *Spartz, Kassel* no. 134 with other examples; *von Saldern, Oppenländer* no. 690; *Auth, Newark* nos. 524 and 526.

342 *Small Flask*

Eastern Mediterranean
Fifth–Sixth Century A.D. or Later
Moore Collection, 1955.6.195
Pres. H. 6.1 cm.

DESCRIPTION: free-blown; similar to cat. no. 341, but with ovoid body; rounded bottom; pinched decoration; pale green. CONDITION: neck missing; hole in body; surface dull and pitted. BIBLIOGRAPHY: *Kouchakji* no. 202.

343 *Flask*

Eastern Mediterranean
Fifth–Sixth Century A.D.
Van Volkenburgh Bequest, 1940.289
H. 15.7 cm.

The tall neck and distinctive handles suggest a late date for this elegant flask. The handles are folded at their corners, a feature most commonly found on late vessels such as the head flasks, jugs, and pilgrim flasks of the fifth to the seventh centuries A.D., although these handles do occur on some examples apparently from the third century. Intentional coloration, such as the yellow of this bottle, again becomes common in the fifth and sixth centuries.

DESCRIPTION: free-blown; rim folded in; concave base; body and handles pale yellow. CONDITION: intact; iridescent. PARALLELS: for the handles, see *Auth, Newark* nos. 87 and 88 (hexagonal mold-blown jugs); *von Saldern, Oppenländer* no. 657 (third century pitcher); Bahir Zouhdi, "Les Verres conservés au Départment des Antiquités Syriennes des époques grecque, romaine et byzantine du Musée National de Damas," *JIV* 3 (1964) 48, no. 47, fig. 33 (head flask); Kamal Mouhandes, "Collection de verres du Musée d'Alep," *JIV* 3 (1964) 36, no. 6, fig. 16 (jug, Byzantine period); *Auth, Newark* no. 181 (jar, sixth-seventh century A.D.).

344 *Flask*

Eastern Mediterranean
Fifth-Sixth Century A.D.
Lehman Gift, 1953.28.15
H. 11.8 cm.

343

In a manner characteristic of late Roman and Byzantine bottles, the tall vertical neck, emphasized by two rings and elaborate handles, dominates the flask. The upper neck ring is a tooled or cut-out ridge similar to those seen in jars of the third to fifth centuries, while the lower neck ring is the trailed thread more common on bottles. The projections at the top and bottom of the handles are somewhat unusual, but they do occur on cosmetic tubes and some flasks of this period.

DESCRIPTION: free-blown; folded foot; rim slightly turned in; cut-out ridge in neck; trailed thread decoration, handles, and body very pale green. CONDITION: intact; iridescent. PROVENANCE: John D. Rockefeller, Jr. no. 55; Duveen Brothers no. 12. PARALLELS: *Hayes, Toronto* no. 348; *Auth, Newark* no. 452; for the handles, see *Hayes, Toronto* nos. 389 and 393.

345 *Bottle*

Eastern Mediterranean
Fifth–Sixth Century A.D.
Van Volkenburgh Bequest, 1940.288
H. 12.4 cm.

A parallel from a sixth century tomb in Jordan suggests a date for this rather unusual form. The handles are similar to those occurring on jars of the fifth and sixth centuries.

DESCRIPTION: free-blown; rim folded in; body and handles yellowish green. CONDITION: intact; brown, white, and iridescent weathering. PARALLELS: Harden, "Amman" fig. 12, from a tomb at Ajlun, Jordan.

346 *Ribbed Jug*

Eastern Mediterranean
Fifth–Sixth Century A.D.
Mansfield Collection, 1930.430
H. 13.3 cm.

DESCRIPTION: probably mold-blown and tooled; faint vertical ribs; folded foot; rim folded out; body, single neck thread, and trailed thread handle pale green. CONDITION: intact; iridescent. PROVENANCE: A. D. Vorce, 1898; Mansfield Collection no. 31.

347 *Jug*

Eastern Mediterranean
Fifth–Sixth Century A.D.
Mansfield Collection, 1930.448
H. 13.4 cm.

The elaboration of the thread decoration and of the

344, 345, 346, 347

multiple handles represents the same Byzantine aesthetic seen in the late forms of the jar.

DESCRIPTION: free-blown; folded foot; rounded rim; pale green with dark green decoration. CONDITION: foot partially restored; flaking iridescent pale brown weathering with a dull, pitted surface underneath. PROVENANCE: J. B. Clarke sale, 1899; Mansfield Collection no. 39. PARALLELS: *Hayes, Toronto* no. 354; *Auth, Newark* nos. 165–67.

MOLD-BLOWN, FIFTH–SEVENTH CENTURY A.D.

348 *Bottle with Honeycomb Pattern*

Eastern Mediterranean
Fifth–Sixth Century A.D. or Later
Moore Collection, 1955.6.200
H. 8.7 cm.

DESCRIPTION: mold-blown, a faint honeycomb pattern; slightly concave base, with a pontil mark and possibly faint mold-blown rays; wide neck; rounded rim; yellowish green. CONDITION: intact; pitted and iridescent. BIBLIOGRAPHY: *Eisen* 614, pl. 151; *Kouchakji* no. 207. PARALLELS: for a similar pattern on a late bottle, see *Cambridge, Fitzwilliam* no. 110b.

349 *Mold-Blown Jug with Christian Symbols*

Eastern Mediterranean, probably Jerusalem
Late Sixth–Seventh Century A.D.
Moore Collection, 1955.6.152
H. 14.0 cm.

This jug belongs to a distinctive group of mold-blown vessels with Christian and Jewish symbols recently studied by Dan Barag. A closely related group has symbols that cannot be assigned to any particular religion. The vessels occur in two forms,

348

349, Sides 1 & 2

350, Sides 6 & 1

bodies are characteristic. The intaglio decoration contrasts with the relief decoration of other mold-blown vessels. Specific symbols recur on vessels of all three groups, as do the dotted ames and other similarities of general appearance. Most of the vessels in all groups are brown.

Barag has established an approximate date of circa A.D. 578–636 for the Christian vessels, based on the occurrence on coins of some of the types of crosses present on the vessels and on events in the history of the monuments of Jerusalem relating to the cross on Golgotha and the destruction of the Church of the Holy Sepulchre in A.D. 614. The Jewish vessels and the unassigned vessels are judged to be contemporary. Only two excavated fragments have been recovered, one from Gerasa and one from Beth She^carim, and neither adds any concrete evidence to Barag's dates.

Numerous vessels in each class are from the same mold, and Barag believes that they were all made in Jerusalem, possibly in a single workshop. It seems likely that they were used as containers for holy oil and sold to pilgrims who took them home as souvenirs of their visit to the holy city. As Barag points out, the frequency of complete examples suggests that they were recovered from graves, having probably been buried with the pilgrims.

This jug clearly belongs to the Christian group, with three different crosses alternating with three lozenges. The lozenges may represent bindings or book covers for sacred texts and appear on the Jewish vessels as well. The three crosses represent different aspects of the Cross of Golgotha. Of these, the cross *fourchée* on three steps is the most significant for dating the vessel, as it can be identified with the cross that stood on Golgotha until the destruction of the Church of the Holy Sepulchre in A.D. 614. A different cross appears on vessels which Barag dates to A.D. 615 or later.

Production of the Christian vessels probably ceased soon after the Arab conquest (A.D. 636) and that of the Jewish vessels after A.D. 629, when the Jews were forbidden to enter Jerusalem.

DESCRIPTION: mold-blown hexagonal jug; each panel framed with a row of impressed dots; side 1—cross *fourchée* on three steps; side 2—lozenge; side 3—cross on concentric circles (*omphalos*); side 4—lozenge; side 5—cross on plant motif (tree of life); side 6—lozenge; trefoil mouth, rim folded in; flattened tubular handle; pontil mark on base; dark brown. CONDITION: intact; surface dull and pitted with some iridescence. PROVENANCE: Moore Collection no. 784. BIBLIOGRAPHY: *Eisen* 505, pls. 126–28; *Kouchakji* no. 159; Barag, "Pilgrim Vessels," Part 1, *JGS* 12 (1970) 55, Class I, no. 4, citing parallels.

350 *Mold-Blown Bottle with Jewish Symbols*

Eastern Mediterranean, probably Jerusalem
Late Sixth–Seventh Century A.D.
Mansfield Collection, 1930.439
H. 7.9 cm.

The Jewish symbols on some panels of this bottle replace the crosses on the preceding vessel. The menorah and the empty aedicula occur exclusively on Jewish vessels, while the other symbols are shared with Christian and unassigned groups. From the similarities of color, form, and decoration in Christian and Jewish vessels, Barag concludes that they are contemporary and the product of a single workshop. They provide yet another demonstration of the close relationship between Christian and Jewish art of this period.

DESCRIPTION: mold-blown hexagonal bottle; side 1—menorah on tripodal base; side 2—X-shaped element with ivy leaf tips, bisected by a horizontal bar with loop ends; side 3—two concentric lozenges with a depression in each corner of the frame; side 4—similar lozenges with crescents in the corners and an outer ring of dots; side 5—empty aedicula; side 6—stylized palm tree; pontil mark on the base; rim folded in; dark brown. CONDITION: rim chipped; light brown and iridescent weathering. PROVENANCE: said to have come from Beit Shean, Palestine; Khayat, 1902. BIBLIOGRAPHY: Baur, *Gerasa* 544, no. 101, pl. 151d; Barag, "Pilgrim Vessels," Part 1, *JGS* 12 (1970) 57, Class V, no. 4, and note, p. 37 (incorrectly as 1930.499), with parallels.

351 *Mold-Blown Hexagonal Bottle*

Eastern Mediterranean, probably Jerusalem
Late Sixth–Seventh Century A.D.
Moore Collection, 1955.6.154
H. 9.0 cm.

Barag's unassigned group includes vessels whose decorative symbols cannot be identified with either Christianity or Judaism. Both the lozenges and the stylized trees that occur on this bottle are also found on Christian and Jewish vessels, but without any more obvious motifs, no attribution can be made. Once again the hexagonal shape, intaglio decoration, dotted frames, and parallel motifs suggest that these unassigned vessels and the Jewish and Christian vessels are contemporary and probably from one workshop.

DESCRIPTION: mold-blown hexagonal bottle; sides 1 and 2—stylized trees; side 3—lozenge; sides 4 and 5—stylized trees; side 6—lozenge; pontil mark on base; rim folded in; dark

351, Sides 3 & 4

352, Sides 1 & 2

353, Sides 1 & 2, 3 & 4

brown. CONDITION: intact; white and iridescent weathering. PROVENANCE: Moore Collection no. 683. BIBLIOGRAPHY: *Eisen* 509, fig. 216; *Kouchakji* no. 161; Barag, "Pilgrim Vessels," Parts 2 and 3, *JGS* 13 (1971) 49, Class I, no. 1, fig. 32, with parallels.

352 *Mold-Blown Jug*

Eastern Mediterranean, probably Jerusalem
Late Sixth–Seventh Century A.D.
Moore Collection, 1955.6.153
H. 16.5 cm.

DESCRIPTION: mold-blown hexagonal jug; side 1—two concentric lozenges with central depression and a depression in each of the four corners; side 2—stylized tree; side 3—pair of crescents and pair of heart-shaped petals forming a cruciform pattern; side 4—amphora on high foot; side 5—diagonal latticework pattern; side 6—uncertain; trefoil mouth, rim folded in; pontil mark on base; dark brown. CONDITION: handle and large part of mouth restored; broken at the shoulder and repaired; iridescent. BIBLIOGRAPHY: *Eisen* 504, fig. 207; *Kouchakji* no. 160; Barag, "Pilgrim Vessels," Parts 2 and 3, *JGS* 13 (1971) 49, unassigned, Class II, fig. 33.

353 *Mold-Blown Jug with Stylite Saint*

Eastern Mediterranean, Probably Syrian
Fifth–Seventh Century A.D.
Moore Collection, 1955.6.149
Max. Pres. H. 14.2 cm.

The Stylites were a group of saints and ascetics whose chief form of austerity consisted of spending many years of their lives on top of a column in prayer and meditation. Their name is derived from the Greek word for column, στυλοσ. The first and most famous of the Stylites was Saint Simeon Stylite (circa A.D. 389–459). Theodoret, a friend and contemporary biographer of the saint, relates that he first ascended a column at Tellnesin, near Antioch, after having been expelled from a monastery for excessive austerities, which were considered to provide a bad example for the other monks. From his perch atop a succession of columns increasing in height to around sixty feet, Saint Simeon Stylite preached, healed, and prayed for at least thirty-seven and possibly as long as forty-seven years. His fame was widespread in his lifetime. Theodoret mentions pilgrims who came from as far away as Spain, Gaul, and Britain, and he notes that small images of Saint Simeon Stylite were frequently set up as protectors in *ateliers* in Rome. After the saint's death, his relics remained in Antioch, and a martyrium was built around the column. The ruins of the martyrium, at the site now known as Qala°at Sema°an, were still attracting visitors in the nineteenth century and were excavated in the 1920s. Saint Simeon. Stylite had many disciples and imitators, notable among these being Saint Daniel Stylite and Saint Simeon Stylite the Younger. Stylites are documented as late as the sixteenth century.

This jug and a number of similar vessels (see cat. nos. 354–58, below) appear to be related to the cult surrounding Saint Simeon and the other Stylites. However simplified, the figure with a pointed hood on a column reached by a ladder is undoubtedly a Stylite, quite probably the most famous, Saint Simeon himself. A cross, a peacock, and a diagonal lattice-work pattern, common symbols on other Christian vessels, appear on the other three sides. It is probable that these vessels were used to contain oil sanctified by the saint or his relics, although none has been found with its contents intact. It is also likely that these jugs were carried home by pilgrims, as they have been found as far away as Egypt. Presumably they were made in Syria, possibly near the site of the martyrium.

DESCRIPTION: mold-blown four sided jug; decoration in relief; side 1—Stylite Saint on column, with ladder to the left, five dots in a vertical row along the right side, and an uncertain object in the field on the left side; side 2—diagonal network pattern; side 3—bird, probably a peacock; side 4—Latin cross, with two dots above and below each arm; trailed-on handle and neck ring; pontil mark on the bottom; light green with dark green handle and thread decoration. CONDITION: mouth restored above neck ring; strain cracks in lower body; light brown weathering. PROVENANCE: Moore Collection no. 776. BIBLIOGRAPHY: *Eisen* 483–84, fig. 200, pls. 121–22; *Kouchakji* no. 156. PARALLELS: from the same mold: Louvre inv. OA 6417, from Egypt, cited by *Eisen* 484, illustrated by Joseph Philippe, *Le Monde Byzantin dans l'Histoire de la Verrerie* (Bologna 1970) 52–55, fig. 25, and Etienne Coche de la Ferté, *L'Antiquité Chrétienne au Musée du Louvre* (Paris 1958) 58 and 111, no. 56. For other vessels with Stylites, see below, cat. nos. 354–58. An inscribed stone relief of the late fifth century showing Saint Simeon, his column, and the ladder is reproduced by Coche de la Ferté, *L'Antiquité Chrétienne* 10, no. 5. See also Jean Lassus, "Images de Stylites," *Bulletin d'Etudes Orientales, Institut Français de Damas* 2 (1932) 67–82. On the Stylites in general, see Hippolyte Delehaye, *Les Saints Stylites* (Brussels/Paris 1923).

354 *Mold-Blown Jug with Stylite Saint*

Eastern Mediterranean, probably Syrian
Fifth–Seventh Century A.D.
Moore Collection, 1955.6.150
H. 12.0 cm.

DESCRIPTION: mold-blown hexagonal jug, two part mold; side 1—Stylite Saint; side 2—diagonal latticework pattern; side 3—palm frond; side 4—uncertain, perhaps a vine growing out of a vessel; side 5—Latin cross with a circle above and below it; side 6—palm frond; trailed-on handle and thread below the mouth; rim folded in; yellowish brown. CONDITION: broken in two at the shoulder and repaired, with a missing piece of the network pattern restored; some iridescence. PROVENANCE: Moore Collection no. 157. BIBLIOGRAPHY: *Eisen* 484, fig. 201, pls. 123–24; *Kouchakji* no. 157. PARALLELS: for Stylite vessels, see cat. no. 353 above; the saint on this example is obviously highly stylized. The unidentified motif on side 4 occurs on other Christian flasks not associated with the Stylites; see, for example, *von Saldern, Oppenländer* no. 504, and Grose, *Toledo* fig. 33.

355 *Mold-Blown Jug with Stylite Saint*

Eastern Mediterranean, probably Syrian
Fifth–Seventh Century A.D.
Moore Collection, 1955.6.148
H. 20.6 cm.

354, Sides 1, 2, & 3; 4, 5, & 6

355, Side 1, Side 4

DESCRIPTION: mold-blown hexagonal jug, two part mold; side 1—Stylite Saint stylized, in monk's hooded robe, standing on column; sides 2 and 5—vertical row of four circles, each with a central dot; sides 3 and 6—diagonal network pattern; side 4—standing full-length, detailed frontal figure in short tunic, presumably male, his left arm at his side, his right hand raised, apparently in a gesture o blessing (unidentified); trailed-on handle and neck ring; pale green. CONDITION: small hole near bottom; small piece of neck ring missing; iridescent, with considerable loss of surface. PROVENANCE: Moore Collection no. 749. BIBLIOGRAPHY: *Eisen* 483, fig. 199, pl. 120; *Kouchakji* no.155. PARALLELS: for Stylite vessels, see cat. no. 353 above.

356 *Fragmentary Stylite Jug*
(NOT ILLUSTRATED)

Eastern Mediterranean, probably Syrian
Fifth–Seventh Century A.D.
Mansfield Collection, 1930.400

A vessel which appears to be from the same mold as the preceding jug but which has been incorrectly reconstructed as a squat jug is being studied and rebuilt by Mr. Ray Errett, Conservator, at the time of writing; correct dimensions are thus unavailable.

PROVENANCE: said to be from near Nazareth, Palestine; Khayat, 1926; Mansfield Collection no. 245.

357 *Mold-Blown Jug with Christian Symbols*

Eastern Mediterranean, probably Syrian
Fifth–Seventh Century A.D.
Moore Collection, 1955.6.147
H. 19.5 cm.

A Greek cross above an altar or column appears on one side of this hexagonal jug, with a palm frond on each of the panels on either side of the cross. Only three arms of the cross are visible; it appears that after removal from the mold the vessel was over-heated as the neck was formed and part of the mold-blown decoration was lost. A jug in the British Museum shows the complete mold. On the opposite side, between two panels of network pattern, is a somewhat obscure figure that is probably another Stylite.

DESCRIPTION: mold-blown hexagonal jug; side 1—Greek cross (3 arms only) over a rectangle with a diagonal network pattern; side 2—palm frond; side 3—diagonal network pattern; side 4—Stylite; side 5—diagonal network pattern; side 6—palm frond; pontil mark; rounded rim; trailed-on neck ring and pinched handle; pale green, with handle and

357, Sides 6 & 1, 4 & 5

neck ring pale green with brown streaks. CONDITION: intact; one side and base iridescent. PROVENANCE: Moore Collection no. 812. BIBLIOGRAPHY: *Eisen* 474, fig. 198, pl. 119; *Kouchakji* no. 154. PARALLELS: from the same mold: BM inv. 1911.5–13.1, from Aleppo, Syria, Harden, *Masterpieces* no. 80; and probably *SPB, Constable-Maxwell* no. 319.

358 *Mold-Blown Jug with Christian Symbols*

Eastern Mediterranean, probably Syrian
Sixth–Seventh Century A.D.
Moore Collection, 1955.6.151
H. 10.5 cm.

The presence of a ladder on one side of this hexagonal jug may associate it with the jugs and flasks showing the Stylite Saints.

DESCRIPTION: mold-blown hexagonal jug; side 1—palm tree; side 2—ladder; side 3—network pattern; side 4—Latin cross; side 5— Latin cross; side 6—diagonal network pattern; concave base with pontil mark; rim folded in; trailed-on handle; brownish yellow. CONDITION: intact; light brown weathering and iridescence. PROVENANCE: Moore Collection no. 771. BIBLIOGRAPHY: *Eisen* 486, fig. 202, pl. 125; *Kouchakji* no. 158.

359 *Mold-Blown Hexagonal Bottle with Greek Cross*

Eastern Mediterranean
Sixth–Seventh Century A.D.
Moore Collection, 1955.6.146
Pres. H. 11 cm.

The palm frond which appears twice on this bottle is an attribute of martyrs, and it probably indicates that the vessel was used to contain oil sanctified by a martyr's relics and taken away by a pilgrim.

DESCRIPTION: mold-blown hexagonal bottle; sides 1 and 4—Greek cross below a lozenge with a dot in its center; sides 2 and 5—vertical line with a row of dots on each side (a plant motif?); sides 3 and 6—palm fronds, one upside down; a horizontal band encircles the bottle below the panels; pale green. CONDITION: mouth and upper part of neck restored; iridescent. PROVENANCE: Moore Collection no. 779. BIBLIOGRAPHY: *Eisen* 473, fig. 197, pl. 118; *Kouchakji* no. 153. PARALLELS: a related jug with a cross on steps rather than a Greek cross and lozenge suggests, on the basis of Dan Barag's dating of the shorter hexagonal vessels, a late sixth to seventh century date for this type as well: reproduced in Sotheby Parke Bernet sale catalogue 2 May 1975, no. 252, ex coll. R. W. Smith, described as having one panel with "a rosette over a horizontal 'H' over concentric circles" (panel not illustrated).

358, Sides 3 & 4; 359, Sides 3 & 4

360, Sides 3 & 4; 361, Sides 1 & 2

360 *Mold-Blown Hexagonal Jug with Two Masks*

Eastern Mediterranean, probably Syrian
Sixth Century A.D.
Moore Collection, 1955.6.142
H. 13.9 cm.

Although similar masks occur at the base of vine-decorated columns in contemporary churches, they seem to have no Christian significance, leaving this vessel among those which cannot be assigned to any particular group or cult.

DESCRIPTION: mold-blown hexagonal jug; sides 1 and 4—masks; sides 2 and 5—network pattern; sides 3 and 6—vertical row of three lozenges with concentric circles; six branch rosette, each branch with a tripartite end, on the base, along with a pontil mark; rim folded in; trailed-on solid handle and neck thread; body, handle, and thread pale bluish green. CONDITION: slightly iridescent, especially at the mouth and handle. BIBLIOGRAPHY: *Eisen* 549, fig. 234a; *Kouchakji* no. 149; *Auth, Newark* no. 89. PARALLELS: *Auth, Newark* no. 89 and *Hayes, Toronto* no. 427, both with other parallels; *SPB, Constable-Maxwell* no. 318. Variants without the masks occur: see cat. no. 361 below.

361 *Mold-Blown Hexagonal Jug*

Eastern Mediterranean, probably Syrian
Sixth Century A.D.
Moore Collection, 1955.6.143
H. 13.1 cm.

A palm frond or herringbone pattern replaces the masks on this jug which, except for a change in the order of the panels, is identical in all other ways to the preceding example. These two variants have come into at least three collections in pairs, and given their stylistic affinity it seems likely that they were produced in the same workshop.

DESCRIPTION: mold-blown hexagonal jug; sides 1 and 4—palm frond or herringbone; sides 2 and 5—a vertical row of three lozenges with concentric circles; sides 3 and 6—network pattern; six-branched rosette and pontil mark on the base; trailed-on hollow handle and neck ring; rim folded in; pale bluish green. CONDITION: intact; negligible weathering. BIBLIOGRAPHY: *Kouchakji* no. 150. PARALLELS: *Hayes, Toronto* no. 426, with parallels; *Auth, Newark* no. 345; numerous parallels in the Damascus Museum, nos. unknown (Dura photos); Harden, "Amman" fig. 12, an excavated pair from a sixth century tomb at Ajlun, Jordan; Crowfoot, *Samaria-Sebaste* fig. 96, no. 8, and what appears to be a bronze mold, fig. 109, no. 9; *Cambridge, Fitzwilliam* no. 108a; for a bucket-shaped variant, see *SPB, Constable-Maxwell* no. 317.

362 *Mold-Blown Hexagonal Jug*

Eastern Mediterranean
Sixth Century A.D.
Moore Collection, 1955.6.145
H. 18.3 cm.

Confronting pairs of birds and animals decorate four of the six panels of this jug. Perhaps identifiable as sheep, goats, and peacocks, these creatures are in any case reminiscent of the birds and animals that frequently inhabit mosaics and column capitals of fifth to seventh century churches and also serve as architectural decoration in synagogues and on Jewish sarcophagi. Lacking any obvious Christian or Jewish symbol, however, the jug cannot with certainty be associated with either group.

DESCRIPTION: mold-blown hexagonal jug; side 1—network pattern; sides 2 and 3—pairs of confronting quadrupeds; side 4—pair of confronting birds or animals; side 5—three globular flasks; side 6—pair of confronting birds, probably

362, Sides 2 & 3

363, Sides 2 & 3, 4 & 5

peacocks; concave base with pontil mark; rim folded in; trailed-on handle and ring below the rim; body, handle, and mouth ring pale green. CONDITION: reconstructed from fragments with considerable restoration; legs of creatures on side 4 missing; iridescent, severely weathered. PROVENANCE: Moore Collection no. 865. BIBLIOGRAPHY: *Kouchakji* no. 152.

363 *Mold-Blown Hexagonal Bottle*

Eastern Mediterranean
Sixth Century A.D.
Moore Collection, 1955.6.144
H. 17.3 cm.

The relief on this vessel lacks clarity, making it difficult to see details and in some cases impossible to identify motifs. Vines growing out of amphorae as seen on the fifth panel are common in relief decoration

and mosaics of sixth century churches; both eagles and peacocks appear with some frequency in mosaic borders in these churches, with the peacock especially seen in association with the amphora and vine in San Vitale, Sant'Apollinare Nuovo, and the Orthodox Baptistry at Ravenna. Once again, however, without a more specifically Christian symbol the bottle cannot be proven to be Christian, although in all probability it is. The sixth side is too indistinct to permit identification of the motifs.

DESCRIPTION: mold-blown hexagonal bottle; sides 1 and 3 —date palm; side 2—network pattern; side 4—grape vine; side 5—amphora with short projecting petals and peacock or eagle on pedestal above; side 6—motifs indistinct; rounded rim; concave base with pontil mark; pale green. CONDITION: intact; iridescent. BIBLIOGRAPHY: *Kouchakji* no. 151. PARALLELS: for the Ravenna mosaics, see W. F. Volbach, *Early Christian Art* (New York, n.d.) pls. 160 (eagle), 140, 161, and 181 (peacock with amphora and vine).

APPENDIX: FORGERIES, IMITATIONS, AND FANTASIES

Two articles have been particularly useful in the identification of the objects in this section:

Axel von Saldern, "Originals—Reproductions—Fakes," *Annales du 5ᵉ Congrès de l'Association Internationale pour l'Histoire du Verre, Prague 6–11 Juillet 1970* (Liège 1972) 299–318 (hereafter von Saldern, "Reproductions"), outlining a system for organization and categorization of different types of reproductions and forgeries based largely on the intention of the maker. Three of von Saldern's classifications, Historicizing Glass, Conglomerates, and Forgeries, will be used here.

Sidney M. Goldstein, "Forgeries and Reproductions of Ancient Glass in Corning," *JGS* 19 (1977) 40–62 (hereafter Goldstein, "Forgeries"), a thorough discussion of the excellent study collection assembled at Corning.

HISTORICIZING GLASS: objects which imitate the style and/or technique of a certain period without actually reproducing a specific object.

A1 *Blown "Sandcore" Amphoriskos*

Probably Venetian
Late Nineteenth or Twentieth Century
Moore Collection, 1955.6.47
H. 10.3 cm.

DESCRIPTION: free-blown; pontil mark on base; trailed-on blue rim and handles; opaque dark blue with white decoration. CONDITION: intact; traces of white weathering. BIBLIOGRAPHY: *Eisen* 230, pl. 5d; *Kouchakji* no. 49. PARALLELS: closest to some of the Venetian examples, as Goldstein, "Forgeries" fig. 11, far right; form close to sixth–fifth century B.C. sandcore, except for the handles.

A2 *Blown "Sandcore" Vessel*

Probably Venetian
Late Nineteenth or Twentieth Century
Moore Collection, 1955.6.276
H. 7.6 cm.

DESCRIPTION: free-blown; transparent dark greenish brown with thin pale green festoon decoration. CONDITION: intact; unweathered. PARALLELS: marvered, somewhat muddy festoon decoration close to some Venetian examples, as Goldstein, "Forgeries" fig. 11, second from left; form unrelated to ancient sandcore vessels.

A3 *Mosaic Glass Bowl*

Venetian, Compagnia di Venezia e Murano
Ca. 1880–1890
Moore Collection, 1955.6.268
H. 3.7 cm., D. 14.7 cm.

DESCRIPTION: mosaic glass; quadrant design with bands and mosaic elements of yellow, white, colorless, dark blue, and light purple. CONDITION: repaired with some restoration; unweathered. PROVENANCE: said to have been found in Olbia in 1908; Chmielowski Collection; sale American Art Association, Anderson Galleries, New York, 1922. BIBLIOGRAPHY: sale catalogue, American Art Association, Anderson Galleries, New York, 1922, no. 551, illus.; *Kouchakji* no. 16a. EXHIBITED: *Bicentennial of the Discovery of Pompeii* MMA, 1948. PARALLELS: *Eisen* pl. 34b, perhaps identical with MMA inv. 40.11.21; Goldstein, "Forgeries" 45, fig. 7, a footed bowl, citing other parallels. Possible ancient prototypes for these vessels include Kisa, *Glas* 520, fig. 213, a hemispherical bowl found at Hellange in 1853, now in the Musée d'Histoire et d'Art, Luxembourg, and, more likely, Naples, Museo Nazionale Archeologico, inv. 13558, a shallow segmental bowl, probably from Pompeii.

A 1, A 2

A 3, A 4

A4 *Mosaic Glass Bowl*

Venetian, Compagnia di Venezia e Murano
ca. 1875–1880
Moore Collection, 1955.6.39
H. 4.9 cm., D. 7.3 cm.

DESCRIPTION: molded ribbed mosaic glass bowl; ribs consisting of alternating single and double twisted white threads in alternating colorless and purple ribs; bowl an agate pattern of gold, green, purple, and brown. CONDITION: intact; pitted, probably acid treated. PROVENANCE: Fahim Kouchakji, 1930. BIBLIOGRAPHY: *Kouchakji* no. 41. EXHIBITED: *Bicentennial of the Discovery of Pompeii* MMA, 1948. PARALLELS: related to a group of reproductions of the Castellani skyphos now in the MMA, for which see Andrew Oliver, Jr., "Late Hellenistic Glass in the Metropolitan Museum," *JGS* 9 (1967) and Goldstein, "Forgeries" 43. Unlike the copies of the Castellani skyphos, this bowl does not seem to reproduce a specific object and therefore falls into the historicizing category.

A5 *Mosaic Glass Jug*

Probably Venetian
Late Nineteenth or Twentieth Century
Moore Collection, 1955.6.18
H. 23.3 cm.

DESCRIPTION: free-blown mosaic glass trefoil-mouthed oinochoe; opaque medium blue and white agate pattern; molded cylindrical foot with recessed bottom. CONDITION: repaired, part of mouth restored; some white weathering, probably acid treated. PROVENANCE: said to have been found in the Danube. BIBLIOGRAPHY: *Eisen* 229, color plate III; *Augustan Art* fig. 50; *Kouchakji* no. 18. PARALLELS: a blown festoon decorated oinochoe, datable to the first–second century A.D., J. Schlosser, *Das Alte Glas* (Braunschweig 1965) 35, fig. 25; *SPB, Constable-Maxwell* no. 31. The foot is not a normal ancient form.

A 5, A 6, A 7 (satyr), A 7 (maenad)

A6 *Pseudo-Mosaic Glass Amphoriskos*

Probably Venetian
Late Nineteenth or Twentieth Century
Moore Collection, 1955.6.35
H. 9.2 cm.

DESCRIPTION: free-blown; dark blue with white marvered spirals on the exterior; blue handles. CONDITION: one handle broken and repaired, part of base missing; unweathered. PROVENANCE: Fahim Kouchakji, 1925. BIBLIOGRAPHY: *Eisen* 221, pl. 43; *Kouchakji* no. 37; *Augustan Art*. PARALLELS: MMA inv. 17.194.283; imitating first century A.D. pseudo-mosaic glass vessels.

A7 *Cameo Glass Bottle*

Venetian, Compagnia di Venezia e Murano
1875–1900
Moore Collection, 1955.6.46
H. 16.7 cm.

DESCRIPTION: free-blown with pontil mark on base; cameo technique, white on dark blue; dancing satyr and maenad separated by a palmette on each side; two palmettes below a band of ivy on neck; laurel wreath below figures. CONDITION: intact; surface acid treated. PROVENANCE: said to have been excavated at the Villa Albani near Rome by Carlo Marchione when he constructed that palace for Cardinal Alessandro Albani in 1760; ex coll. Baron Wladimir von Greuneisen; Fahim Kouchakji, 1925. BIBLIOGRAPHY: *Eisen* 156, color plate I; *Kouchakji* no. 48. PARALLELS: A. C. Revi, *Nineteenth Century Glass* (New York 1959) 157, second from left, a virtual duplicate of the Yale example, with others, now collection of Pauly & Cie., Venice and published more recently by A. C. Revi, "Venetian Cameo," *Spinning Wheel* (May 1966) 10–11. I am grateful to Dr. Leonard S. Rakow for providing this last reference. The satyr reproduces almost exactly a figure on the marble Borghese Vase in the Louvre.

FORGERIES: objects made with the intention of deceiving the buyer as to their age and importance.

A8 *Fused Glass Plaque*

Egyptian or European
Twentieth Century, ca. 1940–1950
Moore Collection, 1955.6.300
H. 4.5 cm., W. 10.3 cm.

DESCRIPTION: flat rectangular fused glass plaque; bull drawing a plow, with three workers. CONDITION: broken and repaired; surface polished or acid treated. BIBLIOG-

A 8

RAPHY: *Kouchakji* no. 16. PARALLELS: one of a group of plaques once in King Farouk's collection; see von Saldern, "Reproductions" 308 and Goldstein, "Forgeries" 55, fig. 33. The subject is from a Theban tomb painting.

A9 *Painted Bottle: Metalworker's Shop*

Egyptian
Late Nineteenth or Early Twentieth Century
Moore Collection, 1955.6.12
H. 9.8 cm.

DESCRIPTION: free-blown; flat base with pontil mark; thick dark green glass; decoration either paint or perhaps glass paste, a scene in a metalworker's shop; figures white, kilts, hair, and shading brown; nonsense hieroglyphs in the field. CONDITION: broken and repaired; surface acid treated. PROVENANCE: said to have been found at Fayum, Egypt; Khayat, 1911; Moore Collection no. 744. BIBLIOGRAPHY: *Eisen* 153, pl. 12; *Kouchakji* no. 12. PARALLELS: John D. Cooney identified this piece in some unpublished notes for an exhibition catalogue. The scene is taken from an early nineteenth century publication of a Theban tomb painting (F. Cailliaud, *Recherches sur les arts et métiers . . . de l'Egypte* [Paris 1831] pl. 16) and repeats certain misunderstandings of the painting preserved in the publication. I am grateful to Mr. Cooney for this information.

A10 *"Gold-Glass" Base: Eros and Psyche*

Probably Venetian
Late Nineteenth or Early Twentieth Century
Moore Collection, 1955.6.266
Max. D. 23 cm.

DESCRIPTION: transparent dark blue glass with molded (?) relief, gilded, covered with top layer of colorless glass; a footed vessel on a pedestal stands between Eros (left) and Psyche. CONDITION: intentional fragment, unbroken; acid

A 9, A 10, A 12

treated. PROVENANCE: Fahim Kouchakji, 1940. PARAL-
LELS: for the subject, see, for example, Berlin Antiken-
abteilung inv. 7806, a fourth century B.C. bronze relief
group from Epirus, and especially Morey, *Gold Glass* 6, no.
15, a blue gold-glass medallion with a variant composition
in which Eros stands on the right, his back to the viewer,
known through published drawings as early as 1716.

AII *Bowl with Wheel-Cut and Molded Decoration*

Early Twentieth Century
Moore Collection, 1955.6.275
H. 5.5 cm., D. 12.7 cm.

DESCRIPTION: colorless bowl with pad base; wheel-cut
wreath below rim with wide molded gadroons in relief near
the base. CONDITION: intact; white and slightly iridescent
weathering. BIBLIOGRAPHY: *Eisen* 255, 276; *Kouchakji* no.
140a. PARALLELS: the combination of wheel-cut and
molded decoration is inconsistent with ancient usage.

AI2 *"Weight" with Two Masks*

Late Nineteenth or Early Twentieth Century
Moore Collection, 1955.6.226
H. 8.2 cm., D. 6.8 cm.

DESCRIPTION: solid cylinder of heavy dark blue glass; two
applied faces of the same glass. CONDITION: intact; dull
surface. BIBLIOGRAPHY: *Eisen* 652, pl. 166; *Kouchakji* no.
232. PARALLELS: *von Saldern, Oppenländer* no. 738. As von
Saldern points out, these "weights" are related to a group
of fake bottles with four masks, for which see von Saldern,
"Reproductions" 309–10.

AI3–18 *"Gold-Glass" Bases with Christian Subjects*

Probably Venetian
Late Nineteenth or Early Twentieth Century

As first noted by von Saldern, *Reproductions* 315, note
77, these gold-glass medallions are forgeries of third
and fourth century A.D. originals of the type frequently found in the Roman catacombs. The forgeries
are made from one or two ancient fragments, whose
original weathering and incrustations lend an appearance of authenticity. The gold-glass design is painted
on the bottom of one of these fragments, and the
second fragment, or a modern one, is glued into
place to cover the painting. The use of painting is of
course completely unrelated to the ancient gold-glass
technique. This fact, plus the frequent addition of
color in the forgeries and the rather Romanesque or
even Renaissance style of some of the figures and

A 11

compositions, leave no doubt as to the nature of these medallions. Other examples are discussed by Goldstein, "Forgeries" 58–59, where the Yale examples are also noted.

A13 "Gold-Glass" Base Fragment: Christ Blessing the Animals

> Moore Collection, 1955.6.207
> Max. Pres. D. 8 cm., D. base 6.5 cm.

DESCRIPTION: base fragment of a shallow bowl; pale green; painted scene outlined in black on exterior shows Christ with gold robes and halo blessing animals in a green landscape with blue sky; gold and black meander border; painting covered by tall foot and round glass disc. CONDITION: some decomposition of gold paint. PROVENANCE: unknown, but compare *Eisen* 573. BIBLIOGRAPHY: *Eisen* 574 and 581, color plate VI; *Kouchakji* no. 214.

A 13

A14 "Gold-Glass" Base Fragment: Christ at Emmaus

> Moore Collection, 1955.6.208
> Max. Pres. D. 7 cm., D. ring base 6.2 cm.

DESCRIPTION: base fragment of bottle; thick pale green glass; painted scene on the exterior outlined in black shows supper at Emmaus, with Christ seated between two apostles in gold robes; red background; meander border; painting covered by another base fragment with a ring base CONDITION: edges chipped; iridescent. BIBLIOGRAPHY: *Eisen* 574, plate VI; *Kouchakji* no. 215.

A 14

A15 "Gold-Glass" Base Fragment: The Trinity

> Moore Collection, 1955.6.209
> Max. Pres. D. 8.5 cm., D. ring base 6.5 cm.

DESCRIPTION: base fragment of plate with ring base; pale blue green; painted scene on exterior outlined in black: God the Father, Christ, and the Holy Spirit in the form of a dove enthroned against a green background; twisted strand border; Greek inscription TPIAC in field to right; colorless disc set in ring base to cover painting. CONDITION: iridescent. BIBLIOGRAPHY: *Eisen* 574, plate VI (reversed); *Kouchakji* no. 216.

A16 "Gold-Glass" Base Fragment: Lamb of God

> Moore Collection, 1955.6.210
> Max. Pres. D. 8.5 cm., D. ring base 5.5 cm.

DESCRIPTION: base fragment of ribbed vessel with ring base;

A 15

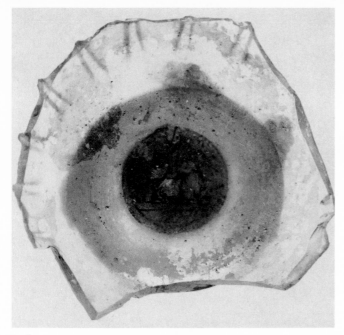

A 16

A 17

A 18

pale green; painted scene on the exterior outlined in black shows seated lamb beneath a red Greek cross on a gold ground; Latin inscription on the reverse in red outlined in black on a gold ground: EC AGNUS DEI; colorless disc fitted into ring base to cover painting. CONDITION: iridescent. BIBLIOGRAPHY: *Eisen* 574, pl. VI; *Kouchakji* no. 217.

A17 *"Gold-Glass" Base Fragment: Christ Enthroned*

Moore Collection, 1955.6.211
Max. Pres. D. 5.6 cm., D. ring base 4.6 cm.

DESCRIPTION: base fragment of bowl with ring base; pale green; painted scene on the exterior outlined in black: Christ seated on a throne holding a book and raising his right hand in blessing; plain gold border; Greek letters A and Ω in the field to the left and right of Christ; colorless disc set in ring base to cover painting. CONDITION: iridescent, some discoloration of the painted surface. BIBLIOGRAPHY: *Eisen* 573 and 574, pl. VI; *Kouchakji* no. 218.

A18 *"Gold-Glass" Base Fragment: Scenes from the Life of Christ*

Moore Collection, 1955.6.212
Max. Pres. D. 7.6 cm., D. ring base 7.2 cm.

DESCRIPTION: base fragment of round-bottomed bowl; pale green; painted scene on the exterior outlined in black; tondo: Three Marys at the Tomb, in a plain gold border; around the tondo, clockwise from the top: Crucifixion, Kiss of Judas, Massacre of the Innocents, Flight into Egypt, Adoration of the Magi, Adam and Eve; another plain gold border; thick ring base and disc applied over painting. CONDITION: upper (painted) fragment broken and repaired, ring base unbroken; iridescent. BIBLIOGRAPHY: *Eisen* 581; *Kouchakji* no. 219.

CONGLOMERATES AND FANTASIES: objects made up of fragments of two or more ancient vessels, which may or may not reproduce a form known from antiquity.

A19 *Small Footed Beaker*

Moore Collection, 1955.6.170
H. 7.7 cm.

DESCRIPTION: two fragments joined: upper neck of fifth-sixth century A.D. bottle with spiral thread plus the foot and

A 19, A 20, A 21

part of stem of a fourth–fifth century A.D. stemmed cup, the stem projecting inside the neck beyond the join; both pale green. CONDITION: some thread decoration missing; iridescent. PROVENANCE: Moore Collection no. 662. BIBLIOGRAPHY: *Eisen* 426, fig. 170 f, pl. 93; *Kouchakji* no.177.

A20 *Footed Beaker*

Moore Collection, 1955.6.129
H. 11 cm.

DESCRIPTION: two fragments joined: neck and small part of body from a large funnel-mouthed flask, and base, apparently from a cup; both pale green. CONDITION: iridescent. BIBLIOGRAPHY: *Kouchakji* no. 135.

A21 *Funnel-Mouthed Vessel with Elephant Heads*

Moore Collection, 1955.6.193
H. 15.7 cm., D. mouth 10.7 cm.

DESCRIPTION: fragments from an unknown number of vessels, probably with some modern additions; separate pieces, varying in color, include mouth, foot, concave central body, elephant heads, and vertical ridged ribs; pale green to yellow. CONDITION: most parts iridescent, some with black and white weathering. BIBLIOGRAPHY: *Kouchakji* no. 200. PARALLELS: imitating Mediaeval German and Bohemian forms; for further discussion see recently Marian Wenzel, "A Reconsideration of Bosnian Medieval Glass," *JGS* 19 (1977) 63–76, figs. 5e, 6n, and 6o.

CONCORDANCE

Accession Number	Catalogue Number	Accession Number	Catalogue Number	Accession Number	Catalogue Number	Accession Number	Catalogue Number
1912.928	266	1930.401	264	1930.454	230	1940.637	180
1912.929	293	1930.402	249	1930.456	303	1940.638	172
1912.931	244	1930.404	192	1930.460	67	1940.639	173
1912.932	207	1930.405	320	1932.1173	95	1940.640	179
1912.933	295	1930.406	268	1932.1174	105	1940.818	272
1912.934	245	1930.408	329	1932.1175	168	1943.50	226
1912.935	27	1930.409	21	1932.1176	171	1943.51	225
1912.936	74	1930.410	7	1932.1177	152	1943.53	224
1912.937	223	1930.411	30	1932.1178	204	1943.54	42
1912.944	219	1930.412	94	1936.50	4	1947.251	269
1912.945	324	1930.413	191	1937.178	19	1947.252	218
1929.629	164	1930.414	241	1937.179	29	1947.253	209
1929.630	294	1930.415	331	1937.180	2	1947.330	193
1930.44	199	1930.416	304	1937.181	3	1953.28.1	89
1930.45	300	1930.417	309	1940.263	23	1953.28.2	90
1930.46	213	1930.418	91	1940.264	11	1953.28.3	176
1930.47	297	1930.420	282	1940.265	9	1953.28.6	155
1930.373	15	1930.422	48	1940.266	243	1953.28.7	166
1930.375	25	1930.423	120	1940.267	246	1953.28.8	161
1930.376	144	1930.424	142	1940.268	242	1953.28.9	81
1930.377	28	1930.425	203	1940.269	281	1953.28.10	58
1930.378	24	1930.426	259	1940.270	189	1953.28.11	151
1930.379	13	1930.427	157	1940.271	215	1953.28.12	153
1930.380	33	1930.428	260	1940.272	291	1953.28.13	88
1930.381	34	1930.429	316	1940.273	160	1953.28.14	138
1930.382	335	1930.430	346	1940.274	149	1953.28.15	344
1930.383	325	1930.432	340	1940.275	169	1953.28.16	93
1930.384	235	1930.433	221	1940.276	167	1953.28.17	92
1930.385	327	1930.435	336	1940.277	174	1953.28.18	140
1930.386	236	1930.436	115	1940.278	61	1953.28.22	80
1930.387	237	1930.438	229	1940.279	178	1953.28.24	228
1930.388	196	1930.439	350	1940.281	288	1953.28.25	183
1930.389	330	1930.440	301	1940.282	177	1953.28.26	60
1930.390	326	1930.441	314	1940.285	338	1953.28.27	323
1930.391	253	1930.442	341	1940.286	233	1953.28.28	321
1930.392	17	1930.445	96	1940.287	319	1953.28.29	107
1930.393	146	1930.446	302	1940.288	345	1953.28.31	285
1930.394	143	1930.447	271	1940.289	343	1953.28.32	98
1930.395	141	1930.448	347	1940.290	231	1953.28.33	108
1930.396.1	158	1930.449	251	1940.292	147	1953.28.34	37
1930.396.2	148	1930.450	275	1940.293	305	1953.28.35	43
1930.398	311	1930.451	50	1940.294	313	1955.6.1	1
1930.399	232	1930.452	84	1940.635	85	1955.6.2	26
1930.400	356	1930.453	263	1940.636	181	1955.6.3	16

Accession Number	Catalogue Number	Accession Number	Catalogue Number	Accession Number	Catalogue Number	Accession Number	Catalogue Number
1955.6.4	22	1955.6.53	122	1955.6.108	175	1955.6.182	258
1955.6.5	18	1955.6.54	127	1955.6.109	170	1955.6.185	322
1955.6.6	20	1955.6.55	128	1955.6.111	238	1955.6.186	328
1955.6.7	14	1955.6.56	121	1955.6.112	290	1955.6.189	337
1955.6.8	8	1955.6.57	125	1955.6.113	106	1955.6.191	292
1955.6.9	35	1955.6.58	124	1955.6.114	252	1955.6.193	A21
1955.6.10	36	1955.6.59	132	1955.6.115	261	1955.6.195	342
1955.6.11	102	1955.6.60	130	1955.6.116	262	1955.6.196	289
1955.6.12	A9	1955.6.61	62	1955.6.117	116	1955.6.197	208
1955.6.13	109	1955.6.62	56	1955.6.118	117	1955.6.200	348
1955.6.14	111	1955.6.64	139	1955.6.120	317	1955.6.201	339
1955.6.15	55	1955.6.65	145	1955.6.121	234	1955.6.202	298
1955.6.16	54	1955.6.66	118	1955.6.122	194	1955.6.203	299
1955.6.17	41	1955.6.67	135	1955.6.123	201	1955.6.204	217
1955.6.18	A5	1955.6.68	134	1955.6.124	202	1955.6.205	257
1955.6.20	53	1955.6.69	131	1955.6.125	113	1955.6.207	A13
1955.6.21	49	1955.6.70	75	1955.6.126	114	1955.6.208	A14
1955.6.22	51	1955.6.71	284	1955.6.127	99	1955.6.209	A15
1955.6.23	52	1955.6.72	286	1955.6.128	227	1955.6.210	A16
1955.6.24	45	1955.6.73	333	1955.6.129	A20	1955.6.211	A17
1955.6.25	46	1955.6.74	190	1955.6.130	200	1955.6.212	A18
1955.6.26	47	1955.6.75	332	1955.6.131	186	1955.6.214	254
1955.6.27	39	1955.6.76	188	1955.6.132	184	1955.6.216	77
1955.6.28	38	1955.6.77	283	1955.6.133	100	1955.6.217	76
1955.6.29	69	1955.6.78	278	1955.6.134	315	1955.6.218	198
1955.6.30	68	1955.6.79	279	1955.6.135	312	1955.6.219	197
1955.6.31	72	1955.6.80	129	1955.6.136	274	1955.6.226	A12
1955.6.32	73	1955.6.81	276	1955.6.137	310	1955.6.237	10
1955.6.33	97	1955.6.83	210	1955.6.140	211	1955.6.238	40
1955.6.34	65	1955.6.84	216	1955.6.142	360	1955.6.240	87
1955.6.35	A6	1955.6.85	214	1955.6.143	361	1955.6.242	185
1955.6.36	70	1955.6.86	247	1955.6.144	363	1955.6.245	78
1955.6.37	71	1955.6.87	250	1955.6.145	362	1955.6.246	79
1955.6.38	66	1955.6.89	270	1955.6.146	359	1955.6.247	318
1955.6.39	A4	1955.6.90	267	1955.6.147	357	1955.6.250	64
1955.6.40	44	1955.6.91	187	1955.6.148	355	1955.6.251	112
1955.6.41	101	1955.6.92	104	1955.6.149	353	1955.6.253	306
1955.6.42	103	1955.6.93	265	1955.6.150	354	1955.6.254	273
1955.6.44	63	1955.6.96	222	1955.6.151	358	1955.6.259	256
1955.6.45	57	1955.6.97	86	1955.6.152	349	1955.6.266	A10
1955.6.46	A7	1955.6.98	150	1955.6.153	352	1955.6.267	110
1955.6.47	A1	1955.6.99	82	1955.6.154	351	1955.6.268	A3
1955.6.48	32	1955.6.101	205	1955.6.157	255	1955.6.270	296
1955.6.49	137	1955.6.103	59	1955.6.162	220	1955.6.271	126
1955.6.50	136	1955.6.104	165	1955.6.170	A19	1955.6.272	123
1955.6.51	280	1955.6.105	162	1955.6.178	239	1955.6.273	133
1955.6.52	119	1955.6.106	163	1955.6.179	240	1955.6.274	277

Accession Number	Catalogue Number	Accession Number	Catalogue Number	Accession Number	Catalogue Number	Accession Number	Catalogue Number
1955.6.275	A11	1955.6.347	6	1955.6.361	159	1955.6.368	195
1955.6.276	A2	1955.6.357	307	1955.6.364	182	1955.6.369	31
1955.6.278	287	1955.6.358	308	1955.6.365	212	1955.6.371	156
1955.6.295	5	1955.6.359	154	1955.6.366	83	1960.2	334
1955.6.300	A8	1955.6.360	248	1955.6.367	206		

INDEX

Lid, 97
Livia, 138
Lotus beaker, 126
Luxor, 1

M

Maenad, 136, 190, A7
Maker's mark, 94, 191(?)
Malalas, Johannes, *Chronographia*, 276
Marbled glass, xvi, 40, 41, 48, 97
Marine motifs, 132
Marvering, xv
Masks, 333, 360, A12
Medallions, 287
Medusa, 188
Meges, 133
Mesopotamia, xi
Metalwork, xii, xvii, 109, 110, 118, 121, 125, 132, 133;
    metalworker's shop, A9
Millefiori glass, 48, 49
Mold-blown vessels, xiii, xv, xvii, 94, 118–48, 188–91, 224,
    258, 276–83, 290, 332–34, 346, 348–63
Molded ribbed vessels, 40–44
Mold-pressed vessels, xv, 34–55, 108, 112, A3, A4, A11(?)
Morgan, J. P., Collection, 133
Mosaic glass, xi, xii, xv, 34, 38, 48, 50–55, A3, A4, A5
Mount Carmel, 91, 122, 303
Mythological subjects, xiii, 127, 258, 280

N

Nazareth, 356
Neikias, 133
Neo-Attic reliefs, 136
Nimrud, xii

O

Oinochoe, xvii, 7–9
Olive branches, 111
Optic blown, xvi, 217, 290

P

Painted decoration, xii, xiii, xvi, 111, 264, A9(?)
Palestine, 34. *See also* Israel *and individual sites*
Palmettes, 125, A7
Palm frond, 129, 131, 133–35, 287(?), 354, 357, 359, 361
Palmyra: sculpture from, 283; Tyche of, 276
Pan, 136, 280
Panels, 119–23, 129
Panther, 136, 137, 280
Parsons, Harold Woodbury, 53
Patella cup, xvii, 45–52, 106
Pattern-molded, xvi, 284–86
Pausanias, 276
Pheidias, xii

Pier, Garrett Chatfield, Collection, 4
Pillar molded vessels. *See* Molded ribbed vessels
Pinched decoration, xiii, xvi, 299, 337, 339, 340–42
Plant motifs, xiii, 119, 120, 121, 129
Plate, xvii, 54
Pliny the Elder, xiii, xv, 276
Pompeii, xii, 55, 62, 63, 65, 96, 109, 111, 125, 126, 138
Poseidon, 137
Pottery: Greek, xi, xii, xvii, 7, 10, 13, 22, 91; Hellenistic,
    xiii, xvii, 118; Roman, xiii, xvii, 104, 106, 108, 136, 188
Praeneste, Bernadini Tomb, xii
Pseudo-mosaic glass, 66–70, 74, A6
Puteoli, 203
Pyxis, xvi, xvii, 121, 124, 125; lid from, 97

R

Rhineland, 111, 200, 278
Ribbon glass, 38
Rockefeller, John D., Jr., Collection, 37, 43, 58, 60, 80, 81,
    88–90, 92, 93, 98, 107, 108, 138, 140, 151, 153, 155, 161,
    166, 176, 183, 228, 285, 321, 323, 343
Rome, xii, 76; Villa Albani, 7
Rosette, 94, 257

S

Sandcore vessels, xi, xvi, 1–3, 7–33, A1, A2
Sangiorgi, Giorgio, Collection, 5
Satyr, A7
Scroll pattern, 129
Seasons, 137
Sedeinga, Sudanese Nubia, 257
Semiprecious stones, imitation of, xi
Shield, 123(?)
Sidon, 118, 119, 145, 284
Signature, glassmaker's, xiii, xiv n. 20, 118, 133
Silenus, 280
Silver, xvii, 111, 126, 136
Siphnos, 135
Skyphos, xvi, xvii, 109
Snake thread decoration, 184
Splash glass, xvi, 61, 109–11
Sprinkler flask, 225–29
Stephane, 190
Strabo, xii, xiii
Strigil, 62, 120
Stylite saint, 353–56, 357(?), 358(?)
Syria, 70, 125, 134, 273, 341, 353. *See also individual sites*
Syro-Palestinian area, xii, 40, 184, 219, 297

T

Tel-el-Horus, Syria, 191
Tel-el-Hoson, Syria, 203
Terra cotta, 80, 188, 235, 282

Thyrsos, 123, 280

Trailed thread decoration, xiii, xvi, 1, 7–11, 13–33, 74, 75, 101, 184, 192, 194, 200–2, 210, 224, 225, 231–33, 235, 239–41, 243–46, 251, 254, 255, 264, 267, 272–75, 294, 297, 303–6, 309–12, 317–21, 324–34, 337, 338, 343, 346, 347, 353–55, 360. *See also* Dragged thread decoration, Feather pattern, Snake thread decoration, Zig zag thread decoration

Trees, 132, 351, 352, 358

Tyche of Antioch, xiii, 276, 277

Tyre, 30, 124, 134, 284

U

Unguentarium, 56, 57, 78, 79, 155, 167, 169–74, 176–77, 179–81

V

Venice, Compagnia di Venezia e Murano, A3, A4, A7

Vessels, as decorative motif, 119, 120, 122, 123

Villa Albani, Rome, 7

Vorce, A. D., 157, 221, 314, 346

Vulture, 5

W

Wave pattern, 292

Weathering, definition of, xvi

Wheel-cut decoration, xii, xiii, xv, xvi, 34–37, 40, 42–44, 55, 60, 80, 86, 88, 91, 92, 96, 98–100, 110, 112–18, 133, 150, 203, 235, 258, 259, 263, 265, 287, 292, 339, A11

Wheel-polishing, xvi, 34, 40, 48, 53

Windows, xii

Workshops, 94, 118, 120, 133, 330, 361

Wreath, 128, 134, 135, 257, A7

Y

Yugoslavia, 101

Z

Zig zag thread decoration, 1, 7–11, 13–15, 17–25, 233, 255, 272–74, 304–6, 318, 327, 329, 338